* * *

ABORTION IS NOT A SIN

* * *

A New-Age Look At
An Age-Old Problem

Pandit Press
24843 Del Prado, #405
Dana Point, CA 92629

i

"For the time will come when you will say... Blessed are the wombs which have not conceived and the breasts which have not given milk."

Jesus Christ,
The Gospel of Thomas

ABORTION IS NOT A SIN

A Pandit Press Book

PRINTING HISTORY
Pandit Press edition published November 1987

Pandit Press Inc.
P.O. Box 7200
1548-D Adams Ave.
Costa Mesa, Ca. 92626

Printed in the United States of America
ISBN# 0-944361-00-5

"The soul within the fetus cannot be destroyed by any kind of abortion."

Seth

* * *

"I know that no soul is ever destroyed. I know that when a soul chooses to be born, it will be born. The soul is wise and would not inhabit a body if it were not to come to term."

Emmanuel

* * *

"In the early stages of conception, the immortal self is not present; nor in the early stages of fetal growth in the mother's womb."

James Perkins

* * *

"On the other hand, souls come into these bodies for needs of their own. Thus, if victimization does occur, it could be said to be happening on both sides."

Karl Schlotterbeck

* * *

"The physical destiny of the doer-in-the-body must fit in with innumerable events in the life of others and with public matters. Time, condition, and place are all-important. To be born too soon or too late would mean a misfit in the social order. The time for the beginning of a certain body must be selected so as to allow the cycles of its own life to intersect cycles in the lives of others with whom it is to be connected."

Harold Waldwin Percival

* * *

* DEDICATION *

To the women of the world — God's own choice for reproductive responsibility

* TABLE OF CONTENTS *

FOREWORD - THE QUESTIONS

CHAPTER 1 - THE FETUS AND THE SOUL

CHAPTER 2 - THE WAY IT IS

* FOREWORD *

There are few more perplexing questions in our lives than the decision to terminate a pregnancy. Unwanted and untimely pregnancies bring into sharp focus the issues of life, death, freedom and responsibility. In these times, violent emotions are often aroused in well-meaning people on issues that really pertain to only one person - the pregnant woman. It is a time when quiet reflection is needed, and a time to examine in depth what the real consequences and responsibilities are going to be in deciding to give, or not give, birth to a child. To be or not to be . . . that is the mother's question. And only she holds the answer.

Ethically and morally we must ask whether we have the right and capacity, the emotional and psychological vigor to bring a child into the world? Is this the right time? Can I adequately provide? Have I had too many children already? Am I just too scared to take total responsibility for controlling my own reproductive behavior? Am I committing murder? Will I go to hell? Am I already in a hell of my own making? Is it a sin to control my own life? The very way we think about the many questions involved in pregnancy termination will most certainly affect our behavior and state of mind.

But a decision must be made, and this book is dedicated to young girls, and all women of childbearing age struggling to make their own "right" decision. And making that decision today, free from coercion of the church or state, is more difficult than ever. The urge by others to control you and your reproductive system in a "free country" is overwhelming. But the deep issues are psychological and spiritual. And these are precisely the areas where we will attempt to take a fresh look, from new perspectives, at these ageless questions.

The question of abortion is as much a question of our freedoms as it is one of life and death. Will it be freedom for the fetus, or freedom for the mother *from* the fetus? Will there be freedom from the state, religious institutions, and the self-styled preachers of the "moral majority" and their many vociferous followers? Is the aborting of a fetus, before it has reached the capacity to survive outside the womb, a crime? Is a young woman's life stillborn by not having an abortion? Is the fetus conscious? Is the fetus inhabited by a soul in the early stages of pregnancy? What is the sin... the act of abortion, or the premature and unplanned pregnancy?

And in an increasingly crowded world, what is the morality of irresponsible parenthood, where parents often do not have the will or the capacity to provide for their babies? Should not we also be morally alarmed at the sight of our beautiful earth being ravaged by irresponsible procreation and overpopulation, when millions already suffer from starvation?

"Thou shalt not kill" says the sixth commandment. In our society we find it difficult to live without killing some form of animal life for the food we eat? And unless we are strict vegetarians and rarely step outside the house we are involved in some form of "killing" for our sustenance. Just as many animals feed on others within Mother Nature's grand scheme so does man. Is this wrong? Who feeds on mankind to control his numbers? And how many "pro-lifers," so righteous about controlling your womb, are strict vegetarians? How many oppose the death penalty? And how many will actually go out and adopt even one of the many babies, born to mostly young, poor, and ill-prepared mothers and all too often destined to a life of poverty, neglect, and disadvantage?

The moral dimension of pregnancy decisions today is as wide and vast as the earth itself. Narrowness of mind, tradition, doctrine and circumstance are more the problem than the solution in our decision-making process. And the many inconsistencies of abortion opponents are often glaring and unexplainable. But when it comes to others seeking to control your body, whatever their motives, their intrusion into your life is neither wanted, nor respectful of your rights as an individual to determine your own destiny and motherhood.

Perhaps the really big question in abortion is guilt. Am I committing murder? Who says that it is murder? And more importantly, who really knows that it is murder? Is there "life" in a fetus? Is the soul present yet? When does the soul inhabit the body? Do I really control conception?

And certainly personal freedom is no less an issue. Do I have any right to control my own body? Am I just a slave to the unborn? Where has our present day patriarchal "morality" come from? What is the effect of the male ethos on women today and where is it leading us? Do not women have the basic right to a matriarchal morality defining a woman's rights and duties in the process of motherhood?

In addition to the crucial and essential problems of individual rights, to examine why the right of abortion is such an important question, we must look at the broader environmental crisis of humanity in the world today. For no woman is an island in today's crowded world. Birth decisions have impact now and in the future on a mother's, a child's life, our community and our world. It is my hope that this book will provide a new frame of reference for the critical decisions about motherhood and personal freedom. Now more than ever, we have obligations to protect our planet, and all future children, from the ravages of overpopulation.

K.B.W.

* Chapter One *

- The Fetus and the Soul -

THE BEGINNINGS OF "LIFE" -

To begin to explore the larger questions of "life" in the womb, we must begin with a brief look at what happens at conception in the woman's body. Our understanding of just what "it" is that is inside the womb, in the early months of pregnancy, is vital to our understanding and discussion of the real meaning of pregnancy termination called abortion.

We know that in the process of a woman's ovulation every month, a tiny bundle of cells, the egg, slowly moves down the fallopian tube and into the uterus. These human "eggs" are microscopic in size - about 130 microns. And this microscopic human egg, having a very brief "life," will soon disintegrate and "die" if not fertilized by the male sperm cells.

Fertilization, or the penetration of the egg by the male sperm, is accomplished by a single male sperm within the first, or possibly the second, day after its "arrival" in the fallopian tube. When a man's army of tiny sperm finally reach the female egg, only one of millions need penetrate to the center of the egg and join with the female cell nucleus. The fusing of these two cells, from the mother and the father, is the beginning of a long journey involving the preparation of a "vessel" capable of containing, or receiving, "personhood."

Now the process of cell division begins according to the instructions in the genetic material handed down from the mother and father. At this stage, we might ask, is this process of cell division, immediately after conception, now tantamount

1

to human life? Is there a "person" present at this stage? Regardless, can we now say that this tiny bundle of replicating cells should take legal and moral precedence over the mother's life at this point?

Before the fertilized egg enters the womb, this tiny microscopic cluster of cells may drift for several days until finally adhering to the wall of the uterus. If, for any number of reasons, attachment to the uterine wall does not occur, the fertilized egg exits the uterus and pregnancy does not occur.

It is only possible to detect pregnancy some three weeks after conception at the earliest. At four weeks the fetus is only one-fifth on an inch long. At eight weeks the fetal material is only one-inch long. Most studies confirm that over 90% of all abortions occur before ten weeks of gestation. But even after three months the relatively undeveloped fetus is only 3.5 inches in length and weighs a mere 1.5 ounces.

It is a fact of life that Mother Nature often has her own unexplainable reasons for aborting an estimated one-half of all pregnancies. In many cases, even after the "conceptus" binds to the lining of the uterus, the embryo may not survive, become dislodged, and result in a case of "natural" and spontaneous "abortion" referred to as miscarriage. Thus, the number of pregnancies terminated by choice is relatively small in comparison to Mother Nature's own unpredictable (and sometimes cruel) program of natural birth control and pregnancy termination.

WHEN DOES LIFE BEGIN? -

Never say the biologists, and in this respect they agree with the mystics - life does not "begin" at conception. Since the origin of the universe and the big bang (pardon the expression) the "beginnning" of time occurred and "life" in the form of cellular (or perhaps soul-ular) information has been passed on from generation to generation. There is no "before life" time in the basic cellular life of human beings or any animal. Every cell gets its life from a preceeding cell in a living continuum. On the more minute and immaterial atomic level some might say that the essential building blocks of our bodies are deathless in that they only change location, or cellular hosts, in the process we now call "death."

But if we choose to call the information in our cellular blueprints life, then every month the woman creates "potential life" in her ovaries. In her reproductive career a woman produces some 10,000 eggs, or "unborn children" in her ovaries, of which perhaps as many as 400 will ultimately reach the womb in her lifetime. And without sexual abstinence or contraception, a woman is capable of producing a baby nearly every month of her post-puberty and adult life. Individually speaking, in most cases, fertility is not our problem. Our ability to produce babies, despite our intentions and circumstances, is *the* problem we must deal with.

"One hundred women are not worth a single testicle."[1]

Confucius (551-479 B.C.)

In addition to the ongoing fertility of a young girl and mature woman, the male of our species is capable of producing approximately 250 million sperm in one ejaculation. And out of that swiftly advancing horde, only a single sperm is needed to fertilize the egg and begin conception. Again, we have an overwhelming abundance of raw potential - Mother Nature invented overkill.

But all this raw potential abundance of cellular "blueprints" is not exactly what we might call fully human "life." If we choose to do so, we can easily imagine the new possibilities and problems arising from the modern alchemist's petrie dish, where multiple eggs from a woman are fertilized, and then only the "best" one is picked to be implanted in the uterus. The other remaining microscopic tissue cultures, or conceptuses, are then disposed of as only one fertilized egg is necessary to create a human being.

In our new age of biochemistry, we have now become the co-creators of life, with god-like powers and truly awesome responsibilities. Today, our procreative powers and the real

3

consequences of that power, whether in the womb or the petrie dish, deserves our full attention *before* the fact and not just after.

Aside from the frightening new potential of petrie dish conception, the possibilities to conceive naturally are limited only by the mother's ability to give birth every year. And just one man, consorting with several women, can smother a neighborhood in children if left without devices. A man and a woman (or should we say Mother and Father nature?) are, by ancient design and neccessity, incredibly fertile. But depending on our current state of affairs, this incredible fertility can be either a blessing or a curse. Our problems stem from the fact that nature is permanently switched on, there is no off-button unless we ourselves push it.

In the "natural" world of our ancient and recent past, where our survival was precarious at best, this incredible fertility was essential. Today, however, due to man's intervention in nature's control of fertility, and growing resource limitations, it is another matter. Our fertility has become the problem. We must now control it.

However, if we choose to look at our fertility problems from the perspective of a "pro-life" morality, are we then to expect that a woman today must attempt to nurture all of this "potential life" and give birth to all 400 of her eggs? Are we to expect, as some would suggest, that it is the duty of all women to remain open to birth every year for the thirty odd years of her reproductive career to avoid killing any potential life? Must every fertilized egg become a chicken? Or a human being? If this is to be the case, what can we say of Mother Nature's own "crimes" against both potential and actual life?

Obviously, when the "morals" of the past do not jibe with the realities of our present time, we will simply be following absurd and self-destructive ethical requirements. There is no question that the logic, and effect, of protecting all "potential life" can become absurd. In our brave new world of created "synthetic" children, should the bio-chemist be obligated to "hatch" all the eggs fertilized in an attempt to give an infertile woman the best chance to have a baby? This is plainly absurd. But this appears to be the logic many well-meaning "pro-life" people would impress upon scientists today as they have upon women for centuries.

And speaking of potential life, we know that of the approximately 100 trillion cells in the human body, almost every one has a complete set of blueprints or information to construct a complete human being - thus the real potential of cloning life. But if we damage any of these cells, even by scraping our skin, brushing our teeth, or removing a cancerous tumor, we are thus killing potential life. And using Garrett Hardin's analogy, if we destroy the blueprints of a house, can we really say we are also destroying the house?

There is no question that "potential life" is almost infinite, especially in an age where the "artificial" creation of life is becoming commonplace. But if we apply a "right to life" to all potential life there is no end to the potential catastrophe. A perfect illustration and satire of the real extremes of this situation is contained in Hardin's brilliant short essay "Truth's day in Court" contained in Appendix A. As Hardin has suggested, the real question cannot be when does *life* begin because no human has ever witnessed the beginning, if there ever was such an event. The essential question is when does *human* life begin?

Certainly we can safely say that all but the most neglectful of mothers are "pro-life." And well within the meaning of the term is a mother's concern for the quality of her own life as well as that of her future children. First, she is concerned about the conscious self-determination of her own life; and second, for the sake of those children she may already have, or others she may choose to have at the right time in her life. And being pro-life is not just giving in to a lack of control, it is taking control of, and responsibility for, one's own reproductive life. The only remaining relevant question is where, when, and under what circumstances, will a woman choose to activate her pro-life potential and become a mother?

In the earliest stages of pregnancy, when fertilization occurs and cell division begins, the blueprints of genetic information in the cells are activated. But can we now say, with any degree of certainty, that a "human being" is present at this point of cellular activity? Is their a soul, or consciousness, in existence and present "in" the molecules at this point? Or is the locus of consciousness elsewhere and completely separate at this stage? When does this bundle of cellular information become life, a soul, a human being? And what are to be the rights of our replicating cells versus the rights of the mother in the early stages of pregnancy? Where is the person? Where is the soul, the mind or consciousness of the new being? These are a few of the essential questions that need more discussion in the abortion debate.

PERSONHOOD? -

The modern debate about pregnancy termination, and when "personhood" begins, has often centered on the argument about the presence of brainwaves in the fetus. Of course, implicit in this argument is that the personhood of the mother doesn't count anymore, even though there is no argument over the reality of her own brainwaves. The old debate over the fetus's ability to feel pain, and the validity of assumptions as portrayed in the anti-abortion film "The Silent Scream," rest on shaky assumptions about fetal awareness.

Many doctors have long argued that premature infants could not feel pain due to the fact that their nervous systems had not fully formed. Thus reflexive fetal movement may not by synonymous with the "conscious" experience of pain. It now appears that this is most probably the case with undeveloped embryonic tissue in the early stages of pregnancy. However, we know for certain that a woman feels pain when she is forced to complete a pregnancy against her wishes. Of this single fact there is no doubt.

During fetal development, different parts of the brain grow at different speeds. In the early months, the midbrain and spinal cord are forming first, followed by the pons and medulla. The

6

development of the cerebral hemisphere, the supposed seat of our cognitive functions, lags behind the other more elementary areas of the brain. At this early stage any reflexive activity represents responses from the lower brain regions and not the cerebral cortex.

But can there be a "person" without a functioning and fully-developed brain? Is it simply a matter of reflexive tissue? Is there a person, a soul, inhabiting the premature body, brain and nervous system? Is the soul, the animating spirit or intelligence, actually residing "in" the embryo from conception? Is it possible for the full spectrum of human consciousness to be within an undeveloped fetus? Or is our essence elsewhere? And where are we before birth if not "in" the fetus?

These are but a few of the essential questions we will explore as they lead us into the meta-physical realms of our mysterious existence, and into regions of reality where our so-called "objective" object-oriented science may not yet have penetrated. Of course, that is to say that there may well be other plausible theories and explanations of the phenomenon of human life, illuminated by human experience, that represent credible "answers" to these cosmic questions. Obviously, in a culture dominated by a rigid scientific-materialism, these metaphysical new-ancient explanations of the fetal-soul-spirit phenomena may differ substantially from what is generally accepted or believed . . . but they cannot be ignored.

It is in precisely in these "metaphysical" and spiritual areas where we will explore alternate "truths" about life and death. And where the fundamental freedoms of motherhood are challenged it is extremely important that we now attempt to redefine the meaning of life *in* the womb and define the new responsibilities of motherhood in an increasingly crowded world. With pregnancy termination, we cannot adequately discuss what is believed to be the "taking" of "life" without fully exploring metaphysics, the science of the soul, in order to define "life" in the womb in a most comprehensive fashion.

But before we attempt to answer these many questions in detail, it will help if we state some of the more generally uncontested facts about the developing fetus in the early stages of pregnancy, as related by physicians familar with fetal development:

> "A fertilized egg has become implanted in the uterus at the end of two weeks. At this point, the product of conception begins to receive nourishment from the mother and is called an embryo. Six weeks later the various organ systems are well defined, and the embryo progresses to the stage of a fetus . . . For the first 24 weeks of pregnancy, the fetus is completely dependent on maternal nutritional support and is non-viable if separated from the mother through a miscarriage or accident."

> "Nowhere in the world would such a fetus be listed in the vital statistics as a still born infant. And a fetus lost in a spontaneous miscarriage during this period is not treated as a human being. No mini-caskets are manufactured, no funeral or burial is conducted. The hospital pathologist then disposes of the fetus as he would any other nonviable tissue. This universal procedure has never excited any comment from the medical, legal or religious communities. Morally and legally, then, the performance of an abortion in the first 24 weeks of pregnancy is not to be equated with the taking of a human life."[2]

Dr. Alex Gerber

* * *

> "The cerebral cortex and the synoptic connections are not sufficiently developed to provide the biological basis of person-hood until the thirty-first week of gestation. The presence of electrical activity is common to virtually all cells and cannot be considered meaningful "brain waves" before thirty-one weeks."[3]

Dr. Dominick Purpura

* * *

"I don't think a 24-week fetus can ever have an independent existence. Fetuses weighing less than 35 ounces are often born with serious defects: learning disabilities, poor vision and impaired hearing. Technological advances have been keeping them alive, not keeping them intact, and the heartbreak is staggering."[4]

Dr. Michael Burnhill

* * *

"If we had an aborted baby below the age of viability that was technically live born, we'ed put it in an Isolette (incubator), keep it warm, give it oxygen and observe it. But we would not actively intervene to protect the baby from dying. To place tubes in a fetus that has no chance of survival, is abusive. It is subjecting the fetus to an experiment . . . To me, that is cruel."[5]

Dr. Richard Stavis

WHERE IS CONSCIOUSNESS? -

Putting aside the questions of viability for the moment, it is important that we begin to explore the nature of life, or consciousness, residing "in" the fetus from conception to birth? It is once again a question whose time has come. Only recently have scientists delved into the previously hidden depths of nature in an attempt to discover the core building blocks of our physical beings and material world.

But the result of tracing the paths of sub-atomic particles and reconstructing the basic building blocks of nature, has not led to our finding the essence of our physical bodies. Instead, we have discovered that all "matter" simply disappears into waves of energy. Our physical bodies are but a mask covering the energy nature of our beings. We are not material. We are energy. We are consciousness itself.

Thus, the physical stuff of human life is, at its core, energy in motion. But despite our attempts we have not been able

9

to pinpoint, in our body or brain, the precise location of the "ghost in the machine." Today, many scientists, from diverse disciplines, now theorize that our discrete unit of consciousness, or life, is only part of a larger energy-field network encompassing the entire universe.

What does this have to do with abortion? Definitions of life are implicit in people's religions and morality. If those who oppose abortion define personhood and the presence of fetal "life" with many unproven postulates, such that the result is to take away the rights of the mother, then certainly those who favor the right to abortion can and must explore and re-define fetal and human life from other less rigid perspectives, allowing us a larger view on our problems and their solutions. Let us continue.

What we normally experience as our "I-ness" is the fact that we are discrete, isolated, and separated beings. But at the most basic levels of existence this is simply not the case. We are here, there, and everywhere connected by the energies inter-communicating on the atomic level of reality. It is now apparent that we are more like interconnected and individualized radio sets tuned in to the same frequencies of stored and evolving thought-programs (of our own making as well as that of others) that penetrate our environment.

Our consciousness, or spirit, is said to be akin to software being radiated to our individual brains from the collective hologram of the larger universal consciousness. However, the brain is not the software, the life content, but only the hardware. Thus our brains are not the site of our consciousness, but only our mechanism for receiving and processing the subtle waves of energy and information about our greater, and subtler, selves. So what we call life, our greater selves or consciousness, is not necessarily located "in" the undeveloped fetal brain or even the fully-human body.

To illustrate the dilemma of scientists today, we find in Michael Talbot's "Beyond The Quantum" a review of the exciting findings of the new physics now beginning to radically reshape our understanding of our "material" world as well as the deeper nature and context of human beings. Talbot cites the recent work of John Lorber, a British neurologist working with anencephalics, or "brainless" individuals whose neural tube never developed properly. What is truly startling about his discoveries is that several of his subjects did not show any evidence of possessing a cerebral cortex - the part of the brain believed to be the seat of consciouness! Despite this condition, they appeared to be normal.[6]

Other research revealed a university student at Sheffield University with a slightly larger-than-normal head. Intrigued, Lorber requested a CAT scan (a new brain-scanning technique) only to discover that he had "virtually no brain." It was revealed that there was only a extremely thin layer of brain cells a millimeter or so thick and the rest of the skull cranium was filled with cerebrospinal fluid - and he had an I.Q. of 126, with an honors degree in mathematics!

Lorber has apparently gone on to discover other people who function normally but do not possess a "brain" as such. So where are "we" then? And where is our mind? If there are those who exist who don't have brains in their bodies, where is their mind, their conscious essence? Is there one, or are there other "locations" for our consciousness? And if the essential "I" is not in the brain, are we "in" the body at all? Are we then "in" the ether or energy fields surrounding the body? And most important to our discussion here, are we actually "in" the fetus prior to ur birth? In other words, are we prisoners in our "material" bodies *or* more free-ranging spirits? What do we abort?

It is now apparent to many that there exist ubiquitous energy-fields, interpenetrating our world and bodies. These fields, like light itself, carry the information of life and consciousness. Some suggest they may even program the DNA and the design of our bodies. No matter how hard we try we cannot confine ourselves to our bodies alone. This out-of-body intelligence, spirit, soul, light, or "morphic resonance" is at work in sensing and shaping our physical world. So our "ghost" may not be "in" our machine machine after all.

> "From certain experiences that I have had of leaving the body while in the isolation tank, I would say that the spirit contains the being that is contained in the brain."[7]

> John Lily,
> Scientist

Thus the revolutionary message of the new physics is that we are not the body. And we are not the fetus as such. We are much more than the building blocks of matter called body, and even the exact location of our "mind" is in doubt. Our consciousness, or the sense of I-ness that we experience as ourselves, is not located in any one body location such as the human brain. It may be anywhere due to the ability of sub-atomic particles to encode and transfer our experience. Thus, we may influence and communicate with one another thru time and over very great distances.

So we are both within and without our physical bodies. We are not either confined, or defined, by the body, or the fetus, in and of itself. We are also the sum of not only the varied genetic information passed on from a multitude of ancestors, but our largely unconscious beings are also awash in our own cellular memories (perhaps of past, present, and future?) as well as the information stored in light waves that constantly intersect with our personal world.

We are not separated but joined by the new revelations of physics. We now find that "we" are here, there, and everywhere - perhaps lost or unconscious of the relativity of both time and space. Life is no doubt a very curious and almost indefinable phenomenon. Today, it is more mysterious than ever - especially the nature of early fetal life as we will see.

Science is now cutting the hologram of our existence into smaller and smaller pieces only to find the whole image of our being still remaining in each minute particle. In a recent book, entitled The Unknown Spirit, french physicist Jean Charon boldly asserts that all of the electrons in the universe constitute the world of spirit, and that all these electrons, both

together and individually, are the location of the "I" of our
existence.[8]

These electron particles, the most abundant in the universe
with nearly a hundred billion of them in each of our cells,
have been in existence since the beginning of time. And it is
these same electrons that are responsible for all of the
underlying electro-magnetic functioning of our bodies and
brains. These same basic "units" of nature may well be the
truly quintessential building blocks of body and soul.

"You could compare these units, simply for an analogy,
to the invisible breath of consciousness. They are
emitted by the cells. They are electromagnetic . . .
following their own patterns of positive and negative
charge. The units are just beneath the range of physical
matter . . . consciousness actually produces these
emanations. Being just beyond the range of matter,
having a structure but a nonphysical one, and being
of a pulsating nature, they combine the qualities of
a unit and a field . . .

"They will draw other units to them, for example,
according to the intensity of the emotional tone of
the particular consciousness at any given "point."
Certain intensities and certain positions of polarity
between and among these units and great groupings
of these units compress energy into solid form
(resulting in matter). Units are the forms that
experience takes when directed by the inner self.
Matter is the shape of your dreams. Your dreams,
thoughts, and emotions are literally transformed into
physical matter purposefully by this inner self.

"Buildings appear to be made of rock or stone or steel.
They are actually oscillating, ever-moving, highly
charged gestalts of EE units. They are solidified
emotions. The powers of consiousness are clearly not
understood, then. And each individual has his part

to play in projecting these EE units into physical reality. Therefore, physical reality can be legitimately described as an extension of the self, as much as the physical body is a projection of the inner self."[9]

Seth (Jane Roberts),
The Seth Material

We are much more powerful than we know. The idea that the body is the sum total of our conscious self is but an illusion. It seems these elemental and ubiquitous "units" are capable of interacting with one another at a distance, communicating with one another across time and space, and regardless of whether or not they happen to be encapsulated within the same larger human body! Information and experience is stored in the locations and spin states of the photons in electronic space similar to the way memory is stored in computers. These memories, from the dawn of time, are stored in our cellular structure and may be accessed when our consciousness and vibration rate is capable of "listening" to and unlocking the atomic records of our past existence.

And even when there is no cellular structure called a human being, the electrons apparently retain the hologram of life-memory information and transplant it to whatever larger being whose energy it becomes a part of. Here, science is plainly leading us into the New Age of understanding of our beings - and "back" into the ageless, timeless, and perhaps simultaneous, past-present-future of the mystics.

"There is a natural body, and there is a spiritual body."[10]

I Corinthians 15:44

In our discussion of the propriety of a pregnancy termination, if we remain pure materialists we will only see the sum total of "life" in the cell plasma of the body alone. But in the now converging viewpoints of the ancient mystics, metaphysicians, and modern physicists, we cannot find life encapsulated only "in" the cell, the body or the brain, but in a larger context surrounding and penetrating physical matter.

14

Thus, other considerations aside, our attitudes toward the termination of a pregnancy will then be shaped by how we view the nature of our world, our very beings, and the always illusive phenomenoa of "life" and "death."

In the western world, due to the new revelations of scientists and a few of the truly startling "channeled" intelligences, we are just beginning to seriously confront the fact that death, as we now understand it, does not exist. The reality of an immortal soul, or consciousness, independent of the body material, is an issue that has not been adequately addressed in the current abortion debate. While verifiable evidence that pregnancy termination does any harm to the immaterial and deathless soul is difficult to establish, so also is evidence of Papal infallibility, or the truth of Catholic and fundamentalist doctrine, regarding the origin of life at conception similarly impossible to confirm.

WHEN ARE WE IN THE WOMB? -

In discussing the presence of "life" in the womb and the moral meaning of abortion, how many of us can really say with certainty when the soul inhabits the body? According to many ancient traditions, the soul is thought to be the energizing or "animating" force that inhabits the being created by the coming together of a man and a woman. And this soul, or energizing force, is not necessarily emanating from within the confines of the "human" fetal body. As we shall see, new evidence from hypnosis studies, as well as out-of-body and near-death experiences, about our spiritual odyssey thru the process of birth, death, and reincarnation reinforces this view and provides us with new perspectives on "life" in the womb. In effect, the wisdom and experience of the ancient sages of many traditions is today being validated.

"Woe to you, for you have not learned the lesson that they rise from death."[11]

> Jesus Christ,
> Gospel of Thomas

* * *

"The Self does not die when the body dies. And Concealed in the heart of all beings lies the atma, the spirit, the self; smaller than the smallest atom, greater than the greatest spaces."[12]

> Katha Upanishad

And what do we know of "Life before Life" or the soul's great number of lives lived in different bodies and different times? There is a growing body of experiment, and many fascinating cases, that we will examine that strongly suggests we are not just our bodies, but living electrical phantoms inhabiting bodies in the material plane. Indeed, the new generation of modern physicists have, in effect, become the new mystics after rediscovering the non-material and energy-like essence of every living thing in the universe.

At "death" our energy-body, soul, or bundle of electrons with a unique set of spin states constituting what we sense to be a unique and isolated self, then exits our "material" and earthbound body. The body then quickly begins to decay due to the loss of its unifying force-field called life. And now, having lost the mysterious animating life force, the cells of the body begin to disintegrate and we "die."

But just when do we re-inhabit the womb or fetus? Is it from the moment of conception, when the DNA cells from the mother and father rapidly multiply to prepare a new body? Or is it later when the fetal body is now well prepared and substantially human? Or is it at the moment of birth? Is the answer locked inside "our" electron memories? Is there only one and the same answer for all?

16

If the soul does not inhabit the fetus until just before birth, how can one say that we are *taking* a life prior to this point? But if the soul is not in the womb, how can we equate abortion with murder? These are critical questions in the abortion debate that few today even bother to address or begin to answer, precisely because they are "objectively" unanswerable. But are they?

> "God built the human body from the sand of earth. Then God blew the breath of life into his nose. So Man became a living soul."[13]

Genesis II:7

Even the Bible, in the book of Genesis, tells us that life is a two-stage process, the building of the body and then the infusion of the soul to animate and bring "life" to the fetus. Similarly, Jesus tells his disciples in John 6:63 that "it is the spirit that quickeneth; the flesh profiteth nothing."

For most of us, the essential question that surrounds the propriety of abortion might be: Once our bodies are forming, or substantially built in the womb, when does the "breath" or soul of life arrive? Today, there are now more answers than ever before to this question. And, most importantly, no one answer may be "right" in all cases.

IF THE FETUS COULD SPEAK, WHAT WOULD IT SAY?

In the current resurgence of interest in banning a woman's right to abortion, why is it that no one ever asks how the fetus, or the soul who eventually will reside in the fetus, would relate to the mother in her decision to terminate a pregnancy? Is the answer so obvious? Could there not be classic elements of christian charity within any fetal being, or soul, indicating sympathy for the plight of the reluctant mother who did not intend pregnancy? Because we can't "hear" the answers from the confines of the womb does not mean we should not ask the questions and imagine the responses.

So in our exploration of the concept of personhood and the location of "life" in the womb, imagine for a moment that the developing fetus could speak. Aside from the where of the soul's pre-natal residence, we may certainly speculate on the how and the why of its circumstance, and its appearance at a particular conception event. And, we might ask, just what would the new soul have to say about the conditions of its new existence?

If the fetus, or soul, were conscious and in control during the conception process, would he/she then choose the mother's particular situation? Would he/she pick you? Would he/she pick now? Would he/she be desirous of your situation, or greatly desire a change of circumstances if he/she were aware of the mother's problems? Does he/she have a choice, or only an "unconscious" propensity, to invade the mother's womb?

Looking at the conception event from other alternative cosmologies and viewpoints, we might ask whether he/she picked the time and circumstances of this birth with foreknowledge of the future and the probable outcome of the pregnancy? And for those of a more deterministic mindset, could not the abortion also be a part of the incarnating soul's karmic package? Or is the "incarnation" totally a result of an unconscious affinity alone where souls are pulled or racing headlong to a conception event like sperm to an egg? Just where did the soul, or "new" consciousness, come from? Is there some previous relation to the mother? Or the father? Or neither?

How do we know that these "new" souls are either conscious, or perhaps not totally unconscious, of their new circumstances until the birth event? Is life only in the confines of the physical matter of the body, or also "in" the free-floating electron consciousness? And regardless of the soul's awareness or karma, should the new soul's fetal rights supercede the living mother's human rights? Are all souls, or only an advanced few, aware of their predicament and capable of choosing their next incarnation? Are they aware of yours? Are things off to a good start? Is this the way you would want your parents to conceive you the next time around? Does a real home, a ready and waiting world, await this new soul? The questions are almost endless?

And what might a tiny bundle of cells, this "hovering" soul or fetus conclude if it were conscious? What might the responses be? If there are those who assume that their particular morality gives them the right to speak for the rights of the pregnant mother, then why can't we also presume to speak for the well-being, and moral perspective, of the fetus or new soul?

Understandably, the comments of these not-yet people would most likely vary with the particular circumstances of their incarnation and might be as follows:

"Hey, I don't want to go where I'm not wanted"

"I'll gladly wait for the right time and circumstances"

"Have me when your life is in order and you are ready, not when you just happen to get it on in the back seat of a car"

"I don't want to be a burden."

"I want the best deal I can get, I'll wait thank you."

"If you don't care enough to do the very best for me, forget it."

"I would like not to be an "accident" that was forced on somebody."

"Take your time, There is no rush. I have all the time in the world."

"Don't ruin your life on my account, there's plenty of time ahead of you."

"I don't want to think that my mother sacrificed her own life for mine."

"I want to be wanted, and have my parents want me and be able to provide for me. Why else would I come? To hurt them? What good does that do me?

Is it so hard for us, the living, to imagine such responses from the beyond? Is heaven so bad, and the impulse for rebirth so frantic, that souls are rushing headlong into any birth opportunity and any conception regardless of its circumstance or outcome? Are they fighting over available wombs in the netherworld, anxiously awaiting any energy-wave-love transaction to ride into the womb without the mother's conscious permission? Or might we assume their is a more orderly and thoughtful process involved in the new soul's descent into matter? But is that process linked with the mother's own thought processes? Can she change her mind?

Aside from the speculations about other dimensions of life, our real problems with pregnancy are here and now, not to mention later on. And in dealing with the here and now, as well as the ongoing problems of responsibility in child care, we must ask whether the young children of many unprepared teenagers, and simply overburdened mothers, will be deprived and abused early on, as well as later in their lives? Will they grow up to ask why their mothers didn't prevent or postpone birth until circumstances were better? Will these children later blame their parents for their mistakes and lack of courage? Will society continue to pay for all these "mistakes?

And will the soul/fetus be thankful for birth under most any circumstances? Or, given a choice, would they have preferred a second chance in a better place and time? And how do we know that every new soul may not be picking the very circumstances of their birth and, more importantly, even the termination of that potential birth with complete foreknowledge of the outcome? Can a fortunate birth only be within the domain of advanced and "enlightened" beings, with the chosen help of advanced or enlightened parents?

If, for a moment, we put ourselves in the position of the fetus, or new soul, wouldn't we prefer to come into the world in a secure environment, thru two people in love and consciously coming together for the prayerful purpose of giving birth to a child that will be greeted with open arms, true love, and respect in a caring world? And can we not say that this is vastly preferable to the idea of being forcibly yanked out of a peaceful limbo into a cold and cruel world under the worst of circumstances, and forced into the arms of reluctant "parents"? What is moral?

Who would seek that kind of birth, assuming they were conscious of their predicament? Or is assuming the worst of births part of the cosmic school we must all attend? Should not the mother, the school marm, determine when the class will begin? And if we are not "new" but old souls, and we are not necessarily conscious as oppposed to floating downstream in a karmic dream, then the duty is even greater on ourselves, as parents, to ensure the best of circumstances for new life.

If we truly respect life then we can only allow it to happen under the best of circumstances. To be "pro-life" is to be for the best of birth, and life, conditions.

Surely, the act of giving birth to a new being must involve more than just the physical act of having sex. And in our increasingly crowded world, birth can no longer be the result of an accident, a one-night stand, or just a callous indulgence of our sexual needs. To do justice to the process of birth, we must be aware before, during, and after the act of conception and creation, consciously desiring and accepting responsibility for a new being, including all the heavy demands of long-term care and nurturance. Only in this way are we truly "pro-life" and do justice to the fetus, the new life and soul, as well as our family and our shrinking world.

Short of this, we are shortchanging new life and selfishly letting a child happen due solely to our indulgence in unconscious, and perhaps selfish, sexual enjoyment. The plain fact is that for many women their pregnancies are all too often an unintended "mistake" in both judgment and timing. Intention and consent to give birth are absent from the minds of both the mother and the father. The act of sex is not, in itself, a consent to give birth and a waiver of the rights of motherhood.

With modern methods of contraception, sex may now be for pleasure. But the highest spiritual qualities of Love should

21

be present in the process of procreation. Only in this way do we "do unto others as we would have them do unto us."

So, in light of the circumstances of procreation, would the fetus, or incarnating soul as the case may be, then choose your situation or would he/she wait for better times, conditions, and/or parents? It is here that we must enter the arena of metaphysics, the only science of the soul, to arrive at a greater understanding, and a higher intuition, of these issues and their relevance to the rightful termination of a pregnancy.

> "Where am I? Who am I? How came I here? What is this thing called the world? What does this world mean? Who is it that lured me here into this thing and now leaves me there? How did I come into the world? Why was I not consulted . . . but was thrust into the ranks as though I had been bought of a kidnapper, a dealer in souls? How did I obtain an interest in this big enterprise they call reality? Why should I have an interest in it? Is it not a voluntary concern? And if I am compelled to take part in it, where is the director . . . whither shall I turn with my complaint?"[14]

> Soren Kirkegaard

DOES "LIFE" BEGIN OR ARRIVE AT CONCEPTION? -

How does anyone know when life, as opposed to fetal movement, "begins" in the fetus? Is it one and the same, or is it not quite an accurate picture of the sum total of our existence? What and *where* is life? Does the soul "grow" "in" the fetus, or does he/she simply "watch" the process from another dimension of our existence? Are the fetal cells fully conscious? Are their degrees of life? Does the soul exist "in" each cell? In how many dimensions do we exist at once? And why do we insist on confining the unknowable and undefinable to a definite space, time, location or body?

To all these many questions, it can be said that we simply don't know the answers with any degree of certainty, especially the kind of certainty that could give some people reason to condemm others for controlling their unplanned pregnancies in accordance with their own unique religious understanding. How many lives do we have? Are we limited to one or a million? And when does the soul inhabit the fetus? The possible answers have been debated for centuries, except that in some centuries certain answers, contrary to dogma, were considered taboo. Some things never change.

> "A human soul is composed of the various unrefined energy rays of the universe . . . There are numberless energy rays in the universe, including the rays of all the stars and spirits of nature. All rays and spirits come from the subtle origin of the universe"[15]

> Lao-Tzu, circa 2500 B.C.

* * *

> "It would seem that the sensitive soul is not transmitted with the semen, but is created by God. But the sensitive soul is a perfect substance, otherwise it could not move the body, and since it is the form of a body, it is not composed of matter and form . . ."

> " . . . It would seem that human souls were created at the same time. For it is written (Genii.2) God rested him from all his work which he had done. This would not be true if he created new souls every day. Therefore all souls were created at the same time."[16]

> Thomas Aquinas, Summa
> Theologica (1259 A.D.)

Though they lived centuries apart, Aquinas and Lao-Tzu agree that our souls do not begin in the womb. Nor do they, as they might also have agreed, end at "death."

And these questions of prenatal life and soul were continually debated in the early annals of the Christian Church. But just as it is today, no one knew for certain and few could agree on the unknown. They eventually dropped the questions

23

because no one knew the answers. No one knew, with any legal or moral degree of certainty, exactly when the soul of a "new" person "quickens" to the womb or takes up residence in the body. In this debate nothing has changed. The situation is much the same today as it was centuries ago when they dropped the questions for lack of answers. But the quantum reality of our new physics, and recent hypnosis research probing the many layers of our beings, is changing the nature of our "western" conception of human life.

In addition to the contemporary Catholic and Christian fundamentalist doctrines there are many other ways, as we have discussed, of looking at the mysteries of life, birth, death and soul. When we examine our own history and the fate of the early Christian Gnostic mystery schools, and understand how they were persecuted by the late Roman emperors, Constantine, Theodosius and Justinian, we find that many early christians with alternate views of the afterlife and reincarnation were exiled and wiped out by the church in the first centuries after the "death" of Christ. Dissent from dogma, and state religions, was not tolerated.

Thus, a part of our western heritage was neatly excised and exiled from our consciousness and our holy book. Not unlike today, many of those in positions of political power felt they had the only answer, the only holy book. In effect, our ability as individuals and as a culture, to freely examine these questions of life and death, as in the case of the termination of a pregnancy, was severely stunted and neatly circumscribed by the elimination of much of our religious heritage due to these religious persecutions and re-writes.

In the early centuries after Christ we now know that other interpretations, truths, and "heresies" were buried and burned out of existence. The very word "heretic" means, essentially, one who is able to choose. Thus, being a heretic and having your own freedom of choice was a sin, much as some abortion opponents would have it today. And so the Emperor Theodosius decreed in A.D. 380, in the Edict of Thessalonica, the only choice his Christian subjects could have without risking their lives for forming their own opinions.

> "And we require that those who follow this rule of faith embrace the name of Catholic Christian adjudging all others madmen and ordering them to be designated as heretics, condemmed as such in the first instance to suffer divine punishment and there-with the vengeance of that power which we, by celestial authority, have assumed."[17]

Theodosious,
Edict of Thessalonica

This edict indicates the severity of the terrifying political-religious climate of early Christianity. But even "madmen" can be persistent in the face of death. And, as we shall see, some of these madmen apparently wrote the recently re-discovered "Lost Gospels" of the bible. Therein, Jesus speaks of reincarnation and the independent life of the soul as separate from the body. Today, it is well understood by most biblical scholars that our modern bibles, having been translated, edited, re-written, and re-interpreted many times over the centuries, are but incomplete testaments of the life and knowledge of Jesus Christ.

And in our new international and inter-connected world, our "holy" books should be inclusive of the many other ancient traditions, and include the counsel of all "enlightened" sages who have walked the earth. Otherwise, our holiness fails by deliberate exclusion. In our jet age of information and travel, ignorance and deliberate exclusion are no longer excuses for widening the circle of religious counsel in the important matters of life, death, and motherhood.

As always, the historical scriptural truth is hard to come by, centuries after the fact, especially where contrary evidence may have been destroyed and alien ideas brutally suppressed. For example, at the Council of Constantinople convened by Justinian in A.D. 553, the final stake was driven into the hearts of the neo-platonists who considered other "heretical"

interpretations of the bible, and pre-biblical holy texts, to
represent valid spiritual realities.

The doctrinal conflict was apparently so bad that the
secular Imperial Councils had to act. And so the formal
recognition of an afterlife, of rebirth and reincarnation, was
voted down in a narrow three-to-two vote by the five council
judges - as if reality or alternate "truths" could be vetoed. And
as a result of the vote, the emperor Justinian decreed fifteen
heretical "anathemas" of which the first read:

> "If anyone assert the fabulous pre-existence of souls,
> and shall assert the monstrous restoration which
> follows from it: let him be anathema."[18]

Thus Justinian saw to it that the teachings of the
neoplatonists, and any pre-christian influences suggesting
reincarnation, were excised from the bible - the word of god.
In effect, the Church decreed that immortality only exists in
the future and not in the past - only forward and not backward.
You can *go to* heaven but you can't be *from* heaven! Resurrection
could only be used once despite what Jesus said about being
"born again."

But this "monstrous restoration" phenomenoa just won't
go away. So it appears that what comes down to us today
in our modern bibles is only half-truth at best, and at its worst,
seriously lacking in the real understanding and message of
Christ.

Today, we have the wisdom of many sages and enlightened
men and women from many cultures, as well as that of Jesus,
to help us understand the phenomenoa of life both in and
out of the womb. The anguish of women around the world,
struggling with the problems of poverty, and their unwanted
pregnancies, is reason enough to seek all the ancient
philosophical and religious understanding we can get. Our days
of one-book religion, and one-book intolerance, are past. After
all, the human experience of transcendence is one, only the
words and interpretations are many and varied.

And with our modern hypnosis techniques and spirit channeling, as well as the near-death and out-of-body experiences, we now have other clues as to what the real process of life and creation may be. In age after age, and culture after culture, the experience of man regarding the separation of body and soul is similar. And, as we shall see, from the ancient shamans to the modern hypnotists, the revealing answers to our many questions about pre-natal life, from many disparate sources, are nearly identical.

The newer revelations about the nature of life and soul, mainly from recent innovative hypnosis research, tend to verify the wisdom of the ancient masters and mystics normally found outside the orthodox church traditions. We shall begin to examine, in the following sections, these interesting new metaphysical phenomenoa in our search for pre-natal "life" in the womb. Hopefully, at the same time, we will find the wisdom we need to deal with the urgent and anguishing problems of baby-making. There is simply no intelligent way that we can discuss the wisdom and morality of the termination of a pregnancy without first exploring the basic question of the nature of "life" "in" the fetus from as many perspectives as possible.

Our problem today is, as always, that the dogma or compassion of any one church is not necessarily completely wrong or infallibly right. But the "hell" we can create in our mind, as a result of our beliefs, is only too real. If our beliefs do not correspond with reality, then our hell is also a fiction. The real "hell" is always our own creation, generated in the confines of our minds. We must not let our imaginary hells, created by a cancerous guilt, spread from our minds to take shape in the outside world. Our conscious and responsible action is the only antidote to the fear of "hell" and the hell of fear. The innocent religious misunderstanding and ignorance that gives birth to an inappropriate sense of guilt, regarding the termination of a pregnancy, is for many women the big problem in taking control of their lives.

27

And guilt over abortion is a hell that many seek to put women thru in furthering their private brand of morality. The only difference between the torturing of women yesterday and today is that, today, we don't burn women at the stake for seeking, believing, or acting in accordance with their own, or others, truths. Beyond that, things haven't changed much in two thousand years when it comes to control of women by our mostly male-dominated institutions.

The question of abortion, of planned parenthood and responsible ecological behavior, is too important to be frozen in a "right-to-life" concept that might eventually prove to be a "right-to-disaster." Your body is your private vessel. All decisions concerning that vessel, and who is to gain life through the vessel, are yours alone. But if we are only motivated by fear, then we may make mistakes for ourselves, and our children, that are irreversible. The very purpose of this book is to give all women, and anyone interested in the consequences of birth control, alternate ways of looking at a most perplexing and mysterious phenomenoa - life.

> "And he (the Pope) is against abortion. Why should these people be against abortion? On the one hand they go on talking about the immortality of the soul . . . then why be afraid of abortion? The soul is immortal so there is no sin at all. All that you have done by abortion is you have prevented the soul getting into this body. The soul will find another body. That's what abortion is. The soul says, "May I come in, Madam?" and you say, "no, the place is too crowded. Knock at some other door."[19]

Bhagwan Shree Rajneesh,
Philosophia Ultima

WHOSE LIFE IS IT ANYWAY? -

When it comes to defining "life" in the womb, along with our own rights in defining our responsibilities toward that life, or cellular development as the case may be, there are many questions we might ask the true believers - those who would use their own particular religion and cosmology to override and interfere in the life affairs of another person. So in the interests of women everywhere, let's pose a few in order to put the question of abortion in a wider perspective.

Does the fact that two people have sex to express their love somehow give the incarnate and unborn spirit the absolute right to take up residence in my body?

Must I make a "body" against my will?

Do I get a "life sentence" for a timing error?

Or is it an error? Are we inextricably tied to the incarnating soul? Did I agree to conceive in some other dimension of my existence?

Just what kind of agreement do we make with a new soul? And why can't we make new arrangements?

Is the soul conscious or just magnetically pulled to any conception event happening?

Does the new soul, by itself, "cause" the conception? And can I not uncause it?

Is this soul part of my greater soul or is it someone else's?

Are we (women) prisoners of a Karmic drama beyond our control? Can we not change it?

Does the state or church have a right, or only a responsibility, to guide me in my procreation decisions and not influence secular law?

Is there any doctrine of a Church or state that is necessarily right or infallible? Is it relevant to our situation or wishes?

Are we individuals or slaves? And who are all these people telling me what to do with my body anyway?

The questions go on and on. But the puzzle of life, both inside and outside the womb, is like a series of chinese boxes and atomic dimensions, one more ethereal and hidden than the next. Where and when does "life" begin? Is it in the womb? Or does life ever end? Do we really die? And are we part of god? Are we divorced from god? And why do we blame "god" when we fail to control our reproductive lives?

We know little of how the mother, father, and any fetal soul interact to produce life? But should the mother lose control over her body by a two to one vote? Or should giving life require a unanimous decision from this holy trinity, all of whom are parties to the act?

First, and most importantly, the great mystics of free and unorthodox wisdom down thru the centuries have hinted at the fact that it is the quality of the love, in the union of man and woman, that determines the quality of the soul that we attract to the womb. If real love and intent is missing in the act of procreation, then the quality of the soul attracted is not as advanced. We only do justice to the miracle of childbirth when we consciously come together with our mate and unite with our higher selves in the act of love with the specific intention of asking a soul to enter our lives.

The act of love is our highest prayer. We merge as one to unite our energies for the express purpose of giving birth. And our procreative love is not just recreational sex for the completely necessary and wonderful enjoyment of each other. It is also a special prayer, a communion between mother and father addressed to the unborn who may come into our lives. In our day and age, it is now possible to know the difference between sexual love and procreative love, to enjoy that difference, and act accordingly.

In fact, the idea of a "virgin birth" prevalent in many religions and mythologies, may have originated in the more ancient ideas that the Buddhas and Christs of this world consciously seek rebirth thru parents of a pure heart and love. The "virginity" is thus one of mind and heart, while in the act of procreation, and not necessarily of womb or vagina. It does not need to mean that a man and woman did not come together to procreate but, rather, that their procreation was surrounded by a virginity of mind - a conscious act.

Every religion needs miracles to make their god or saint appear superhuman, otherwise there may be little reason to believe. But in the human species, nature has only one way of uniting the male and female forces. When we try to make our god or savior special, by implying a virgin birth, we fall victim to the ego-disease of having the one and only true faith or savior. The idea of a virgin birth may simply derive from the idea that sex was often thought to be dirty, or bestial in past ascetic and patriarchal eras. Thus, out of doctrinal necessity one's savior must somehow be divorced from this earthy and natural process in order to remain pure and clean.

But if sex is not dirty or sinful then there is no need for a virgin birth. Enlightened men, or women, hardly need a "virgin birth" to justify their existence. The act of conscious and "pure" love in conception will surely suffice.

In effect, the virgin birth idea only serves as a barrier for a man or woman to realize their own christ-like potential. Joseph and Mary, as well as the parents of other enlightened beings, were obviously special as people, and in their procreation, or they would not have given birth to such extraordinary human beings. In effect, the virgin birth story not only de-humanized Jesus but became an intrinsic part of the psychology that has led to centuries of sexual repression and guilt. Only in recent years has our thinking about sex, and related matters like abortion, been released from many centuries of moralistic hysteria over sexual expression.

LIFE BEFORE LIFE -

"Life before Life" is the intriguing title of psychologist Helen Wambach's extraordinary book exploring the answers to questions asked of some 750 subjects under hypnosis about their life experience before birth. Thru new approaches to the mysterious process of hypnosis, researchers are just now beginning to find other methods of coaxing out the memory imprints buried deep in our soul consciousness, our energy-bodies, or our atomic structure as the case may be.

> "90% of the people who come to me flash on images from a past life. I am now convinced that the time has come to study rigorously the plausibility of reincarnation."[20]

Dr. Helen Wambach

Dr. Wambach found that by leading her subjects to an apparent brain-wave cycle of five cycles per second, this brain-wave state deepened the subject's trance, facilitating the unusual responses. What is apparently demonstrated here indicates the reality of the deathless soul and our continuum of soul consciousness thru death and re-birth. We can now examine buried memories indicating the soul's "presence" or absence in the fetal state, as well as critical pre-natal and post-natal experiences of the birth process.

In this respect, the commments from Dr. Wambach's subjects in reliving past-life experiences are revealing as to when the soul or life-force actually inhabits the womb. The participants responded as follows:

> "I attached to the fetus when I decided to meet it in the womb of my mother just before birth."

> "I was attached to the fetus only when I was ready to be born."

> "I was not attached to the fetus until the last breath and expulsion from the womb."

> "I attached to the fetus only after it was fully formed, just before birth."

> "My attachment to the fetus was kind of on and off; it wasn't clear to me when I was actually part of the fetus"

> "I seemed to become aware of the fetus when Mom was five or six months along"

"I was looking down to earth at a fetus. My feeling about
the prospect of being born was that I was waiting and
anxious to see if the body would be okay this time."

These reports indicate a whole new dimension to the
question of "life" "in" the fetus. If such hypnotic recall is valid,
or suggestive of the real state of affairs of the soul or spirit,
then the soul may not be "attached" or "quickened" to the fetus
until the very end of pregnancy. If this is the case, then we
cannot say that aborting a fetus, in the early stages of
pregnancy, is the taking of a life, but rather the postponement
of an incarnation and the halting of cellular development.

Our knowledge of the nature of our being is so limited
as to what the actual reality may be, that we cannot say for
certain what is the true moral meaning of abortion or
preventing birth. Other than our "subjective" reports from the
world of hypnosis, there is absolutely no certainty as to the
presence of life, or consciousness as we know it, residing *in*
the fetus. But based on these reports, we might conclude that
pregnancy represents a vigorous fetal cellular development
taking place in the womb, preparing the way for "life" to enter
the fetal body at the proper moment, at the discretion or
unconscious inclination, of the soul.

As expressed by Dr. Wambach's patients, the time of this
"animation" or ensoulment may not be occuring until our birth
itself or, at the very earliest, when the fetus is fully developed.
With this new information, our viewpoint on the termination
of pregnancy may be liberated from the fears that we are
committing a "murder" or "death" of the life that might have
connected with the body in our womb. It now appears that
this is simply not the case as it applies to a fully conscious
human life. Fetal material is not synonymous with "life" or
consciousness as we know it. Life *enters* the fetal material but
does not grow from it - this is the essential point.

Those who oppose abortion assume the creation of life
"in" the fetus. In fact, it appears that life is not so easily

encapsulated. Our definitions of the morality of abortion must not either be so mistakenly encapsulated.

Some of today's scientists seem convinced that we are just now emerging from a modern spiritual dark ages where a strict materialism dominated "rational" thought. And only now, in the late twentieth century, after the theology-jarring discoveries of relativity and quantum physics, are we again exploring the subtle energies of the unseen realms. After three hundred years of rigid and myopic Newtonian materialism, we are now able to look deeper into the true nature of life, or our series of lives as the case may be. One day perhaps we will come closer to "objectively" measuring the subtle energy realms of spirit vibration, as well as measuring or observing the actual entrance and exit of the soul from the human body - a fact purportedly witnessed and mediated by shamans of many ancient and varied cultural traditions.

Speaking of different dimensions, it is true that humans cannot hear the same high frequencies as a dog, but this does not mean that those other frequencies don't exist, or that they may not be just slightly beyond the realm of our normal comprehension or measurement. And so other realms of conscious existence, like the many and varying frequencies and vibration spectrums of all energy-matter, now appear to us to interpenetrate one another and "exist" in many different dimensions, frequencies, and vibration levels. But they are verifiable only to a capable sensing mechanism, whether human or machine.

In attempting to define our existence in other realms, Ruth Montgomery, the respected journalist with a life long interest in psychic affairs, uses an apt analogy to illustrate the vibrational nature of different dimensions. For example, we can see the blades of an electric fan at rest, and even as they start up they are still visible. But as soon as these revolutions become rapid the blades "disappear" and are now "invisible." And so it is with our bodies and spirit as they change form and vibration rate, like water to steam, in the transition from material to immaterial states of being. If we only experiment with what we can presently see, measure or quantify, we would never reach any further than our current understanding, which may be nothing but ignorance of other more subtle realms of the spirit.

"You and I, Arjuna, have lived many lives. I remember them all. You do not remember."[21]

Krishna,
Bhagavad-Gita

If, in the abortion decision, women believe that they are "creating" a soul at conception then it follows that they are destroying one in the process of abortion. But if this is not the case, and it is true that souls cannot be destroyed, then any societal structure that institutionalizes guilt and prohibits abortion must give way to new realities in which women are responsible, as well as morally blameless, for the regulation of their motherhood.

The exploration of reincarnation is now essential in any abortion debate that attempts to define and understand life while, at the same time, proposing to set moral and legal limitations over a woman's right to terminate a pregnancy. To justify a fetal "right-to-life" must firstly mean there is a fully human animating force, a life or soul, present within the fetus justifying any limitation on the mother's right to reproductive freedom. Without that proof there is no crime, either moral or legal.

And now even the problem of remembrance of past lives might be explained in part by the discovery that the hormone oxytocin, which controls a woman's labor contractions, is known to cause anmesia and loss of memory in laboratory animals. The fetus is bathed in this hormone prior to birth. And just as the chemical ACTH apparently enhances memory, so the relative balance between memory and forgetfulness may be the relationship between the amounts of these chemicals and hormones at birth.

In effect, this dose of oxytocin at birth is then the physical equivalent of the "cup of forgetfulness" from the "River of Lethe" as well as other metaphorical explanations given to this phenomenoa. In this way nature mercifully prepares a clean slate for our conscious memory, leaving past-life memory buried deep in the cellular sub-conscious, to be accessed when our vibrations are subtle enough to digest the information contained.

Dick Stuphen, another innovative and experienced hypnosis researcher and Director of the Hypnosis Center in Scottsdale, Arizona, is the author of numerous books on hypnosis. He has regressed thousands of subjects to their between-lives state-of-being. In his book, "You Were Born To Be Together," he states the following in response to the question; "When does a soul enter a baby's body?"

> "At the time of birth. I often carry an individual forward in regression to the time of his birth in his present lifetime. The situation is always the same. For a long time prior to birth, he/she (the soul) will always be close to his parents-to-be . . . invisible to them, but constantly around them."[22]

In this regard, Dick Stuphen's experience is similar to that of another "past-life therapist," Karl Schlotterbeck. In "Living Your Past Lives" Schlotterbeck relates his experience in this matter:

> "Some of my clients spoke of moving in and out of the body during pregnancy. One man insisted that his soul entered the body at five months of gestation, although he also had memories from conception."[23]

Once again, Stuphen and Schlotterbeck indicate in their research that the soul or spirit is not "in" the fetus but apparently in another dimension intermingled with our own. Rather than pretending that an elephantine consciousness is forced into an atomic pinhead at conception, we might say that the unification of the male and female energy forces at conception may simply create an electro-magnetic attraction enabling a soul to become aware of a potential body in the making. This push-pull, or positive-negative electrical energy charge of attraction or repulsion, may then move a particular spirit to "hover" near the womb. Others might conclude the soul may actually "cause" the conception in a more active way.

Aside from mere speculation involving the nature of our sub-atomic reality and arcane karmic theory, we can move on to examine the strange experiences where people have suddenly, and with a unique objectivity, experienced the separation between body and soul . . . and lived to tell us about it.

NEAR-DEATH EXPERIENCES -

This indication of our being deathless spirits and apart from the premature body in the womb, derived thru the hypnosis experience, is consistent with other more unusual human experiences. For example, many people who have undergone surgery and were supposedly "out" under anesthesia, have been able to recall, and not necessarily under hypnosis, the exact happenings and conversation that occurred between doctors and nurses in the operating room. Even when their eyes were closed things were seen, leading us to conclude that our senses are not necessarily confined to our physical bodies but part of a larger conscious energy field that more adequately defines our true being. And even when our bodies are immobile and "unconscious" we are still "there" as a functioning, yet bodiless consciousness.

In other words, we are not the body. We are more than the body . . . and we are more than the fetus.

As reported in George Gallop Jr.'s book "Adventures in Immortality," and based on his 1981 Gallop poll covering religion, some two million Americans described an out-of-body experience in connection with a near-death. Those people that have had an "NDE" near-death experience, have reported being completely divorced from their bodies and "hovering" over the scene of a severe accident. And in case after case similar stories were told.

37

Due to the extreme trauma and shock of the various accidents experienced, these people had the unique experience of witnessing, in an aware state, their lifeless and then apparently unconscious body being placed in an ambulance, receiving artificial respiration, and seeing the grieving of friends and relatives, etc., even at locations remote from the accident! All of these people were able to recall the exact events and conversation that occurred, and yet here they were supposedly "unconscious" or not "in" the body at the time.

To those who have had such experiences, their concepts of life and death are forever changed. The dis-identification and displacement from the body at those critical and lucid moments opens the possibility of new realms of being like few other human experiences.

For years most western scientists have ignored, rejected outright, or simply refused to take seriously these human events and experiences. In the age of quantum physics, however, this is no longer the case. Our knowledge and our conception, and thus our experience, of events and "reality" has changed. These vivid and real human psychic events, the out-of-body experiences and memories of past lives, all lead us to the conclusion that our minds and consciousness are intermingled with our brains and bodies, for the duration of our earthly life, and not solely resident in the body. The ability to observe ourselves, from another point in space, while we are supposedly unconscious, as in operating table OBE's, is our "objective" evidence of this subjective reality.

> "Better than the life of a hundred years of a person who does not perceive the death-less state, is the short life of a single day of the person who senses that death-less state."[24]

> Buddha,
> The Dhammapada

* * *

"Men occasionally stumble over the truth but most of them pick themselves up and hurry off as if nothing happened."[25]

Winston Churchill

To further elucidate the reality pointing to the separation between the life consciousness and the early fetal material, we can examine one of the most interesting of near-death "OBE" experiences that happened to James Perkins. On a cold and windy day in 1948, while walking along a country highway not far from Chicago, Perkins turned the collar of his coat up against the cold wind as he walked while absorbed in a meditative state. The road was devoid of traffic as he walked along the grassy shoulder of the road on the side that faces traffic. Absorbed in his walking meditation and feeling the wind in his coat, he did not hear the speeding car as it approached from behind at high speed, careening over onto his side of the road and striking his body with tremendous force. In his own words:

"Suddenly, with no note of warning whatsoever, the vehicle struck with tremendous impact, shattering leg bones and hurling me back upon the radiator. The back of my head hit the car's hood with such a loud crack. This sudden force catapulted my body onto the paved highway, landing it on the forehead and face . . ."

"After such a smash, and judging from all outer appearances, I was surely dead. But the compelling interest at this point was not the body, it was my state of consciousness. An ambulance conveyed my body to a hospital where I remained unconscious for five days. The question was whether or not I would live. So far as I was concerned, I had experienced the death of my body in full free action."

"The astonishing truth is that my stream of consciousness, which was engaged in meditation, was not interupted at all! The continuity of my mental pursuit remained unbroken during, and following, the violent change in my physical condition."

"This state of being continued throughout the five days that the physical body, and physical brain, were immobilized and inert. "I" remained consciously alive. The bond with the physical body had not been completely severed . . . the experience was essentially reincarnation in miniature."[26]

James S. Perkins,
Experiencing Reincarnation

For James Perkins, the life of the soul in the state of a formless consciousness, free from the body and consciously experienced during his near-death coma, is no longer a theory. Author of the unique books "Experiencing Reincarnation and "Through Death to Rebirth," Perkins' own experiences lead to his energetic exploration of these new realities he had experienced. Watching his own body being transported to a hospital and operated on, from a mental vantage point outside his body, changed his life. For James Perkins, and many others who have experienced these similar mini-deaths, their concept of reality is forever changed.

With regard to our topic, Perkins also continues with information about the probable realities surrounding the birth process, based on his extensive metaphysical studies and illuminating experiences. He states:

"In the early stages of conception, the immortal self is not present; nor in the early stages of fetal growth in the mother's womb; although there is usually a higher spiritual rapport between the soul of the child and that of the mother throughout the pregnancy period."[27]

In order to be truly "pro-life" we need to examine the nature of this "immortal self" that doesn't die, and that is apparently not "in" the fetus, and who is apparently not capable of being destroyed in the process of abortion. The nature of this "higher spiritual rapport" between mother and fetal/soul is really what we must attempt to analyze and define in order to expand our understanding of the larger implications of the termination of a pregnancy.

There is another fascinating case that reveals the questionable demarcation between death and rebirth, and is expecially pertinent to our own discussion of "life" in the womb. In their exhaustive study on reincarnation, Sylvia Cranston and Carey Williams report the case of William Martin. In 1935, Martin reported this strange experience that happened to him in 1911 at the age of sixteen.

"I was staying about twelve miles away from my home when a high wall was blown down by a sudden gust of wind as I was passing. A huge coping stone hit me on the top of the head. It then seemed as if I could see myself lying on the ground, huddled up, with one corner of the stone resting on my head and quite a number of people rushing toward me. I watched them move the stone and heard all their comments. All this time it apppeared as though I was now disembodied from the form lying on the ground and suspended in mid-air and I could hear everything that was being said . . .

"As they started to carry me, I was then immediately conscious of a desire to be with my mother. Instantly I was at home and father and mother were just sitting down to their midday meal. On my entrance mother sat bolt upright in her chair and said "Bert, something has happened to our boy." She had hardly left the room when a Porter from the railway station knocked at the door with a telegram saying I was badly hurt."

"Then suddenly I was again transported - this time it seemed to be against my wish - to a bedroom, where a woman whom I recognized was in bed, and two other women were quietly bustling around, and a doctor was

41

leaning over the bed. Then the doctor had a baby in his hands. At once I became aware of an almost irresistible impulse to press my face through the back of the baby's head so that my face would come out at the same place as the child's."

"The doctor said, "It looks as though we have lost them both," and again I felt the urge to take the baby's place to show him he was wrong, but the thought of my mother crying turned my thoughts in her direction, when straightaway I was in a railway carriage with her and my father. I was still with them when they arrived at my lodgings and were shown to the room where I had been put to bed. Mother sat beside the bed and I longed to comfort her, and the realization came that I ought to do the same thing I had felt impelled to do in the case of the baby and climb into the body on the bed."

"At last I succeeded, and the effort caused the real me to sit up in my bed fully conscious. Mother made me lie down again, but I said I was all right, and remarked it was odd she knew something was wrong before the porter had brought the telegram."

"She and Dad were amazed at my knowledge. Their astonishment was further increased when I repeated almost word for word some of the conversation they had had at home and in the train. I said I had been close to birth as well as death, and told them that Mrs. Wilson, who lived close to us at home, had had a baby that day, but it was dead because I would not get into its body. We subsequently learned that Mrs. Wilson died on the same day at 2:05 p.m. after delivering a stillborn girl."[28]

The phenomenoa of stillbirth, of babies born dead without the breath of life brought by an animating soul, is often a medical mystery. The fetus can develop for months and then nature, or the soul, calls a halt to the process. In other words, souls may very well have their own reasons for not showing up for their own birth! Can we not say that it takes a willing mother, and a willing soul, to produce life. But that neither mother, nor soul, has the right to entrap the other against their conscious will. Without the conscious consent of the mother to give birth, a fetus in the womb is essentially a parasite . . . an unwanted soul.

Another classic case somewhat similar to Perkin's experience is reported in Ian Wilson's book "Mind Out of Time" and summarized in Colin Wilson's book "Afterlife."[29] In May of 1957, Joanna and Jacqueline Pollock, two sisters aged eleven and six, were walking along a road in a small town in England. A car rode up on the pavement and struck the girls, killing them instantly along with a nine-year old boy. The father of the girls, John Pollock, became obsessed with the idea that their death was a sort of punishment for him but that somehow the girls would be reborn again to his wife.

Amazingly, some eighteen months later, on October 4, 1958 twin daughters were born. Jennifer, in fact, had a thin white line across her forehead exactly where her dead sister Jacqueline had a scar - the result of falling off a bicycle. She also possessed a birthmark on her hip identical to the one Jacqueline had in the same spot. Inexplicably there was no similar mark on the other twin even though they were monozygotic twins - formed from the same egg! In these highly unlikely circumstances a theory of coincidence fails. The force of spirit enabled the return . . . what else can we say?

Colin Wilson goes on to relate that three years later, the father took them back to Hexham, the scene of the previous accident, and from where they had moved when the twins were four months old. They behaved as if they were quite familiar with the place. One suddenly said to the other: "The school's around the corner." "That's where we used to play in the playground" "The swings and slides over there." They correctly identified the house they had lived in as well.

Also, the toys of the dead sisters had been stored in an attic and when the twins were four they let them play with them. The Pollocks were further convinced when Jennifer replied immediately: "There's Mary . . . And this is my Suzanne." Jennifer had correctly named the names of "her" dolls. Wilson goes on to relate that the Pollock's were relieved when at the age of five the past life memories of the twins began to recede allowing for a more normal childhood.

APPOINTMENT WITH A SOUL? -

It appears that the rapport between a woman capable of giving birth, and the discarnate soul seeking rebirth, may be looked upon as an agreement that takes some form of consent on both sides. If it is right for both parties, and the timing is right, then the mother can begin to form a body for the soul's incarnation. And if the time is not right for the mother, then she is free not to form a body, or be forced to form a body in her womb. The soul can wait. And even if a body is formed, if it is not right for the soul, then the soul may also leave, thus leading to miscarriage or stillbirth.

We might say that the soul aborts itself, in effect, if it doesn't like the conditions, or if it is there to suffer some karmic fate. In that case, we can then say, in all fairness, that this process must work both ways or the mother is just a used and abused bystander. The mysteries of conception, birth, and karmic relation, may be considerably beyond our present and "normal" comprehension, but we can certainly learn from the revealing experiences and perceptions of others as to what the rights and responsibilities of prospective mothers might be given these new insights into the nature of the fetal-soul existence.

And speaking of perceptions, Harold Waldwin Percival is a little-known western mystic whose masterpiece, "Thinking and Destiny," ranks with the greats of eastern literature. Over a twenty-year span between 1912 and 1932, the book was dictated to an associate after his enlightening experiences and metaphysical research created a particularly vivid and exact insight into the nature of our beings. Percival states:

"Every human body that comes into this world is fashioned in its mother according to the form, the soul, which enters her body through her breath and causes the conception of the body which is to be fashioned. At birth the physical life-breath of the breath-form enters the infant body, thereupon the breath-form performs its function as the "living soul" of the body."

"The selection of a family and of the time for building the body often involves many problems. The physical destiny of the doer-in-the-body must fit in with the innumerable events in the life of others and with public matters. Time, condition, and place are all-important. To be born too soon or too late would mean being a misfit in the social order. The time for the beginning of a certain body must be selected so as to allow the cycles of its own life to intersect cycles in the lives of others with whom it will be connected."[30]

Harold Waldwin Percival

Indeed, time, condition, and place are important! And can we not say that it is the mother's duty to determine what the right time, condition, and place are to be?

In Percival's description, the breath-form, or unit of nature containing the hologram of the old/new form, is then carried on the pranic winds of atomic particles that invade and permeate our bodies. And at, or near, the completion of the sexual act, the sub-atomic dance of energies is set in motion. And whether completely chaotic and random, or due to the karmic affinity and relation of some greater part of our beings involved, the woman is now pregnant.

But of even more importance is the fact that the new soul has a duty to fit in with the mother's life plan, and the mother also has a duty, in her own time and place, to provide the best possible circumstances for the soul. If it is otherwise, one or both are abused. We might also conclude that it is not our duty, or society's, to intervene and take charge of these cycles of relationship, of which we have so little understanding, for the supposed "benefit" of either mother or child.

We might say, then, that to avoid a sort of cosmic rape by a soul eager for life, the mother should consciously consent to the presence of new life in her womb. If thru ignorance, or faulty birth control, or sheer pressure from one's mate, a woman finds herself pregnant, there is then an important lack of conscious and deliberate consent to become a mother. If she is not a willing participant, but rather a forced guilty one, there is an important lack of a spiritual bond, or agreement, implicit in the pregnancy.

This message of conscious consent is an important ingredient in successful and responsible motherhood. If a Church or government attempts to force consent on the mother, and insist that by engaging in sex she has already tacitly assented to birth, then the mother is, in effect, raped for the benefit of another soul. The penalty for sex is an unwanted child. But does the soul wish to come into the world where it is not wanted, as a penalty, as a result of faulty contraception, or irresponsible and maybe even violent sex? In the absence of prior consent to motherhood, will the mother want to nurture an unwanted soul?

> "On the other hand, souls come into these bodies for needs of their own. Thus, if victimization does occur, it could be said to be happening on both sides."[31]
>
> Karl Schlotterbeck,
> Living Your Past Lives

Precisely. By forcing women to undergo pregnancy, thru fear, guilt, and "religious" artifice, we simply destroy any voluntary contractual consent between the parties, the mother and the new soul. Is this moral or compassionate? Perhaps we can safely say that this other-worldly "agreement" may not be part of our normal conscious mind, but that is not to say it should not exist on our everyday plane of existence upon which we are fully conscious. How many dimensions are we? How many "mansions" in our souls? On what basis can society justify intervening in the spiritual relationship between mother and fetus? Regardless of the answers to these seldom considered questions, we must live, and live rightly, in our world as it exists today, with adequate consideration for the world of tomorrow - a world of limited resources.

And can we not say that we must be conscious and responsible for the conception and incarnation of a soul according to our best instincts and life plan? Should not new life be brought into this world under the best and most loving of circumstances, and not dragged in under the worst of life conditions, as in the many cases of teenage pregnancy?

If we assume the fact of this ethereal, and perhaps unconscious, communication between the mother and the new/old discarnate soul, we are certainly justified in saying that it is not moral for a soul to rape his or her way into existence by taking up residence in the reluctant mother's womb. There must be some form of mutual agreement, however intuitively that fact may impress itself upon the mother's psyche. The fact that conception accidentally occurs does not give another soul the inalienable right to enforce motherhood upon the unsuspecting, unwilling, and unprepared. The choice must be the mother's.

> "The soul within the fetus cannot be destroyed by any kind of abortion."[32]
>
> Seth

what about reg. death?

And if a soul does not die, then we cannot say that we "take a life" by the act of abortion. Who has been killed? We can delay the incarnation of the soul, but "death" here is impossible. In this cosmology, the act of terminating a pregnancy is quite a different affair from that of people who believe that life begins at conception and ends at death.

The information that we obtain from the disembodied and "channeled" intelligences such as Seth (Jane Roberts) and

Emmanuel (Pat Rodegast), among others, is both persuasive and compassionate in a larger sense. And whether these beings are separate entities, or a larger and "deeper" god-like aspect of their channel persons, is not of the utmost importance. As Ram Dass comments in the preface to "Emmanuel's Book," using the words of Sri Ramana Marharshi, "God, Guru and Self are one." In this sense, we are all connected to the ultimate wisdom, only some hear it better than others. On the act of abortion Emmanuel states:

> "One must be fully aware of every act in one's life, the act of conception no less than the act of abortion . . . But when, after profound prayer and consideration there is a need to terminate a pregnancy it is not an unforgivable act. If it is done with willingness to learn, it then becomes a useful act . . ."

> "I know that no soul is ever destroyed. I know that when a soul chooses to be born, it will be born. The soul is wise and would not inhabit a body if it were not to come to term."[33]

Emmanuel

From Emmanuel's cosmic viewpoint, a soul is not subject to karmic torture by the termination of a pregnancy - he/she is not *there* to suffer! In a larger sense, the compassionate soul is certainly not there in the womb to see the mother suffer thru an unwanted birth. A mother is a part of nature. Indeed, she is nature - gone wrong or gone right. For this reason, the expression, and timing, of the mother's creativity must be firmly in her control.

And to the extent of their participation in the act of conception, we can say that the soul too must accept part of the blame for unintended pregnancies *and* their termination.

> "For a human soul, the greatest of self-inflicted wrongs is to make itself (so far as it is able to do so) a kind

of tumour or abscess on the universe; for to quarrel
with circumstances is always a rebellion against nature
- and nature includes the nature of each individual
part"[34]

> Marcus Aurelius,
> Meditations

But perhaps another larger misunderstanding in this
mysterious process is our assumption that this "new" soul is
not a part of our own greater personhood or "triune" self. Is
the new being just more of our "stuff" or solely his own? Or
will he/she be a mixture of cells and consciousness from many
distinct and separate consciousness's and countless previous
incarnations? Are we truly distinct persons, or a blend of
previous being's consciousness's and particles that defy our
notions of complete individual discreteness and separateness?
What and who remains and endures within us? Are we just
"I" alone? How many I's are we? If we state "I am" are we
just indulging in an earthbound illusion? Is the fetus/soul just
another part of our larger selves, rather than a discrete and
unrelated entity? On other levels, the beings, or being, may
be as varied as the stars or as singular as the sun.

We might say that we are not our children in the sense
that we are not comprised of the exact same components or
units of nature. We may have been constructed from the
elementary particles previously in use by other levels of
existence, whether it be a rock, an animal, or another human.
The imprints or "memories" upon those minute units, from
which our physical bodies are built, may be different and
distinct, or they may share and blend the information and
experience of existence thus blurring the lines of selfhood. The
particles and cells in our bodies may carry memories that are
not "ours" but also the undigested experience of others. And
just as the astral body of the new life is within, or surrounded
by the astral body of the mother, where our "I" begins and

leaves off is hard to discern. Whose life are we anyway? And whose greater-being will eventually reside in the fetus?

In this sense, our ideas about the uniqueness of our personhood and individuality may not reflect reality in a larger sense. If such is the case, we may not be "killing" a "new" or "old" unrelated soul in the act of abortion, but merely postponing the incarnation of another greater and related part of ourselves, another identity spun off from our own greater consciousness. Here, our earthbound legal notions of discrete "personhood" become increasingly fuzzy as do the metaphysics.

But just as sub-atomic particles, or consciousness itself, seem to have no boundaries, we cannot say where the "I" or "Thou" begins and the "we" ends. How many I's are we? Are we each unique souls or, perhaps, just unique sub-souls of greater selves? How much unique individuality, apart from ourselves, is in the womb? Is the new life in the fetus another one of our "own" persons from our greater self? Or is the fetus a unique new self from another discrete and greater self? As Seth states in this regard:

> "Each greater personage takes several parts, or brings forth several psychic children, who spring to life as human beings."

> "The soul, or this greater personage, does not simply send out an old self in new clothes time and time again, but each time a new, freshly-minted, self that then develops and goes its own way. That self rides firmly, however, in the great flight of experience, and feels within itself all of those other fully unique versions that also fling their way into existence."

> "Now remember: You are one earth version of your own greater personage."[35]

Seth

We might ask whether these new "parts" of ourselves always come into our own wombs, or those of other greater selves, for the pure sake of experience. Does the "other" actually exist?

50

Is the expansion of each greater self in conflict, or harmony, with others? Are they not simply multiplying, for experience sake, at my expense, as a reluctantly pregnant woman might ask? And can we not then prayerfully ask them, or our own greater selves as the case may be, to "fling their way into existence" in another time and circumstance? Or into another womb?

Along with the voices of the old and new mystics, and the disembodied channel entities like Seth and Emmanuel, the "mythologies" and experience of "primitive" peoples on planet earth have much to say about soul relations on other planes of our existence. Perkins relates this revealing story about the Australian Aborigine's views on birth and incarnation:

> "With primitive people ... sometimes their own mythologies represent tried and true memories of nature's processes. An interesting example is provided by certain Aboriginal people of Australia. Among some tribes, the mythology of birth is linked with a "DreamTime" agreement that is literally an appointment between a reincarnating soul and the parents who are to give it a physical body ...
>
> "The belief is held by some, that children are not born merely of sexual intercourse, but by means of the parents going into the "dreaming," or into the bush, and then contacting the soul who wants reincarnation through them ... the belief is that only through such an appointment does pregnancy become possible."[36]

If, in other realities, it is an appointment we are making with the soul, then deciding to terminate a pregnancy is merely cancelling the appointment. And certainly, in good conscience, we must do so at the earliest possible date. But, most importantly, we can change the date, taking control of our lives and choosing to give birth when circumstances are better. Thus, in good conscience, we may decide to give birth when we are able to more adequately provide and care for the new soul. This is a necessary, positive, and moral step in a

51

motherhood career, both for the mother and for the lives that we eventually bring into this world. The soul, after all, has all the time in the world for its purposes. But we mortals, bound by space and time, have a relatively short time span in which to create a meaningful earth-life.

WAITING TO BE BORN -

Helen Wambach, Dick Stuphen, Karl Schlotterbeck and James Perkins are by no means the only investigators of the validity of reincarnation and the after-death-before-birth states of consciousness. Dr. Joel L. Whitton, former Chief Psychiatrist of the Toronto school system, and his journalist colleague, Joel Fisher, have published the intriguing results of Dr. Whitton's own life-long interest in hypnosis research. Although "objective" proof is impossible in wholly subjective internal situations, the similarity of results, from various researchers working with a variety of patients in various cultures around the world, is significant and today lends considerable credibility to the rediscovery of much ancient knowledge about the many levels of our spiritual reality.

In this "new" age of scientific and philosophical enlightenment, it appears we are only rediscovering other dimensions of life previously explored and chronicled by such ancient and venerable texts as the Egyptian and Tibetan Books of The Dead, wherein the process of death and rebirth, having been experimented with and observed over thousands of years, are described in detail.

Using his particular brand of past-life therapeutic techniques, Dr. Whitton inadvertently came across a patient's between-life disembodied state. In one session, in response to an unusual inquiry, he noticed a very sudden and complete change, a total relaxation in the facial expression of one of his patients. As his subject's body relaxed totally, her voice changed to a dreamy monotone and the session continued with the following exchange.

"I'm in the sky . . . I can see a farmhouse and a barn . . .
it's early, early morning. The sun . . . is low and making,
making . . . making long shadows across the burnt
fields . . .'

Dr. Whitton could hardly believe what he was hearing.
She wasn't supposed to be "in the sky." "What are you
doing up in the air," asked the puzzled hypnotist?

"I'm . . . waiting . . . to be . . . born. I'm watching,
watching what my mother does."

Dr. Whitton continued. What is your name?

"I . . . have . . . no . . . name."[37]

Life Between Life

This state of "metaconsciousness" and recall of the soul's
life in the bardo plane (cosmic limbo), occupied by the "dead"
soul after death and prior to rebirth, is, with present day
methods and attitudes, not what we would call objectively
verifiable. And these experiences may forever escape the realm
of verifiability and may never be measured by anything other
than personal experience. But, again, that is not to say that
some forms of our "subjective" experience may not indicate
the true nature of things.

"It is likely that the Roman Catholic idea of purgatory
is derived from the ancient Greek interpretations of
a discarnate life between incarnations. According to
Rudolph Steiner, the founder of Anthroposophy, the
purgatory of the Catholic Church is a recognizable,
if seriously inaccurate picture of the between-life state
where the soul weans itself of all desires, appetites,
and passions."[38]

Dr. Joel Whitton/Joel Fisher,
Life Between Life

53

Regarding the entire question of reincarnation, Fisher relates: "To disbelieve is, of course, not to disprove, and to believe is not to prove." We can also say this is the case with the proof of life "in" the fetus, especially for those who discount the hypnosis studies as "verifiable" proof of animation or ensoulment. Belief that life, as opposed to fetal development, somehow "begins" at conception is, like reincarnation, difficult or impossible to verify.

However, in Dr. Wambach's hypnosis experiments, her subjects responded to the question of "When does your soul enter the fetus?" The responses of her 750 subjects, who were carefully selected in various locations known *not* to be hotbeds of "new-age" credulity, were nearly unanimous on one essential point. She explains:

> "They felt that the fetus was not truly a part of their consciousness. They still existed, fully conscious, as an entity apart from the fetus . . .

> "89 per cent of all the subjects responding said they did not become a part of the fetus or involved with the fetus until after six months of gestation. Even then, many subjects reported being "in and out" of the fetal body.

> "The largest group in the sample, 33 per-cent, said that they did not join the fetus, or experience inside the fetus, until just before or during the birth process."[39]

So according to the knowledge gleaned from our greater selves, our inner recesses accessed via hypnosis, we exist as an entity apart from the fetus, as a consciousness too vast to occupy the limiting confines of the premature fetal material. The new soul then chooses to enter at his or her "right" time at or near the birth event.

In light of this information, we must ask who, and more likely what, it is that is being harmed in the more than 95 per cent of abortions that occur before sixteen weeks of gestation?

To continue, the list of serious investigators of the mysterious before-between-after life states also includes the well-known psychic Edgar Cayce. Also known as the "The Sleeping Prophet" from Virginia City, Cayce's depression-era readings from the trance state truly astounded many medical observers around the world. And, more importantly, his trance observations coincide neatly with the later results from Dr. Wambach's and Dr. Whitton's research. Consciously commenting on life in the womb at a church forum, Cayce once stated:

> "I do not believe that a soul enters the body until the breath of life is drawn. The soul doesn't enter at conception."[40]

Edgar Cayce

And yet another sceptical hypnosis researcher, Dr. Alexander Cannon, regressed 1382 volunteers to explore these past-life "theories." In 1950, after years of research, Dr. Cannon related in "The Power Within" the following:

> "For years the theory of reincarnation was a nightmare to me and I did my best to disprove it and even argued with my trance subjects to the effect that they were talking nonsense. Yet as the years went by one subject after another told me the same story in spite of different and various beliefs. Now well over a thousand cases have been investigated and I have to admit now there is such a thing as reincarnation."[41]

* * *

> "It is no more surprising to be born twice than it is to be born once."[42]

Voltaire

* * *

"Reincarnation is making a comeback."[43]

Anonymous

The relevant ideas from reincarnation research, and past-life therapy, all seem to corroborate the point that the soul does not necessarily enter the fetus at conception, but at a much later stage, either after a fairly complete fetal development, or at birth with the first autonomous breath by the new soul. But notions of *where* exactly "life" resides prior to birth are not really possible for us to decide. We simply do not know the answers to these most important questions. And that is precisely the point. We cannot then prohibit abortion on the basis of unverifiable assumptions about "life" in the womb.

The reincarnation research certainly calls into question, if not totally contradicting, the hard-line Church position that "life" somehow "begins" at conception, and therefore that abortion is the "taking" of a life, the destruction of a soul, and unquestionably wrong. It would appear that this is simply not the case. In light of this research, it appears that there is no verifiable legal or moral justification, other than a blind religious dogma, that can truthfully serve as a basis for prohibiting the termination of a pregnancy in accordance with the mother's wishes. At most we might say that we are all, by the very fact of our existence here, truly ignorant in the ways of the spirit and the many mansions of our greater existence.

Although the subject under examination is not exactly the validity of reincarnation, once again, I only hope to call into question the rigid dogma and "truths" that so many fundamentalist churches propose as the only reality concerning the "life" of the fetus. No one is requiring "moral majority" members to convert to new-age cosmologies. And certainly Catholics and other fundamentalist christians are perfectly free to act in private matters in accordance with their own beliefs. But too many today appear unwilling to allow others the right to act in accordance with their own personal and alternative understandings, or experience, of life's most mysterious processes. Theological fascism has no legitimate place in our bedrooms, our hospitals, our courtrooms, our schools, or inside a mother's womb?

WHO IS IT THAT DIES? -

> "Thirst for life is inherent in the very nature of life, which is absolute existence. Although indestructible by nature, by false identification with its destructible instrument, the body, consciousness imbibes a false apprehension of its destructibility. Because of that false identification it tries to perpetuate the body, and that results in a succession of rebirths. But however long these bodies may last, they eventually come to an end and yield to the self, which alone eternally exists."[44]

Sri Ramana Maharshi

One of the great indian sages of the twentieth century, Sri Ramana Maharshi, thus succinctly explains our own myopia in understanding the relation between body and soul. If we are immortal souls, occupying a succession of bodies in our journey back to the source, who is it that dies when the fetus is aborted? And if there is no "death" there can only be a postponed "life." The concept, or reality, of an eternal self makes the taking of pre-natal life impossible by definition, especially where is not yet a connection, or at best a tenuous connection, between body and soul as is the case in early fetal development.

What is important in our discussion is how religious doctrine affects the judgment of women in their decision to exercise their legitimate right to terminate an unwanted pregnancy. But fundamentalist religious beliefs, with their questionable doctrine of one life combined with the mentally torturing threats of eternal damnation to life in a fiery hell (for mostly sexually-related "immoral" acts), most certainly affects the pregnancy decisions of millions of women. Does fear alone produce good judgment? Is this fearful decision, to avoid a questionable future retribution, not essentially selfish? Is this atmosphere of judgment and damnation conducive to concern for the child, *or* is it simply fear for the moral status of the mother?

Today, each birth decision begins to ultimately affect each one of us thru the subtle interactions in our limited biosphere in an already crowded world. A fatalistic and irresponsible approach to ceaseless human reproduction, for "religious" reasons, will only serve to perpetuate human misery and environmental problems.

Also of great import is how legislators, working with only one religious interpretation of "life" and "murder" infuse the actions of the state with a particular religious viewpoint. With a wide variety of religious insights now available to today's global citizen, and many new scientific revelations regarding the nature of our human universe, the abortion decision can be seen in a new light, free from the paralyzing guilt of "sin" based on parochial and dubious religious realities.

This is not to say that life be taken lightly, on the contrary, I propose that it be taken *more seriously*. We must take it so seriously that we only bestow it purposely, in the best of circumstances, and as conscious and consenting adults in accordance with our own understanding of fetal life and responsible parenthood. Otherwise, we may be asking the new soul to stew in our own juice, and suffer our own fates instead of setting the stage for compassionate conception and life-long caring.

For purposes of our discussion, I use the examples of these unique human experiences to illustrate the notion that the fetus in the womb may not actually be all that we call "life." If our pre-natal consciousness does not reside in the fetus, especially in the early months of pregnancy, how can we have a sin in the act of abortion if no "person" is affected? It is this crucial point in our argument about the unknowables of "life" in the womb that should give pause to those who consider abortion to be "murder" and who, because of that belief, then condemm or prevent others from acting in their own best interests based on one's own cosmology and understanding of the rights and duties involved in motherhood.

In attempting to outlaw abortion, how can we legislate against the unknowable and the unproveable? How may churches condemm women seeking abortion, particulary if their own dogma may obscure or deny the true nature of reality? If the existence of a fully-human "life" in the fetus is not subject to verification, and thus unknowable and unprovable, then it is most certainly unlegislateable; and because it is unknowable and unproveable, we cannot condemm abortion. We can't refuse others the right to their own cosmology. But those who seek to protect "life" "in" the wombs of so many reluctant mothers may not understand, or even wish to allow others to recognize, the facts of life as others see them.

This lack of compassion and human understanding translates into efforts by others to make their own belief, your belief, thru the force of law. By focusing on the abstract principle of a fetal right-to-life, we deny the rights of a fully-human being . . . the mother. But should a democratic and pluralistic society enforce only one religious version of life and "compassion" on innocent women where the outcome can be so tragic? And then call it moral?

If these "mystic" experiences and revelations do indeed represent the true nature of our reality, then what can we say about the nature of life in the womb in the early months? And again, if there is no soul residing within the fetus well into the middle months of gestation, whose rights are being violated and what entity is being harmed?

> "Your soul is not inside your body . . . your body is inside your soul."[45]

> Alan Watts

* * *

> "Consciousness does indeed evolve form . . . form does not evolve consciousness."[46]

> Seth

Is there a soul consciousness, on a par with a living human being, *within* the fetus whose "life" we can say we are "ending" by terminating a pregnancy?

The fact that a fetus may move or respond to an electrical stimulation, like the "reactive" flesh of a severed frog leg touched by an electric current, does not necessarily indicate the presence of a person or soul "in" the fetus. And if our full consciousness is outside the body prior to birth, how is it affected by abortion? How do we know that a soul would (or would care to) inhabit a "body" in the uterus before the fetus is completely formed? And speaking of god's plan, how do we know that the mother, in having the abortion, is not acting in accordance with some higher and pre-ordained karmic plan? The truth is, we don't know. But many pretend that they do, and they intend their pretense to become law.

Will the Supreme Court judge who can "objectively" answer these questions please stand up and place your right hand on the Bible, the Koran, the Dhammapada, the Bhagavad-Gita, etc.? Can we not say that only with all religious perspectives sworn in and considered may we even begin to judge, if judgment is to be in our hands, and in our realm. It is said that some gods are well known to have reserved vengeance and judgment unto themselves.

How then can we only have one holy book and, in effect, one-religion justice? In the cosmic court of law, how can we swear in only one religion, and one parochial "truth" as the sole witness against the moral integrity of the mother? We can do so only if we wish to discriminate against others and subject them to our own moral opinions. But motherhood must remain a private affair or all manner of injustices will occur in the name of religion and morality.

These questions of soul and "life" are difficult and present perhaps "objectively" unanswerable questions. And the concept of personhood in the womb is, by human definition and sheer difficulty of detection, certainly subjective. But that is the point. We have now seen that there is a great deal of research, human experience, and a wide variety of religious understanding that does not validate the idea that life, or soul, or spirit, either begins with conception or ends with abortion.

In fact, life as soul may not begin or end at all. And science is now beginning to piece together the new paradigm illustrating that life, as consciousness, endures endlessly, only changing its form and vibration rate as it moves thru "death" from a gross material to a more gaseous and immaterial state. The countless ghostly "visitations" by "dead" people to their loved ones at the moment of "death" are too numerous to recount. In times of crisis, the sheer force of spirit is beyond our present comprehension.

Thus, in the after-death and before-birth state the I-ego-desire-memory comlex of our soul comes to occupy regions beyond the measurement capabilities of today's science. And just as the "laws" of thermodynamics state that no matter is ever destroyed but only changes form, so the soul continues with or without a body. And, as we have seen from the memories evoked in hypnosis research, it is clear the soul-mind may not be "within" the fetus until birth, or shortly before. It is precisely for this reason, the sheer uncertainty of our determining with any precision the time of ensoulment, that the drive to regulate abortion has been shelved so many times in past centuries, even by the Catholic Church.

> "In actual fact, the time of ensoulment or hominization has never been definitely fixed by the Catholic church and is still argued about today. According to one authority, Father John Mahoney, the Second Vatican Council deliberately set aside the question of when the spiritual soul was infused. Also, the Roman Congregation for the Doctrine of Faith acknowledges disagreement about this point and does not adjudicate, yet Roman Catholics are required to behave as though ensoulment occurred at fertilization."[47]
>
> Edwin Kenyon,
> The Dilemma of Abortion

The Church itself has often not even been able to decide what it is they believe (as if they could make nature conform to their decision). And yet they are willing to tell a poor and scared young girl, one who is totally unprepared for motherhood, that she will go to hell if she obtains an abortion. The real "hell" and sin may very well be her having the baby at the wrong time and in all the wrong circumstances. This may be a hell not only for the mother but also for the child and society as well. The "hell" of being pressured into having the unwanted baby is so often a reality in our world today. In preventing abortion, society only punishes the unwanted unborn, and condemms the unwilling immature mother?

Thus there are times when religious dogma can be a cruel mother. But motherhood must be its own religion and the mother must be her own inspiration. The mother is the best judge of what is right and wrong in her own unique set of circumstances. However, without the knowledge of alternative realities and religious viewpoints, many women, and especially young girls, are the psychic prisoners of a guilt-stricken conscience created largely thru a limited, or even censored, religious perspective. After the fact of unwanted pregnancy and before abortion, women are stuck in hell . . . a world full of intolerant people.

> "This is why it is so important to develop self- awareness
> to the depths of your ability so that no creation can
> come into your life without your having made the
> choice."[48]

Emmanuel

Even the channeled voices counsel us that *we* must be the ones who decide about our creativity. Awareness in all our acts will, by its very nature, help us to self-correct the course of our lives and strengthen our future behavior. We can decide the seasons in which the seeds fall from our tree.

"Trees bear seeds. Some fall nearby. And then others are carried by the wind some distances into areas that the tree itself, for all of its height, could not perceive. So identities throw off seeds of themselves in somewhat the same fashion. Identities have free choice, so they will pick their environments or birthplaces . . ."

"And that arithmetic of consciousness is not annihilated. It is multiplied and not divided . . . your own identity sends out strands of itself constantly. These mix constantly with other strands. And the constant interchange that exists biologically means that the same physical stuff that composes a man or a woman may be dispersed, and later form a toad, a star- fish, a dog or a flower. It may be then distributed into numberless different forms . . ."

"You can draw the lines where you will for convenience's sake, but each identity retains its individuality and inviolate nature even while it constantly changes."[49]

Seth

* CHAPTER TWO *

- THE WAY IT IS -

MEDICAL MARVELS AND MODERN PROBLEMS -

Aside from the spiritual arguments about the timing of the "ensoulment" of the fetus, in the deciding to give birth, or complete a pregnancy, we must examine the world we live in and, in good conscience, evaluate our abilities to provide for new life that we intend to bring into our world. When we do examine the changes in our world mankind has wrought in just the last century we have more than enough reason to ponder our responsibilites to our children and the world around us.

With the medical marvels of the twentieth century, we have almost eliminated most of mother nature's "killer" diseases. By controlling the death rate of children and the elderly, and compassionately saving millions from disease and starvation, we have intervened in Mother Nature's own natural process of population control. From the beginning of time, diseases have functioned as her primary method of population control. But now we have worked miracles in both saving and extending the lives of infant children and older people. As a result, there are now more people surviving than ever before at both ends of the population spectrum.

In effect, planet earth's natural birth control has been rendered useless as a result of our medical miracles. Disease after disease had been curtailed and is no longer in nature's arsenal of population control devices. At the same time, we humans must not fail to understand and assume responsibility

for the other half of that control . . . birth control. We are
playing god on one side, that of death control, but closing our
eyes to the other side, that of birth control. We are not taking
our god-like responsibility, for the proper management of
planetary population, seriously enough.

A world that is now in the midst of an unprecedented
environmental crisis, and adds a billion people to the earth's
population in just thirteen years is simply not facing its
responsibilities. The truth may be that there are no gods but
us, as individuals, to make the crucial one-by-one, birth by birth,
decisions about overpopulation.

ARE WE NOW THE GODS? -

"Then the Lord God said, "Behold the man has become
like one of us, knowing good and evil."[1]

Genesis 3:22

* * *

"One God and Father of all, who is above all, and through
all, and in you all."[2]

Ephesians 4:6

* * *

"And the serpent said unto the woman, Ye shall not
surely die . . . For god doth know that in the day ye
eat thereof, then your eyes shall be opened, and ye
shall be as gods, knowing good and evil."[3]

Genesis 3:2,5

Knowledge itself (waiting to be plucked off the tree that
God himself put in our garden), and the awareness of our
human responsibilities, must open our eyes to the realities
around us and the condition of our garden - planet earth.

In centuries past, mother nature, or if you prefer, God,
"killed" millions of both living and unborn children thru disease,
famine and disaster. In past centuries, the average life-span

66

was brutally short. And with incessant warfare many more died in battle. Under these circumstances, the ultimately dangerous population explosion we are witnessing today simply could not take place.

In our recent past many children died in childbirth or early infancy. It was not uncommon for only two to four children, out of ten or twelve, to survive past their tenth birthday to become adults, often to lose their life in wars. Mother nature had to be both fertile, for survival's sake, as well as cruel and vigilant in her population control. But in our modern era, we have now short-circuited Mother Nature's controls over human life in more ways than one. Like it or not, we are now co-gods in both the creation and destruction of life, including all species and not just our own.

"The average life-span in the United States has increased twenty six years in this century forty-seven years to seventy-three."[4]

United Press International

Along with the decrease in the age of fertility of today's young women, and the tremendous rate of increase in infant survival, there has been an incredible change in the average life-span of the older person. People everywhere are living longer than ever before. The incidence of families with four living generations is becoming commonplace. Our global population is under pressure from both ends of the age spectrum.

As man has intervened and stopped the process of natural control, we have taken on a responsibility for the control of our population that we have yet to fully recognize. We cannot prevent death without preventing birth. There is no death control without birth control. We are now fully responsible for the balance and quality of life on earth - God has been removed from the equation. We are now responsible for the arithmetic of population and poverty.

"A society which practices death control must also practice birth control."[5]

Dr. John Rock,
Catholic Physician

So we have already played god on one end, the end of preventing death and overcoming mother nature's "natural" methods of population control. Man's intervention in nature has upset the ages-old natural balance and we must now begin to act on our new duties, that of preventing unnecessary and unwanted births. If we don't population will continue to careen out of control and the world will degenerate year by year at a frightening and accelerating pace. And this comes down to the decisions that you and I, and now billions of others, make regarding bringing new life into being on our already crowded planet.

Wisdom now requires that we assume our godly roles in order to create and maintain the best possible environment for life on our small planet. In the absence of responsible birth control, we must not shirk from the thought of pregnancy termination out of fear, guilt, or superstition. Otherwise, billions of private "moral" decisions will simply add up to the ultimate immorality - the destruction of god's green earth.

"Let this mind be in you, which was also in Christ Jesus; who, being in the form of God, thought it not robbery to be equal with God."[6]

Philippians 2:5,6

THE EARTH EXPLODES WITH PEOPLE -

To answer any of our many questions about the growing effects of population on our small planet, it makes sense to put some historical perspective on the matter. On our shrinking island called planet earth, there is no question that we live in a new and different world from that of just a few decades ago. We need only consider that in 1960, for example, the population of the world was 3 billion people, and by 1998, at present rates, the population will soon pass 6 billion. In 38 short years, the earth's population will have doubled again, and with staggering environmental consequences. At this rate, we are adding nearly a billion people every thirteen years! This rate of increase is now catastrophic for mankind and for the future of humane living standards.

Consider for a moment the impact of every additional billion people on the earth. The following may help you realize the magnitude of these numbers.

FOR EVERY BILLION PEOPLE ADDED TO THE EARTH'S POPULATION, WE ARE ADDING ONE THOUSAND CITIES OF ONE MILLION EACH.

Each year, at present rates of growth, an estimated 85 such "cities" are now appearing on the globe. Never has the earth been in such a suicidal race to outright ecological catastrophe and large-scale famine. In many countries, we are already well down the road to ecological ruin via excessive population growth. And without population control, today's children may grow up in a hopelessly crowded world competing for already scarce and overburdened resources. The incredible technological promise of the twenty-first century is quickly being aborted by the rapid doubling of the world's population and nature's limited ability to cope. Just how scary this phenomenal rise in population has become can only be seen by reviewing the historical timing of our world population growth. The following chart is instructive in this regard.

"Estimated Timing of Each Billion of Population"

First Billion	2-5 million years	1800 A.D.
Second Billion	130 years	1930
Third Billion	30 years	1960
Fourth Billion	15 years	1975

| Fifth Billion | 12 years | 1987 |
| Sixth Billion | 11 years est. | 1998 est. |

United Nations Population Studies[7]

At this rate, given today's trends and conditions, our future is out of control and chaos is fast approaching. It took millions of years to reach the level of one billion persons. It is estimated that the next billion may be created in only eleven years! By the turn of the century, given the huge numbers of people at reproductive age, we may be adding another billion people in just 7-10 years!

This is madness on a planetary scale. And population grows geometrically, two becomes four, four becomes eight, eight becomes sixteen in what we are seeing are shorter and shorter generations, and yet the food supply only grows arithmetically, not doubling like population. Other resources like air and water don't increase at all. Malthus, the original dismal economist, recognized years ago that at some time in the future we will soon be on the verge of suicide by overpopulation. Given the current state of our most sensitive environmental indicators we now know that that time is fast approaching, if not already here. In every country, each decision about birth, especially above that of replacement value, is now critical.

"Population growth is the gravest issue that the world faces."[8]

Robert McNamara

As the world shrinks thru overpopulation, we must learn to see the consequences and the effects on all future generations of our behavior today. Murder on a very large scale will occur, especially in the southern hemisphere, when we set people against people for precious food, water, shelter and jobs. What will the world be like when the population is, god forbid, 12 billion or 25 billion? But we must act now to bring the balance of births and deaths into alignment at the earliest possible date or, tragically, we will find out.

It is now imperative that population growth cease until we have only population replacement. Our generation must act to bring to a halt the madness of our past reproductive behavior. If we do not act, both as responsible individuals, and governments committed to population balance, the odds are very high that we will simply not live in a peaceful world free of war, mass starvation, and ecological ruin.

The 1987 report of the Worldwatch Institute warns that our unbridled exploitation of the earth's air, water, land, forests, and other natural life support systems, are now pushing the "thresholds" of destruction and alteration beyond which recovery may prove impossible. We are caught in a trap of attempting to improve living standards when those efforts themselves are beginning to threaten the health of our global economy. Today, we need immediate international cooperation, not only as nations but primarily as mature and responsible individuals, to offset the negative effects of our competitive self-interest economies upon the earth's resources.

"The course corrections needed to restore a worldwide improvement in the human condition have no precedent. No single generation has ever faced such a complex set of issues requiring immediate attention. Preceding generations have always been concerned about the future, but we are the first to be faced with decisions that will determine whether the Earth our children inherit will be inhabitable."[9]

1987 WorldWatch Report

As responsible citizens of this now fragile planet earth, we can no longer justify bringing more children into the world who cannot be cared for, loved, and raised in the best possible environment. To have a child because one is simply too lazy or afraid to use contraception, and too afraid to take responsibility for ending an unwanted pregnancy, is now the "sin" - a sin against both the unwanted child and against a world struggling to feed the already born. Today, it is contraception and abortion that are the solutions to our problems, not problems in themselves.

Obviously, contraception, or abstinence, is a much preferred method of population control. But where the church prevents contraception and sex education, abortion too often becomes the only alternative for mothers around the world with untimely and unwanted pregnancies. Yet, there are those who want to limit, or even eliminate, your right to control your reproductive life and your motherhood. But we have seen the dark ages of illegal abortion, and it doesn't work.

Our views of "life" and spiritual realities may differ, but there is no mistaking the tragedy of excess population. Five thousand years ago, Lao-Tzu, one of the greatest of Taoist sages, remarked succinctly:

> "The blind and ignorant multiplication of population degrades the quality of humanity."[10]

> Lao-Tzu

I can't say it better than Lao-Tzu. the quality of humanity, and the quality of life experienced by that humanity, is now being degraded. Today, many concerned scientists are studying the multi-faceted and inter-linked environmental problems, created by the pressures of over-population, that now demand our immediate attention.

> "As the tide of population rises higher and higher, it spells less freedom, less mobility, peace, recreation, culture, opportunity, foreign travel, adventure and all of the things that make life superior to that of an ant.[11]"

> A. Wright,
> The limits of Mankind

* * *

"No matter how unfortunate or distasteful, abortion is instrumental in promoting a serious population growth control effort and will remain so for at least another twenty years . . .

"Even today, abortion plays a most significant role. Each year there are seventy to ninety million more births than deaths, and each year there are an estimated forty to fifty million or more induced abortions, one-half of which are performed illegally . . .

"Had there been no abortions over the past thirty years, starvation would now probably be far more widespread, and our world far more chaotic."[12]

Steven Mumford

IS FREEDOM OF CHOICE IMMORAL? -

These are new times. And we are no longer living in a world of only several hundred million people. It will soon be six billion people and more. It took mankind millions of years to reach the level of one billion people. And now that science has largely removed mother nature's hand from the scene, the earth's population has exploded, and in the last century alone, at an unprecented rate. Mankind's miracles of disease control and food production, while solving some problems have created others. To date, our technology has proved itself to be a two-edged sword.

In a brief moment of historical time, we have now filled the earth with our human species beyond our present political, economic, and perhaps environmental, capacity to properly care for all these individuals. Abortion in this setting is no longer a crime, it is a necessity. Freedom to choose *not* to give birth is essential, and no choice but to give birth may be called immoral. Today, many of the more progressive and aware church congregations are coming around to a new understanding and compassion regarding a woman's rightful termination of an unwanted pregnancy.

"Abortion should be taken out of the realm of law altogether and be a matter of careful ethical decision of a woman, her physician and her pastor or other counselor . . . we do not think that abortion should be relied upon as a means of limiting family size . . . but when contraception fails and an unwanted pregnancy is established, we do not think it either compassionate or just to insist that available help be withheld."[13]

> Statement, 182nd General Assembly
> of the United Presbyterian Church

Since the advent of the pill and other modern methods of contraception, we now have options in our sexual lives that mankind never had before. Sex has come out of the closet. The genie is out of the bottle. With birth control, we have divorced the reproductive process from pure amative love and our raucous genital copulation. In other words, we can enjoy one another now, provided we act like responsible human beings occupying a fragile and overcrowded planet. But those who do not act responsibly, or for other reasons find themselves unwillingly pregnant, must not then be forced to aggravate our population problems in the name of short-term mercy and compassion that only adds to our larger problems.

"But if God had wanted us to think with our wombs, why did he give us a brain."[14]

> Clair Boothe Luce

Even with the current wave of sexually transmitted diseases, which has often been another one of Mother Nature's ways to control population, we will sooner or later discover the cure for these problems. And even severely altered social mores, as a result of sexually transmitted diseases, will not eliminate excessive population growth and the real need for terminating unwanted pregnancies. The sexual revolution unleashed by the birth control pill, and newer devices on the horizon, is here to stay. But "accidents" will always happen.

As men and women, we were made to love one another. God even gave us children to show us we were doing it right. The problem is that we just don't need so many proofs! The sexual revolution and modern technology enables us to fulfill our human needs in intimacy and sexual contact. It has also given us the ability to plan our future and prepare for one of life's great gifts - a loved and wanted child.

Today, in these new and different times, each birth must be given the utmost care and forethought. We must do unto others as we would have them do unto us in bringing our children into this world. If we care so little about the birth of a child that we let it happen by accident, and at a time when we are not prepared, or mature enough for the daily and almost life-long demands of parenthood, then we need to deeply consider the process of delaying a soul's incarnation into our lives.

And this is not just for selfish motives, but for the bests interests of the unborn and our world. Our being considerate of current conditions, and attentive to the long-term interests of the unborn cannot now be said to be selfish. On the contrary, it is compassionate. As one young woman, on a radio talk show, expressed her feelings about her abortion years before at an immature age: "I feel good that I am not being a bad parent."

And even in the absence of the important social and environmental considerations, who is to say that we don't have a right to plan the entrance of the new soul into our bodies, which he or she will use for their own reincarnation. We are not slaves to the unborn, we are their mothers and fathers. We might say they borrow our genetic material and use the womb for their own purposes - it is the new soul's staging ground. But can we not also say that it is both our duty, and an act of compassion, to set the stage and prepare, in our own time, for the right occasion to give birth.

The act of cancelling an unplanned and unwanted pregnancy is a way of saying to that soul that their time has not yet arrived. It is a prayerful and respectful assuming responsibility for unplanned and untimely pregnancies, and we might well say for the good of the soul's eventual life to be. There is nothing wrong in taking control of one's reproductive life. And yet women are still punished by the Church, and many countries of the world, first for exercising their own sexuality, and secondly for taking responsibility for unwanted procreation. Why?

> "The first right of every child is to be wanted, to be desired, to be planned with an intensity of love that gives it its title to being."[15]

> Margaret Sanger

Only when the mother isn't forced into motherhood can she truly love and nourish her child. If we assume a fetal "right-to-life" we also assume the new soul is wlling to make a slave of the mother against her will. And any outside interference or coercion in this intuitive connection can only sour a delicate relationship between mother and child. After impregnation by a male who did not intend to become a father, and when a woman seeks help with her problem pregnancy, the reluctant mother often encounters the phalanx of moralist male ideologues . . . hypocrites without wombs seeking to enforce motherhood. Going "underground" for help is a necessity in some countries even today.

> "Consider Italy. A Roman Catholic country, its official face is set solidly against abortions; but it is generally estimated that the abortion rate is equal to the live birth rate, which makes Italian abortions four times as common as American. Italian men write the laws of Italy, and men write books on theology; women have the abortions and the children, with scarcely a glance at the literature of the other (male) subculture . . .

> "The written analysis of our sexual problems has been carried out by males with no experience of having children, or even the experience of living and sharing

76

with the childbearing culture. Women have children, and men write books on theology. Women midwives are also disappearing because women have become literate and are taking up men's occupations but their place is being taken by men physicians who try to enforce the mores of the male subculture."[16]

Garrett Hardin

Unfortunately, the role of the Church has been to prevent and frighten young women from using contraception, almost insuring that they will have unwanted babies in their early sexual experiments. And just as the Church, in effect, unwanted pregnancies and therefore abortions, it then condemms the young mothers and tells them they will now be excommunicated and go to hell if they have an abortion. Is this trap moral? Also, in too many cases, the Church does little or nothing to provide for these unfortunate children that their policies have helped to create!

Millions of families, and the many children that result from unregulated procreation, are becoming dependent on public assistance in cities around the world. Millions now grow up in poverty and miss an equal chance in life. And the sad fact is they are likely to repeat the mistakes of their parents at an even earlier age, thus intensifying the pace of irresponsible demands upon their community and the world.

Often it appears that in all too many cases the only mission of the Church seems to be to baptize the children and train them to be good Catholics, who will then go on to repeat the same sad experience of not using birth control, getting pregnant at an age when they are unable to properly provide for the child, and thus creating another disadvantaged being on the earth who will most likely require public and private assistance in his or her life. Whatever the intent, this is the unfortunate effect of policies.

The cycle goes on year after year and Mother Earth, in many countries, is now breaking under the assault of new life. This is unconscious, unplanned and largely unwanted humanity, that in the spiritual scheme of things will most likely not provide us with the strong, healthy, and properly cared for future stewards of spaceship earth. This truly vicious cycle must stop if we are to see any progress in our world. Only contraception, abortion and family planning are the realistic weapons in our continuing battle for population balance.

MANDATORY MOTHERHOOD -

The Catholic church, and all other fundamentalist religions around the world that still oppose and prevent the use of contraception and abortion, in effect, favor "mandatory motherhood." For whatever reason or mistake the conception has occurred, where abortion is outlawed, a woman is effectively condemmed to give birth against her will. It wasn't long ago tht women were burned at the stake for attempting to define their own feminist cosmology. It seems that in past ages, as is somewhat true today, a "witch" was any who had the guts to tell the Church to stay out of her life.

Today, the Church cannot burn women at the stake, but its doctrines are mental torture enough on those who choose to disagree but lack the necessary philosophical strength and independence to combat the guilt and condemnation. The real problem is that young women are, in effect, punished into giving birth for having engaged in sex. Thus does the child become the punishment. This is not compassion for the unborn but control of the living, a distinct lack of compassion for the woman's right to choose and control her reproduction. And this policy, as we will later see, is why so many women today are leaving the Church.

> "How can we justify compulsory pregnancy? Here we are strapping down a living and breathing creature (the mother) and then forcing her to give birth in the unproven belief that we are saving a 'life.' In many causes we are ruining two lives, the mother's and the baby."[17]

> Garrett Hardin

A MOTHER'S INSTINCT -

Is not this one-sided definition of compassion, that commands the birth of unplanned and unwanted children, not ruining the lives of the mother and the child as well? What really happens to these mostly unwanted and unplanned babies, after the birth event, when the moralists have faded away to spread their compassion elsewhere? As might be expected, many studies from around the world now indicate that all is not well with unplanned and unwanted children. There are far too many teenage "parents" now coerced into aborting their own futures, and their children's, by giving birth when they themselves are still dependent and unable to provide a decent home for the newborn.

"In a Swedish study 120 children born after refusal by the authorities to grant permission for abortion were compaired to paired controls of the same sex born either in the same hospital or district to mothers who had not applied for abortion.

"After a close observation for 21 years, the former group of children were found to have higher incidences of psychiatric disorder, delinquency, criminal behavior, and alcoholism. They were more often recipients of public welfare, were more unfit for military service, and received less schooling than those of the controls."

"In another study of 213 children born to women who had been refused therapeutic abortion, the unwanted children were shown to be physically as well as mentally impaired."[18]

Forssman, Hans and Thuwe,
The Abortion Experience

It is not hard to understand why these studies appear to confirm the real disadvantages of children born from unwanted pregnancies. They also tell us something about the instincts of mothers. Might we not say that most mothers intuitively sense when the time is not right, or even that the baby may not be well, and thus decide to terminate an unwanted and unplanned pregnancy? And subconsciously, in her intuitive maternal wisdom, a pregnant woman may sense that something is wrong with the pregnancy, for whatever reason. However, if society attempts to crush a woman's instincts, and prevent the best of all possible births, we do a great disservice to the woman, her children, and all of humanity.

And what can we say of the mentality, and morality, that demands that a woman have a baby simply because she has become pregnant? Is not the how and the why of the pregnancy of any importance? The panicked and unprepared "mother" is now doomed to motherhood against her will - and her child is her punishment. In the case of teenage pregnancy this is especially reprehensible and counterproductive. And what are we doing for, or to, this new child in the most negative of circumstances? Are we saving his or her life? Are we saving the mother's life? Or ruining them both?

In the African nation of Zimbabwe, where population problems are currently swamping any possibility of economic progress, the killing of newborn babies has become a serious problem. A lack of contraception, legal bans on abortion, tribal prohibitions against adoption, the low social status of women, and the sheer pressures of urbanization on the family all combine to create the ugly environment in which young girls are doomed to immature pregnancy. Without the right to contraception, abortion, or adoption, women of this poor african nation are resorting to the killing of their newborns as the only alternative to escape from the cycle of unwanted reproduction. Is this the moral alternative? Where all the family planning options are closed off to women this is the inevitable and tragic result of "pro-life" morality.

With unwanted pregnancies, abortion saves the life of the mother, giving her the chance to position her children in her life so as to maximize the conditions for the welfare of the child, the mother, her village and our world.

We might also consider that, from the viewpoint of the new soul, the mother is unwittingly providing a staging ground for the new soul who may be incarnating because of their karmic ties to the father. In this case, the woman is just a vehicle for another relationship, that of the father and the incarnating soul. Certainly, the mother has some rights in the use of her body for this purpose.

The act of sex, and the failure of contraceptives or menstrual timing, is not, in and of itself, a consent to give birth and provide womb-space for the incarnation of your partner's spiritual in-laws. And depending on the time of the month, sex is only the potential for birth given the right circumstances. But a mother's instinct as to what is "right" in these situations has to be primary. Without question, and by nature's design, it is the mother alone who is responsible for the new being. Birth is a mother's choice.

Say what?

ABORTION AROUND THE WORLD -

Approximately 40 million abortions are performed yearly around the world, chiefly because contraception is either unavailable or improperly administered. About two-thirds of the world population now live in countries where abortions are readily available and this number is increasing as the reality of population problems causes more grief and suffering. In the remaining countries, where laws forbid abortion, birth rate's continue at very high levels even as more and more women seek abortion.

Unfortunately, in these same countries where the population problems dictate an urgent need for contraception and abortion, these services are against the law. Even today, in many overpopulated nations, women are forced to seek "illegal" medical services at great risk to their health. The outlawing of abortion has never stopped the need or prevented women from obtaining abortions, it has only resulted in women being unnecessarily injured or traumatized in the process.

"First, Natural abortion - spontaneous abortion is very
common. A multitude of studies now indicate that
approximately 69% of conceptuses are spontaneously
aborted."[19]

> Garrett Hardin, Biological
> Insights Into Abortion

Mother Nature herself aborts the vast majority of early
pregnancies. Despite Mother Nature's work in causing a great
many spontaneous miscarriages, women around the world are
often confronted with the urgent problem involving a decision
about pregnancy. Can we not say that, if Mother Nature herself
can say no and induce miscarriage, all women also have the
right to say no? Aren't all women also a part of Mother Nature
and capable of their own decisions?

Pregnancy termination, as we shall see, is an important
fact of life, experienced by millions of women for a variety
of legitimate reasons. In California, for example, even before
the U.S. Supreme Court's Roe vs. Wade decision and after
liberalization of abortion laws began in 1962, it was estimated,
in 1971, that one out of three pregnancies was ended by a
legal abortion - a frequency also experienced in most other
states. Whether legal or not, the numbers of abortions remained
similar. Questions of legality only seemed to affect the
atmosphere and environment under which these operations
were performed.

"Over 90 per-cent of all abortions are performed during
the first fourteen weeks of gestation."[20]

> Edd Doerr

There is no question that the vast majority of abortions
performed occur well before the threshold of viability, or
sentience, is reached. The most troublesome and emotional
problems often occur in very young girls when their own lack
of understanding, fear, and shame often contribute to late
diagnosis and relatively late-term abortion.

82

"forty-four per cent of abortions done after the 21st
week of gestation are performed on teen-agers, who
may not realize that they are pregnant until they feel
the baby kicking"[21]

Newsweek Magazine

It is this very fear in young girls, whether engendered by
religious precepts, legal restrictions, or the simple lack of
counseling facilites, that is one of our biggest problems. The
message of sex, via the media, is widely perveyed, but the viable
alternatives to childbirth are often restrained from view.

"Abortion is rarely a psychologically traumatic event,
even if it is socially disproved and legislation is
restrictive. If there are any psychological sequelae the
most commmon one, by far, is that of relief."[22]

Henry David, Abortion In
Psychological Perspective

* * *

"When abortion was illegal, women often found the
experience traumatic. But in the current environment,
with supportive physicians and clinic staff, we've found
that the overwhelming response to abortion is one of
relief."[23]

Susan Shaw, Clinic employee

Once abortion came out of the closet, and up from the
underground, we began to see the sheer numbers involved in
the new statistics and understand that many women, and young
girls, required the option of pregnancy termination. And one
thing is certain, as long as there are unwanted pregnancies
the demand for abortion will be there.

But how can the "moralists" say that young mothers should
have no choice, at the critical point when they learn they are
pregnant, and their whole being fights the very thought? It
is a cruel logic to prevent abortion, especially, when you

83

consider that the very prevention of sex education and contraception has contributed to the lack of knowledge about their bodies and thus indirectly led to the pregnancy and need for abortion! Women, especially the young and poor, are caught in a knowledge and lack-of-services trap. Beyond that, if fully 69% of all pregnancies result in some form of natural miscarriage, then we might say that in the case of many early abortions, the odds are great that the doctor is often just doing nature's work a little earlier . . . in the mother's best interests.

Especially in a setting of suppressed information and clinical services, it is apparent that the necessity of abortion is left to those women for whom ignorance of their bodily functions and cycles is not all their fault, for whom contraception has failed, for whom nature performed no favors, and those whose own antipathy to the pregnancy was not strong enough to engender a "natural" miscarriage. From another perspective, the reluctant mother is a victim of a fetus/soul who was not kind enough, or conscious enough, to respect the wishes of the mother, consider the circumstances, and find themselves another womb. In all of these circumstances, the woman is a victim anyway you consider the situation.

The fact that a woman sought a little warmth and companionship in sex is not a one-way ticket to birth. If we consider the bleak perspective that she is punishing herself in karmic fashion by getting pregnant, giving birth against her better judgement, and perhaps victimizing the new baby by not being able to care properly for the new life, then we are swimming in a worldview which is clearly self-destructive and irresponsible. Can we always blame it on God? Can we then assume that this is the way God wants births to occur . . . in the worst of circumstances?

> "In today's society, abortion is a life-saving procedure in a broader sense: Young women and men have a second chance for self-determination of their personal lives."[24]

> J. Lieberman & Ellen Peck,
> Sex & Birth Control

A recent magazine article states that the largest group of recipients, especially of late-term abortions, are poor women struggling to raise the money required, and those who simply do not know where to go for the operation. Because a large number of women, of all ages, experience irregular periods at times, the non-occurrence of menstration does not automatically alert women to the need to visit a doctor. Add to this the agonies that young girls experience in telling anyone, including their parents, about their suspected sexual predicament and you have the environment in which the now postponed decision becomes harder, but no less necessary, for everyone involved, physician as well.

YOUNGER WOMEN? -

In just the last century, we have witnessed a new phenomenon in relation to the age at which the capacity to conceive occurs. Today, we have a new class of child-women in our midst, vastly increasing the problem of pregnancy abuse. The average age of the onset of menarche continues to drop into the pre-teen years of childhood.

> "In our country, the average age at which menstruation begins has declined from 17 years in 1840 to 12 years today. This increased fertility period, plus a woeful lack of corresponding sex education in our schools, has resulted in over one million teen-agers becoming pregnant out of wed-lock eack year, usually with unhappy results."[25]

> Dr. Alex Gerber

Indeed, the mind trap of ignorance and guilt has sentenced these children to premature motherhood. These "unhappy results" are the result of our social milieu as well as better nutrition in childhood. We now see many girls as young as 11 or 12 years of age beginning their ovulation and menstruation. This lowering of the age of menarche is an incredible change in nature's natural control of fertility within a very short period of historical time. In only one hundred years, nature and our society have created a new class of child-women, between the ages of 11 and 17, whose bodies are now capable of giving birth.

We now have many underage "mothers" who cannot legally drive, vote, or even work at many jobs! Can we sanction, and even require, this tragedy? These young girls are not old enough for any adult functions and yet we allow them to give birth - the most demanding of adult responsibilities!

Also within a short historical time frame, society has lengthened the age of adolescense requiring dependence on the family. But these awesome biological changes, combined with a general climate of sexual liberation, within an even larger context of prolonged adolescent dependence, have now given us millions of young women who, while capable of giving birth, are still a great distance from being ready to become a responsible and independent mother with full capacity to provide for their child in an increasingly competitive world. And what kind of society are we creating in this context where children beget children?

Another alarming trend contributing to the need for abortion services is the steadily declining age of sexual experience. A recent study in the largely white middle class suburb of Culver City, California revealed the following:

"29% of the 397 middle schoolers and 54% of the 800 high schoolers surveyed say they are sexually active. Middle school (ages 11-13) boys who admit to sexual activity, the average loss of virginity was 11.1; for the sexually active girl 11.7. And according to the sexually active high school boys (ages 14-18), the average age at which they lost their virginity was 13.2; average age for the girls 14.6."[26]

If such figures can be believed, and such activity is occuring without adequate sex education and availability of contraception, then our high-school children will continue to manufacture unwanted pregnancies. In today's society, sexual abstinence until marriage at a mature age, does not appear to be a viable option any longer. The sooner we recognize that fact, the sooner we can act to prevent the flood of unwanted pregnancies amongst teenagers.

When, out of a myopic sense of morality, the Church or state forces motherhood on these under-age girls we steal their childhood and rob them of life's opportunities to build a better foundation for the children they may have in the future. At the same time, where "shotgun" marriages are then enforced to legitimize the birth, the future of many a young "father" is also jeopardized by these new responsibilities for which he is normally ill-prepared and unwilling to face. The reality is that society pays, and in more ways than tax-money alone.

Certainly we can say that premature marriage is no solution to immature motherhood and premature pregnancy. The reality is that it is nearly always a tragic solution to a mistake - two wrongs seldom add up to a right. In unwanted pregnancy situations today, all young women must have the courage, and societal support, to take control of their lives and terminate an unplanned and unwanted pregnancy. This is now the moral solution, and the population imperative.

We no longer have the eden-like luxury of welcoming every birth into a tribe-like setting where every father is an uncle because life and sex were communal, and space, food, and shelter were abundant. Even in these primal settings Mother Nature had to be cruel to keep the human species under control. When nature was in firm control these arrangements worked and did not require human intervention. However, in the already crowded world of today it is a recipe for disaster - and the population disasters, in many locals, are already well under way. Regardless of our particular societal format, we humans are now responsible for balancing our numbers.

"Critics of abortion see it as an almost exclusively negative thing, a means of non-fulfillment only. What they fail to realize is that abortion, like other means of birth control, can lead to fulfillment in the life of a woman. And a woman who aborts this year because

87

she is in poor health, neurotic, economically harassed, unmarried, on the verge of divorce, or immature, may well decide to have some other child five years from now - a wanted child. The child that she aborts is always an unwanted child. If her need for abortion is frustrated, she may never know the joy of a wanted child."[27]

Garrett Hardin,
Stalking the Wild Taboo

Indeed, particularly in the case of early teenage prgnancy, we can safely say that abortion today is a pro-life decision in the sense that the lives of both the baby, and the parents, are being saved from their mistakes and now have a second chance to procreate responsibly, at a proper time and place in their lives. Can we not say that this is the larger moral and compassionate nature of the act of abortion in many instances?

The real consequences of the bringing to term of most unwanted pregnancies is that it ends up destroying two young lives, sanctions the birth of a child into an immature mothering environment, forcibly creates a "home" by still-birthing the educational opportunities of the young parents, and shifts the ultimate financial responsibility upon the grandparents and/ or the community, neither of whom approve of the arrangement or want the responsibility. The real life long-term *effects* of "pro-life" morality and compassion are often devastating.

Yet this forced parenthood is what many of those who espouse a "right-to-Life" call compassion. In effect, it is a slavery of forced servitude to childbirth resulting from irresponsibility. And all of the victims of these unwanted pregnancies, (including many more people that just the new baby and the young parents) are now paying the price for lack of sex and contraception education, so vehemently opposed by fundamentalists Churches and "moral majority" groups in many countries around the world.

"Consider the grim statistics. In the United states each year, 96 out of 1000 girls between 15 and 19 become pregnant, four out of five of them by mistake. This gives the United states one of the highest teen-age birth rates among the world's industrialized nations . . .

"The future for them is frightful. And in California, about eight out of ten pregnant teen-age girls drop out of high school. If the teen-agers marry, their chances of separating or divorcing are three times greater than couples in their 20's . . . because they drop out of school, they can expect much lower incomes for the rest of their lives, and taxpayers can expect to help pay the cost of that . . .

"Babies born to teen-age mothers are more likely to die in the first year of life than those born to older women. The death rate for teen-age mothers is also considerably higher, and their attempted suicide rate is seven times greater that the national average."

"Nearly 60% of California's total welfare budget goes to women who had teen-age pregnancies! About half of the state's teen-age mothers choose abortion to end unwanted pregnancies."[28]

Los Angeles Times

* * *

"Teenage pregnancy is providing us with almost an unlimited supply of new welfare recipients."[29]

Carl Williams, Director,
Workfare-Welfare Program

PREMATURE PREGNANCY - A LIFE SENTENCE? -

These are the unfortunate facts on the continuing tragedy of teenage pregnancy. And behind each new unwanted pregnancy are often scared and confused women and young

89

girls trying to balance the strident voices of counsel. They are uniformly unprepared for their encounter with motherhood, as well as the various religious and political ideas regarding pre-natal "life" and "murder" that prey upon the pregnant women's mind. Those who want to prevent abortion and free choice seem much to willing to condemm these young girls to the slavery of unwanted motherhood. Is this moral? Is this compassionate? Is this a solution to our problems?

But not every country has the same experience in teenage pregnancy and unwanted premature motherhood. When we look at the experience of European countries, we begin to see the value of sex education in our schools.

"In the five European nations, the rate of teen sexual activity is similar to ours - but rates of pregnancy and childbirth are far lower . . . The reason is birth control. In all five, it is cheap and easy to get. Not so for our teens . . .

"Welfare benefits don't necessarily encourage teen-age pregnancy. All five European nations have higher welfare benefits but lower teen birth rates. Our head-in-the-sand attitude about sex is a big part of the problem. While European society says "Don't get pregnant" we say "Don't have sex" and expect the problem to go away. When adults face up to teen sexuality, pregnancy rates decline where contraceptive counseling is provided in school clinics, births to unwed mothers fell dramatically."[30]

USA TODAY

But should a mistake in timing result in a a life sentence of motherhood because of religious dogma? Is the life penalty appropriate for an unprepared young girl? More and more of today's teenagers are frightened into giving birth against their wishes by unrelenting pressure from sincere people who, once the act of abortion has been prevented, will disappear from the scene leaving the reluctant young mother with no help or concern for the destiny of her child.

"Most women who would have abortions want them, and for the best of all possible reasons: because they love children. For the sake of children already born, a woman wants desperately to avoid having one too many. For the sake of other children she may have several years later, she wants an abortion now. She knows that her time, her patience and her love are not infinitely divisible. The straw that breaks the camel's back does not break the legislator's back nor the theologian's. It breaks hers."[31]

Garrett Hardin

Today more women must understand that they have a right to use abortion to control their own lives. Otherwise, they are imprisoned by men, the family, and the state. As one woman interviewed in Kristin Luker's "Abortion & The Politics of Motherhood" stated: "If I hadn't had that abortion early in my life, my life would have been a disaster. I never would have gotten to medical school . . . it's really a life-saving thing for many people."

THE NEW WORLD -

In the real world of today, where young girls are developing earlier, and where the impact of television and the media is so pervasive, the age of temptation as well as sexual maturation has fallen significantly. The only counter-balance to this younger age of sexual experimentation seems to be the current threat of sexually-transmitted diseases. And sooner or later, even fear is conquered by the sexual drive. So the only relevant question remains; are young people prepared to avoid pregnancy and disease in pre-marital sexual experience?

91

"The average American sees 9000 prime time scenes of suggested sexual intercourse or innuendo each year."[32]

Time Magazine

Consider for a moment this new world of today's young people. In most cases, they have more money, more freedom, and more mobility than previous generations. The vast majority no longer live the bucolic farm life of past centuries, where young children were isolated on a farm and fearful of societal standards. In today's increasingly urban world, education is the only prevention for most ills of life, including unwanted pregnancy. Those that seek to prevent sex and contraception education end up acting to prevent sexual responsibility. Those that argue for no sexual experience outside of marriage are asking for a return to a past that no longer exists and is highly unlikely to ever return.

Prior to the world of birth control technology and contraception people had little choice. Many women found themselves sexually unfulfilled in loveless marriages and then condemmed to "hell" or excommunicated if they sought divorce. To return to the days of no choice, and no sexual experience prior to marriage, is to ask women to step back into the cage of male-dominated exploitation and domestic slavery. But with the freedom to pursue our sexual impulses comes the absolute responsibility not to give birth outside of a marriage, or a long-term relationship, rooted in love.

"Birth control is an immensely beneficent invention which can and does relieve men and women of some of the most tragic sorrows which afflict them: the tragedies of the unwanted child, the tragedy of unsupportable economic burdens, the tragedy of excessive child-bearing and the destruction of youth and living in an unrelenting series of pregnancies."[33]

Walter Lippman,
A Preface To Morals

"I know many pregnant teenagers, and teenagers who are mothers. They realized that getting pregnant was a big mistake, but lots of them do it to keep their boyfriends. They just don't understand the situation until after they have the kid. It's sad, girls having babies just to keep their boyfriends."[34]

Sidorrie Brown, 19

* * *

"82 per cent of those girls who gave birth at age 15 or younger were daughters of teenage mothers."[35]

Time Magazine

And the sad undeniable fact is that teen mothers have more children who go on to become teenage mothers, thus leading to the skyrocketing births rates and doubling of populations in 15 or 20 years. This tragic cycle of premature pregnancy and poverty is almost impossible to reverse once it gets started. And the tragedy is that everyone loses from this vicious circle; the mother, the baby, and society.

When one considers that society does not allow a young person to drive before the age of sixteen, or to vote before the age of eighteen or twenty-one, it is quite alarming that we allow, even encourage, immature youngsters to have a baby! It is truly the dilemma of a free society. But it is even more amazing that we consider it may be necessary for young women to get permission to have an abortion while no such permission is necessary to have a baby!

As far back as 385 B.C., Plato, describing his own ideal republic, concluded that men should reproduce only when they are over thirty and under forty-five; women only when they are over twenty and under forty. And any offspring born of any unlicensed matings, or deformed, were to be exposed and left to die. Before and after the legal ages specified for procreation, mating was to be free, on the condition that the pregnancy be aborted. These were the essential conditions to ensure the stability of the ideal republic.

> "If a man either above or below this age meddles with the begetting of children for the commonwealth, we shall hold it an offence against divine and human law. He will be begetting for his country a child conceived in darkness and dire incontinence, whose birth, if it escape detection, will not have been sanctioned by the sacrifices and prayers offered at each marriage festival, when priests and priestesses join with the whole community in praying that the children to be born may be even better and more useful citizens than their parents. We shall say that he is foisting on the commonwealth a bastard, unsanctioned by law or by religion."[36]

Plato, Plato's Republic

Stopping sex was not Plato's concern. But the act of preventing overpopulation, the real threat to the stability of the ideal community, was most important. A citizen's duty was not to procreate and push population beyond an ideal size; a city-state was not to exceed 5,040 persons, each holding one inalienable lot of land - a size dictated perhaps by the fecundity of the local bioregion. This is an ethic which may need to be re-examined in our own time.

Stopping sex is something that cannot be done. Mother nature is such a powerful force, and our sex drive so basic and forceful that all efforts in the past to suppress it have been a dismal failure, resulting in nothing but the reality of too many unwanted children. We can only hope to raise the consciousness of young people about their sexual expression as well as the critical necessity of contraception, restraint, or complete abstinence. Today, that fear function is being accomplished partly by the current wave of herpes and AIDS, two very good reasons to be extrememly careful about our sexual partners. But even with such dreaded diseases hanging overhead, sex goes on. The question is what will materialize out of these laisons - love, or heartbreak and unwanted children?

We are fertile little devils. Just one shot of sperm contains the potential to create millions of children if enough wombs could be found to accept the largesse. With a woman producing an egg every month for thirty years, one man and several women can create a small army of children. But can they produce jobs, food, clothing, comfort, attention and love? It is no miracle to produce a child, almost everybody can do it. But in this crowded world, it is now our duty not to produce a child until we are mature adults, and prepared emotionally and financially for the burdens.

In our modern world of contraception there is only education and availability, there can be no suppression of sex, and sex education, that will not result in ignorance about contraception, more illegitimate births, and a great burden to society. When young couple's hormones begin to fire and they go off cocked and loaded, the result is a population explosion because of lack of restraint, lack of contraception, and most of all, fear of abortion.

"Each year there are approximately one million teenage pregnancies (ages ten to nineteen) in the United States, accounting for one out of every four pregnancies. About 300,000 of these result in induced abortions, 100,000 in hasty and premature marriages and 600,000 in births. These births cost American taxpayers over $8.3 billion dollars each year . . ."

"This is an average of $13,833 for each birth and is only the direct cost, that is, cash support payments, food stamps, social services, free medical services. The indirect costs are not included in this figure. For example, children raised by teenage parents - little more than children themselves - are far more inclined to become delinquents and criminals and are disproportionately represented in our penal institutions."

95

"We must adopt the posture that teenagers should not have the freedom to reproduce unless they can handle all the direct cost and indirect cost and, of course, none can. The welfare of all these accidental births places an overwhelming and unnecessary drain on the nation's domestic economy."[37]

Stephen Mumford: Population,
Growth and Global Security

These are tragic figures. Even more tragic are the individual lives behind the statistics. And yet for each one of these accidental unplanned births by teenagers, we pay enough each to send a poor, but *wanted*, child to college. We simply cannot afford to continue to pay for irrresponsible parenthood. The demands don't end with birth but continue thru into the adult lives of many unwanted children.

Clearly, a birth "right" must also imply a birth "duty" upon the parents. But if the "parents" are unwilling, or incapable, of meeting the birth duties, can they now have the birth right? Why is it that we discuss the abolition of abortion and not the requirement to meet the basic conditions of responsible parenthood? Can we say that one is in the interests of the child and not the other? However, both of these options involve control of the individual by the state.

But whether or not we come to the dismal state of affairs, where we are someday required to show evidence of responsibility to qualify for a birth, depends upon the actions of people today. Irresponsible parenthood will force such undesirable state requirements. Hopefully, technology, education, and parental responsibility will rescue us from the abortion dilemma and state controls over our private lives.

FRIGHTENED INTO CHILDBIRTH -

Undeniably, fear is the real mother of too many unwanted children born today.

Why do nearly 600,000 teenagers per year, in the United States, wind up having their babies? The main reasons are that they are prevented from getting a proper education about birth control and contraception by the political power of the Catholic church, and other fundamentalist religious groups. Second, they may have nowhere to turn once they are pregnant and often wait too long to seek any counseling. On top of that, they are burdened by "religious" doctrines that imply that they will "go to hell" or "commit murder" if they have an abortion. So the pregnant teenager is paralyzed with guilt and fear at a time when she most desperately needs adult compassion, understanding, and mature judgement.

In effect, many women are thus frightened into childbirth, exactly the worst circumstances and psychological state-of-mind for bringing another life into being. As a consequence, they are robbed of their childhood and normal opportunities by the early onset of adult responsibilities which they are hard pressed to meet. Given the almost always tragic long-term outcome of birth in these circumstances, can forcing young women into giving birth really be the present dismal state of compassion and morality in our country? In our world? If the adults involved in premature motherhood situations are paralyzed by the same guilt and indecision, the tragedy will certainly continue.

"It must be regarded as a natural catastrophe in our midst . . . a threat to the future of Black people without equal. In ever-growing numbers, the black teenagers who have babies never do marry. They head their own households, depend on public assistance and find themselves at age 30 grandmothers to their unwed children's babies. So preventing children from having children must become a major priority for our community and the society. The problem must be faced by all - individuals, families, organizations, as well as churches, which are the backbone of our community."[38]

Dorothy I. Height, President,
National Council of Negro Women

The tragedy in the world today is that millions of young unwed mothers give birth to children that they have no capacity to care for. They seem to expect that others will, or should, help them. Who are the others who must pay for their child? Here, we have basically selfish and immature young women who have selfish motives for giving birth other than wanting a child. The child is a passport to getting out of the house, or going on welfare, or "playing adult" with their friends. These are the sad realities of today. How long will the rest of society pay for these tragic mistakes in maturity and judgement? How far can our compassion and our resources be stretched? In these circumstances, encouraging birth only promotes immorality and irresponsibility. And what happens to the children born of this morality?

Depending upon your religious upbringing, the fear of taking control of your life, of terminating a pregnancy, may be so deep-seated that one is paralyzed and unable to follow their more sensible instincts. But right and wrong do not take place in a vacuum. Your decision is in a context, the context of your life, the life of a newborn, and the fate of the earth with its limited ability to provide for new life.

The Church's position of allowing sex only within the confines of marriage is a nice idea, but the problem for years has been that unwanted pregnancies are causing the marriages! And this type of forced matrimony is anything but holy. Love doesn't happen under pressure, only divorce and heartbreak for all concerned are likely to occur. In effect, our preventing abortion, and forcing premature motherhood and marriage upon unprepared teenagers, is just another form of rape.

The real need is to see this growing and tragic problem of premature motherhood from other religious and philosophical perspectives, particularly those that will encourage personal responsibility for the condition of our increasingly overcrowded world. For the sake of women, and their wanted children, all over the world, we need to liberate the solutions from the fears of the past.

"Fears are educated into us, and can, if we wish be educated out."[39]

> Dr. Karl Menninger
> The Human Mind.

* * *

"Fear is never a good counselor and our victory over fear is the first spiritual duty of men and women."[40]

> Nicholas Berdyaev
> Towards a New Epoch

* * *

"When people feel threatened and anxious they become more rigid, and when in doubt they tend to become dogmatic; and then they lose their own vitality. They use the remnants of traditional values to build a protective encasement and then shrink behind it; or they make an outright panicky retreat into the past."[41]

> Rollo May,
> Man's Search for Himself

What the world can no longer afford is millions of women in a "panicky retreat into the past" and suffering from questionable "religious" ideas about guilt and sin over the termination of a pregnancy. And yet this is the unfortunate reality of many young girls and mature women who are unable to escape the dogmas of yesterday. Motherhood is always serious business, requiring sober judgement as to its proper timing and place in our lives, as well as our world. Fear and guilt are the real enemies of sober and responsible action.

But until technology comes forth with the safe "morning-after" pill, which could be sooner than most people expect, abortion remains the only alternatives available to women wishing to control their reproductive destiny after the fact of pregnancy. Those who would abolish your right to seek an abortion, abolish your right to control your destiny. And instilling fear in women is one of their major weapons.

THE FUTURE OF ADOPTION? -

In past years it has been fortunate that there have been many childless couples eager to adopt children and thus provide the loving and secure homes for unwanted and abandoned babies. But will these homes be available in the future for the many unwanted children that need homes?

Science has now made it possible for all childless couples to have "their own child" thru surrogate mothers, or by implanting a fertilized ovum in the infertile woman. Some scientists say we are rapidly developing the ability to create an "artificial womb" in which babies can be "born" from the sperm and egg of the childless couple. An electro-mechanical womb is now reportedly being developed. The era of the made to order test-tube baby has arrived and, unfortunately, with it the probable demise of the adopted child. The new era of "Designer Babies" spells more trouble for the unwanted and unadopted child of the future.

> "A woman who has no eggs of her own can be made pregnant with another woman's egg that has been fertilized with any man's sperm in a petri dish. The little "conceptus" could be frozen to grow in other wombs in the future."[42]
>
> Genoveffa Corea,
> The Mother Machine

100

surrogate parent?

Who will adopt when they can make their own? How many will risk assuming the unknown genetics and temperament of unknown parents, embodied in an abandoned and embittered child? These are sad new realities. And it means that these orphans and unwanted children may no longer have a chance at homes where adoption was once the only alternative. Today, making your own test-tube baby is going to be the choice for many infertile parents. Where there was some hope of adoption yesterday, with test-tube babies and surrogate motherhood, the chances of adoption for unwanted children today are rapidly disappearing.

Today, many young pregnant girls who feel that they can go ahead and have the child, in the belief that adoption will occur, are clearly not doing the child a favor. The real chances for adoption are worse than ever before. And yet, even today, we hear of abandoned babies left in trash bins and on doorsteps. Prospects are now much greater that the reality for these unwanted children will be a life in various state institutions at public expense. This is a direct consequence of many young and mostly ill-prepared pregnant "mothers" who, fearing the abortion alternative for whatever reason, are only failing to come to terms with their responsibility for bringing unwanted life into this world.

With the chances for adoption becoming worse and not better, the young mother is playing roulette with her baby's future and her own. Is this her only compassion? The unwanted and unplanned child will arrive because of paralyzing fear and guilt, caused by religious dogma, that prevents the mother from controlling her own reproductive destiny for the benefit of all her children. Our fear of abortion, along with the vague ideas of religious retribution, is simply no excuse for an immature mother bringing an unwanted child into the world. How can we come to the conclusion that the "mother" is doing the child, the soul, a favor under these circumstances?

> "Compassion not combined with wisdom is ineffectual in relieving suffering."[43]

>   Rimpoche Tara Tulku

BABY AND BIRTH ABUSE? -

Despite the fact that we now live in a world of the birth-control pill, enjoying our sexuality freely without the superstitions and moral straight-jackets of past centuries to cripple our minds, we have a new problem - baby abuse. Not the slapping of two year olds, but the unconscionable giving birth to unwanted babies. And not because they were wanted, planned, or needed, but simply because of a quirk in menstrual timing, the lack of sexual education, or simply not having the courage or sense of responsibility to abort an unwanted and unplanned pregnancy.

We might call this birth abuse, a crime reaching across time and space to mug an unsuspecting soul and thrust he/she into a world in which they have no chance for a decent existence. Of course, this viewpoint presumes that we aren't arranging all these events in advance, abortion included, within the context of our larger cosmic beings. If such is the case, what can we then say about these events that may not have already been considered on other planes of existence?

"Melissa, 21, a single mother with four children was complaining about the lack of shelter run by a Venice evangelical church. Melissa and her children, 15-month old twins, a 4-year old and a 7-year old had left their home for a better life in California. They found lodging and free meals at the church, where each night more than 100 homeless parents and children sleep on the floor. All her children seem depressed, Melissa said, as she held one baby and at the same time tried to coax food into the other twin's mouth. "My babies . . . they have a tendency to cry lots." Now hoping for bus fare home, Melissa wondered . . . "It's not like I thought it was going to be."[44]

Los Angeles Times

Starting motherhood at fourteen years of age, Melissa's future was sealed shut. How many Melissa's and their deprived children, whose lives are short-changed by premature pregnancy and are now struggling desperately for mere subsistence, will society continue to procreate if we value the unborn over the wretched existence of the already living? How many children are manifested by women in need solely to increase their welfare allotment? And while the moralists talk about the sanctity of life in the womb, the streets become ever more crowded with desperate and deprived individuals who arrive via unplanned and unwanted pregnancies.

With sexual freedom has come a greater responsibility - to make certain that all our additions to the world are wanted and planned and arrive at a time in our lives when we can provide the most beneficial environment for a new child. Babies are not toys. Young women and men, especially, must exercise that freedom in a manner that does not call upon others to pay for their irresponsibility, and their progeny to resent the circumstances of their birth.

"Cruel is your creative act, bringing innumerable sorrows to all who are endowed with life."[45]

A Tamil Poet

Consider that some young women even seize upon the opportunity to get pregnant as a way to keep their boyfriends, as if entrapment could ever be a basis for a good long term relationship. Here, we might say that a young girl is taking a soul hostage to ensnare a husband. What good can come out of these motives? And bad motives do not make good futures. Termination of a pregnancy pales in comparison to the ugly motives underlying many teenage pregnancies.

Teenage "mothers" are vulnerable to all of the worst motives for unplanned chilbirth and also the worst results: failure to abstain; failure to contracept; failure to recognize and acknowledge early symptoms of pregnancy; failure to tell a boyfriend of the secret intention to get pregnant; failure to tell anyone including the new soul that he-she is being used as an instrument to get on welfare or keep a boyfriend; and, most importantly, failure to quickly terminate a pregnancy caused by the above reasons.

The impure motives of motherhood are as ancient as the relationship between men and women. They are aptly chronicled in the one of the "Lost Gospels" discovered in 1945. In the Secret Book of John we find the story of Sophia, the Gnostic Great Mother and the embodiment of female wisdom. Only in this case the wisdom is that of afterthought. Her story is revealing:

> "Now Sophia . . . who is the Wisdom of Afterthought and who represents an eternal realm, conceived of a thought. She had this idea herself, and the invisible spirit and Foreknowledge also reflected upon it. She wanted to give birth to a being like herself without the permission of the Spirit (The spirit had not given approval), without her lover, and without his consideration . . . Her partner did not give his approval; she did not find anyone who agreed with her; and she considered this matter with-out the Spirit's permission or any knowledge of what she had decided . . .

> "Nonetheless, she brought forth a child. And because of the unconquerable power within her, her thought was not an idle thought. Rather, something came out of her that was imperfect and different in appearance from her, for she had produced it without her lover. It did not look like its mother, and had a different

shape. When Sophia saw what her desire had produced, it changed into the figure of a snake with the face of a lion. She threw it away from her, outside that realm, so that none of the immortals could see it. For she had produced it ignorantly."[46]

The Secret Book of John,
The Secret Teachings of Jesus

According to the legend, Sophia, thru her own selfishness and cunning, gave birth to Yaldabaoth, a being of mindlessness and "ignorant darkness." And later it is also revealed that Yaldobaoth's progeny included Cain and Abel. Clearly, the message here speaks of the importance of our forethought, consciousness, and purity of motives in the creation of new humanity. Our procreation is not only sacred, but may be profane when love and mindfulness are missing.

We might say that the fact that pregnancy occurs does not necessarily make it, or its creation, holy. The brutal circumstances of rape would indicate this fact. Only the motives, maturity and purity of the mother and father involved, as the story of Sophia illustrates, will sanctify the union and its progeny. Of course, once in the real world, we can only love and provide for the children that arrive, but it does not change or better the circumstances of creation.

In his excellent book, "The Kingdom Within," John Sanford, an Episcopal priest and a Jungian analyst, relates the story of a young couple whose ulterior motives led to the classic trap of young adulthood, a pregnancy resulting not from love but from selfish ulterior motives.

"An all-too-typical case from my pastoral experience illustrates the point. A young man and woman decide to live together without benefit of marriage, then justify this on the basis that sexual feelings are to be freed from conventional restraint. All this time the young man knows that he does not love the girl and corresponds with another girl whom he hopes to

105

marry. The young woman with whom he is sleeping, meanwhile, tries her very best to get pregnant . . .

"Neither loves the other, either romantically or as a human being. The young man uses the woman as an object, a body through which to gratify himself; he finds pleasure through using her and satisfying his doubts about his own masculinity. The young woman also uses him. She hopes to get pregnant to force a marriage that is against his will and is willing to prostitute herself to him rather than face the anxiety of being without a man. So the arrangement is not free love but free sex, for there is no love in it . . .

"It destroys eros . . . there is only manipulation in the relationship, not eros. It is now a dehumanizing relationship to both because each uses the other for egocentric purposes. And spirit is denied absolutely, for neither partner scrutinizes his or her behavior in the light of any value system other than egocentric goals. The sin in all this is not sex as such but the unconsciousness of two people that leaves them victims of their egocentricity."[47]

John Sanford,
The Kingdom Within

Sanford's moral inquiry stops with the motives of the "unconscious" and emotionally immature "parents." But what can we say of the children produced by such loveless liasons? Should society force the product of such a relationship on both parties and society by forbidding the termination of a pregnancy? Are we compounding sin when we force the bringing to term of the products of such wrongful relationships? Does the sex act alone, devoid of real love or compassion, sanctify birth?

For too many years the Victorian morality dictated punishing the participants in sex with parenthood, no matter how inappropriate, or how loveless and exploitive the union, or even how disadvantageous to the new life - the bastards could be sent off to the orphanages. Forcing parenthood in these circumstances is to punish and sentence the new life into a calamitous union. What kind of society, and what kind of life, do we propagate under such inferior circumstances?

The ideas of karma aside, do we have the right to punish new souls into an earthly existence for the "sins" of their irresponsible parents? What good can come of such behavior? Are we "dehumanizing" mankind with such a policy? Can we not "restart" their lives at a later date under better circumstances with a willing and ready mother?

The current epidemic of "babies having babies" where unwed teenagers produce children because they are afraid to take responsibility for their actions is now a serious worldwide problem. We see immature teens getting pregnant simply because they want to go on welfare, get out of their parents house, entrap their boyfriends into marriage, or they have simply been browbeaten by religious extremists into a paralyzing sense of guilt over abortion. They wind up, for any number of illegitimate reasons, proceeding with premature motherhood, resulting almost inevitably in untold harm, sorrow, and regret for everyone involved. This is birth abuse - and it cannot be called sacred.

If these are the real, and mostly negative, reasons for the occurence of a pregnancy, then we could say that the child from that union might have a right to be abusing toward such selfish and irresponsible parents. And the unfortunate criminal statistics of children born into many of these tragic situations is indeed testament to the unconscious rage of the individual against his parents for his unwanted status. In study after study, it has been amply illustrated that being born at the wrong time, under the wrong circumstances, is not beneficial for either the baby, the parents, or society.

"John Doe, a child of scorn
For he knew hard times since the day he was born
An unfriendly life of pain he live,
perplexed, rejected and sordid.

The monopoly of life filled with sin,
was a game too selfish to allow him to win.
John Doe, a child of scorn,
What was the purpose of him being born?"[48]

Michael Hatch

The tragic case of Michael Hatch is a case in point. In his own poem he questions the very purpose of his existence. His life began with the rape of his mother who was 14 when Michael was born. Shuttled between relatives from the age of 2, placed in a foster home at 10, labeled "emotionally disturbed" at 11, arrested at 15, homeless at 17 and shot dead at 20. Michael was killed by the father of his former girlfriend as he sought revenge for a rape arrest just one month prior to his death. Michael Hatch's story is just one of the many tragic outcomes of unfortunate birth circumstances. The newspaper reported that he lived as he died . . . "an unwelcome guest." A former foster mother related: "I think he was destined to die . . . I think in some spiritual way Michael killed himself."

ANCIENT BIRTH CONTROL -

Our modern medical and moral dilemma with abortion contast sharply with attitudes in many older "primitive" societies. For thousands of years, in village cultures all over the world, midwives using herbal mixtures and other methods induced abortion in young and old women alike. Almost without exception, the men were uninvolved, or excluded, from women's affairs. For the most part, pre-industrial women were in control of their sexuality, without fear of men in funny robes shouting slogans of eternal damnation on the one hand and, on the other, expecting the eternal satisfaction of their urges. Most of today's trouble around the issue of abortion and free choice stems from the involvement of men meddling in women's minds and bodies. This was not always the case.

For centuries, people of all nations and cultures have sought after and used various methods of contraception to prevent the birth of additional children. Through trial and error, "primitive" peoples discovered substances and various techniques to prevent birth. And long before "modern" times and organized church morality brigades, women were in control of their sexuality.

Norman Himes, who has studied the long history of contraception, catalogues the vast number of methods and attitudes involved in childbirth and abortion. While not commenting on the efficacy of these methods, he cites East African women placing certain roots under their heads at night and wearing a magic cord tied tightly around their midsection. Other tribal cultures around the world used herbs, and in Central Africa women would plug their vaginas with chopped grass or rags. Cherokee indian women would chew the musquash root, and women in South America would douche with a solution of lemon juice and the juice from mahogany nuts. The bush native women of Dutch Guiana use an okra-like seedpod about five inches long with the end snipped off and insert it into their vaginas to serve as a condom which is held in place by the vagina and not the penis. Australian natives made an incision above the penis so that the semen seeps out of this exit and does not enter the female body.

Himes relates that an old Egytian papyrus, from around 1850 b.c., advises women to use crocodile dung with a pasty substance to block the sperm. A later papyrus tells of a medicated tampon covered with honey and gum from the acacia shrub. But probably the oldest method, that of coitus interruptus, where the male attempts to escape the vagina just before ejaculation, is undoubedly the least successful, and least satisfying, method known to men and women in heat.

"The cure for starvation in India and the cure for overpopulation - both in one big swallow!"[49]

Erica Jong,
Fear of Flying

Of course, the practice of abortion has always been widespread in older societies, and for numerous reasons. In his study of abortion in primitive societies, George Devereaux chronicles the widespread practice of abortion in numerous cultures around the world. He lists the numerous and familiar reasons often cited; medical, therapy, extreme youth, advanced age, improper paternity, social pressure, family dynamics, adultery, marital discord, protection of youthful beauty, dreams and omens, etc.

And the primary emotions that motivated abortion, regardless of culture, were nearly always shame, fear and anger. Shame was often the most important in inhibiting disapproved conduct in primitive societies and motivating young women to seek abortion. In these instances, the real shame was not the abortion but the pregnancy.

> "The very young Suau girl is aborted by her mother's sister. Among the Owambo a girl is not supposed to give birth before she undergoes her puberty rite. Among the Masai it is shameful for a warrior to impregnate an uninitiated girl. And Masai women must abort the children of alien, old or sick fathers. Among the Chagga, women must not bear children after their daughters are married. In Fiji, the Christianized Fiji girls abort in order not to be expelled from the Church. The Gilbert Islanders abort because their soil is barren. In times of famine Ngali and Yumu women abort to feed the fetus to the children already born."[50]

The practice of abortion is as old as the coupling of man and woman. And the reasons have been as varied as the cultures of man. In cultures that did not experience the normal loss of life due to disease, famine, and war, continual pregnancy was the norm. Infanticide, killing the born baby, was often the unfortunate technique used, where girl babies were not allowed to live and grow up to produce more children than could be handled by the tribe or village.

In many older cultures, women simply refused sexual relations during pregnancy and lactation, a period of from two to six years for each child. As with the Hunza and the Semai of Malaya, pregnant or nursing women did not sleep with the husband, and thus long periods of abstinence enabled these societies to prevent over-population and the exploitation of the female.

> "In most primitive societies it was unthinkable that male sexual desires should take precedence over the needs of the mother. Patriarchy everywhere sought to change this, through religious sanction. Women were to serve men's sexual urges even when preoccupied with motherhood. The church then interpreted the fable of Genesis as God's mandate to compel women to bear as many children as possible, even at the cost of the children's or the mother's physical health and welfare."[51]

Barbara G. Walker

In older cultures women needed help to space their births at reasonable intervals. In some tribal cultures it is said that, when children were breast-fed by the mother until five or six years of age, continuing breast-feeding altered the hormone balance and supposedly served to keep women from getting pregnant again. However, in our modern industrial age we may well have lost the knowledge of any such psychic techniques of birth control - if, in fact, they existed.

Regarding the more ancient and tribal environment of childbirth within the "natural order" of things, Seth had this to say:

> "A child born to two parents is also an offspring of the earth . . . a new creation arising not just from the two parents but from the entire gestalt of nature . . . psyche and earth cooperate on a birth that is human, and in other terms, divine. Historically speaking, there was always more land, early man could not run out of land, trees, forests, or food supplies. It was literally a limitless world." "Children came from women's wombs and many were stillborn, or naturally aborted . . . this also was in the natural order of things.

111

All flower seeds do not fall on fertile ground. The seeds that do not grow go back into the ground forming the basis for other life. Only those children perfectly attuned to their environment in time and space survived. This does not mean that the consciousness of a child was annihilated, for example, if it was naturally aborted. It did not develop . . ."

"There was a close biological relationship between the species and the earth, so that women naturally conceived when the situations of climate, food supplies, and other conditions were beneficial. So, biologically, the species knew ahead of time when droughts would appear, for example, and it automatically altered its rate of conception to compensate. Such knowledge resides in the psyche."[52]

> Seth, The Nature
> Of The Psyche

Are many of today's disadvantaged children so "perfectly attuned" to their environments? Or has our species just stymied the natural process and potential to maintain balance? Seth reminds us of the need to conceive only when conditions will be beneficial. Nothing is lost.

In other circumstances of traditional village life before modern contraception it was necessary for women to have as many children as possible to replace the infants that died prematurely, as well as loved ones lost thru disease and war. Other were born to placate the male ego, and as a source of "free labor" to maintain a stable family and strong village economy. In this context, the thought of women voluntarily preventing a potential birth was, pardon the expression, inconceivable. Add to this the fanatic credos of the various religions whose only interest was to have more believers, more soldiers, more of the faithful to rule over, and you have a climate for active procreation. But this took place in times where, in most cases, there was not yet a shortage of land, water, fuel, and food as we are experiencing today.

In the past, women were often little more than child-bearing machines. But for the last several thousand years of patriarchal domination women have been fighting back against the male establishment and clergy to regain control over their own bodies. The odds have always been stacked against women, considering the many chauvinist male legislators, judges, inquisitors, doctors, priests and self-proclaimed moralistic crusaders invading their bodies. For centuries, women have solved their own problems concerning childbirth in traditional village societies. Why do we need a change?

But not until the rise of large city-states, where the prejudice of men was codified into law, did women find it necessary to fight back, or go underground, only to find themselves again at the mercy of male doctors and priests. To stop the brutal unending wars in ancient Greece, for example, Aristophane's heroine, Lysistrata, lead the women of Athens on a crusade against men and their dangerous and infantile behavior - we might say in reproduction as well as war. The only weapon they had was sex - withholding sex. Wine goblets firmly in hand, Lysistrata proposed the following oath for the women of Athens:

"To husband or lover I'll not open thighs,
Though he bring proof-of-love of monstrous
    size,
But still at home, ignoring him, I'll stay,
Beautiful, clad in saffron silks all day,
That so his passion I may swell and pinch,
I'll fight him to the very last inch.
If, spite of hostile knees, he rapes me
    there,
I'll put him out, so frigid and aloof,
Nor wriggle with my toes stretched at the
    roof,

Nor crouch like carven lions with arse in
   air,
If I keep faith, then bounteous cups be
   mine,
If not, to nauseous water change this wine."[53]

Lysistrata's Oath

If it were not for the ready availibility of contraception, Lysistrata's oath might even now become a necessity. Today, woman must demand control over their reproductive rights and assume more responsibility for the control of population growth - or the Athens of the world will again be overrun.

THE PILL - NOW A CHOICE -

The advent of the modern birth control pill is one of the most revolutionary inventions of all time. The pill, and other devices, have finally made it possible to separate sex from procreation, and "amative" love from "procreative" love. We can now enjoy sex without fear of unplanned pregnancies. It is no small historical coincidence that the latest women's liberation movement gained considerable force when women were unleashed from the fear of pregancy and emboldened by the free expression of their own sexuality and creativity.

And all sex, whether amative or procreative, is sacred to the degree that love is present in the act. But that is not to say that women must always be vulnerable to pregnancy, out of some mistaken sense of doing god's will by continually avoiding contraception. Many Catholics seem to feel that any interference with unrestricted reproduction is somehow synonymous with profanity. Is interference, by condom, with the transmission of AIDS immoral?

Nineteenth-century Victorian morality is still prevalent in most fundamentalist religions today. In an age when sex was considered a "vile neccessity" for procreation, people were punished with childbirth if it occurred out of wedlock. A woman's only justification for sex was procreation and so "bastards" and orphans were created with a vengeance when

114

abortion was prevented. The idea that sex was bad unless it occurred within marriage most certainly led to many miserable marriages. Any information that encouraged sexual activity was suppressed, thus leading to the punishment of people for out-of-wedlock births that would most surely happen in the absence of education and contraception.

This was the nineteenth-century catch-22, when pleasure was a dirty word. Early in this century, Bertrand Russell, commenting on this warped morality, observed: "It is illegal in England to state in print that a wife can and should derive sexual pleasure from intercourse." So sex was sin, pleasure was against the law, and the "bastards" were quickly sent to distant orphanages. Naturally, due to this pervasive sexual suppression, the pornography industry reached new heights during these years.

Of course, unplanned pregnancies and the question of abortion will always be with us, unless we enter another dark ages of church-sponsored morality legislation turning individuals, and any unborn children, into the property of the state. If each and everyone of us do not exercise responsible control over our reproduction, then out of desperation and environmental necessity, the state surely will. Fortunately, science is closing in on solutions to birth control that will soon make the "morning after" pill a reality.

CHEMICAL ABORTION -

Already in development in several countries are estrogen and prostaglandin hormone-based "morning-after" pills that may have the potential to return complete control over pregnancy to women acting alone in the privacy of their own bedrooms. The only remaining questions are those of safety and whether the political-religious climate in each country will allow women to have a choice. But regardless of the fate of legalization of abortion, if these new pills are developed, they will be used and, if necessary, a significant black market will develop to make them available to women in need.

"Since a woman would take the pills before any diagnostible pregnancy, they might very well have the potential to ease the abortion controversy. The drugs can either prevent implantation or trigger the discharge of an already implanted egg."[54]

Mac Lean's Magazine

For all practical purposes, these new morning-after pills, given that there are no serious side-effects, will have the potential to end the abortion debate in favor of women's rights.

* Chapter Three *

- The Environment and Morality -

THE MORAL DILEMMA -

"The dilemma is this . . . all the impulses of decent humanity, all the dictates of religion and all the traditions of medicine insist that suffering should be relieved, curable diseases cured, and preventable disease prevented. The obligation is regarded as unconditional: it is not permitted to argue that the suffering is due to folly, that the children are not wanted, that the patient's family would be happier if he died. All that may be so; but to accept it as a guide to action would lead to a degradation of the standards of humanity by which civilization would be permanently and indefinitely poorer."

"Some might take the purely biological view that if men will breed like rabbits they must be allowed to die like rabbits . . . most people would still say no. But suppose it were certain now that the pressure of increasing population, uncontrolled by disease, would lead not only to widespread exhaustion of the soil and of other capital resources but also to continuing and increasing international tension and disorder, making it hard for civilization itself to survive: Would the majority of humane and reasonable people then change their minds?

117

Abortion Is Not a Sin

> "If ethical principles deny our right to do evil in order that good may come, are we then justified in doing good when the foreseeable consequence is evil?"[1]

> A.V. Hill,
> Promethean Ethics

ENVIRONMENTAL MORALITY -

In a crowded world, our decisions about childbirth take on new meaning and significance. Every decision to give birth, beyond simple replacement, has long range implications for the planet. We cannot afford a short-term outlook or, worse yet, no outlook at all. Ignorance and irresponsibility in childbirth now present real problems to our village, our nation, and our planet. In essence, environmental morality asks the basic question do we abort fetuses or civilization itself? Do our private and "moral" individual acts of motherhood, with each of us acting alone in our private universe and without due consideration for the whole, only add up to total immorality and catastrophe? This is the essential question. Are we capable of understanding our moral obligations to the people of the earth as a whole? Never in the history of the world have we faced this dilemma. These are new times - we have entered the age of "Promethean Ethics."

> "We should not hesitate to say that where over-population exists there is a human evil . . . A family, or a nation, condemmed to a mere vegetable, or even animal existence, by the sheer pressures of overpopulation is living in a state of destitution, in an inhuman condition . . . and if reason and medicine bid us take off excess weight, surely reason and humanity bid us reduce overpopulation."[2]

> Frederick Flynn, Natural Law And
> The Problem of Over-Population

* * *

"Many people ... are concluding on the basis of mounting and reasonably objective evidence that the life of the biosphere as an inhabitable region for organisms is to be measured in decades rather than millions of years. This is entirely the fault of our own species."[3]

G. Evelyn Hutchinson

The essential resources of our planet earth are not inexhaustible. There are limits to fresh air, water, ozone, topsoil, forest cover, ocean fish and the largely invisible species that perform vital functions of which we are only now becoming aware. In recent decades we have seen the catch of ocean fish, for example, decline as man becomes more efficient in farming the oceans. The pressure for more fish from more fishermen increases the likelihood that these commercial species will disappear altogether. Consider the whalers, who with their new technology of tracking whales, have wiped out species after species of the world's biggest mammal.

We add to this eco-pressure with the billions of tons of pollutants dumped into the ocean each year. In this deluge of effluent, toxic metals and substances move inexorably up the food chain causing cancers in fish and man. The contamination of the oceans is now well under way with some species now exhibiting a 30-50% organ cancer rate. The insidious process of bioconcentration means that small amounts of pollutants in small species become great amounts of bio- poisons in larger species that provide the food for billions of people.

The earth's rather small supply of fresh water is being rapidly reduced as man draws from the continental basins faster than the hydrologic cycle can replace it. Along with diminishing supplies of fresh water, we reduce the oxygen content of the atmosphere when we cut down trees in the world's forests - our oxygen factories.

Wholesale destruction of the earth's forests is now well underway in many countries accomodating the huge growth in human population. Half the world's population uses wood to cook their food. Shortages of firewood are threatening their very survival. Historically, this process of deforestation has been the prime cause of desertification, famine, and the collapse of civilizations. Today, with a larger population, the rate of forest destruction is accelerating.

Consider that Panama has reached the point, where due to the rapid destruction of their forests, there may not be enough water captured to fill the canal. Lakes are filling up with silt due to topsoil being washed away by too many subsistence slash-and-burn farmers. These destructive farming practices in the fragile rain forests are the poor man's only subsistence, and the rich man's source of cheap products. But they are the death of our common environment. With population out of control we cannot replant and regenerate our forests faster than destruction takes place.

And as the carbon dioxide builds up in the earth's atmosphere, man's brain will be gradually dulled from the lack of proper oxygenation and nourishment, perhaps compounding an already astonishing insensitivity to the natural environment.

A recent joint study by Brazilian and United States scientists, sponsored by NASA, found that the Amazon jungle has an impact on air quality throughout the world. And what happens to our worldwide air quality as that reserve is being progressively eliminated by man? In an interrelated ecology, the remaining forests are everybody's forests, thus creating problems of national and international conflict over usage of resources.

So our excess population growth accelerates the day when we will see these tragic resource conflicts. The new religion of "growthism" must not become the pathway to our planetary suicide, the excuse not to act responsibly. As someone aptly remarked, "growth for its own sake is the ideology of the cancer cell." Today, balance for its own sake is our only cure. Consider that there may be more people alive today than have ever lived in the past history of the earth.

"How dense can we get?"

Bumper Sticker

We have already approached the limits of our food derived from the sea, and in some locations we are approaching the limits of food sources from traditional agriculture. And where soil is depleted thru constant use and overgrazing, and underground water sources drained, the dust begins to blow and people begin to go hungry. Starving people in desperation, like hungry animals, will cut down the last tree, eat the last seed and drink the last water, thus ensuring their demise. If we are able to understand our impact on the land, the limits of nonrenewable and renewable resources, and the need to control our population, we will have a chance to florish. But without that knowledge or restraint, we are destined to self-destruction, repeating the same mistakes of earlier bygone civilizations.

At this stage in our planetary "development" it remains to be seen whether mankind will be able to work in concert, in global community, to protect the very staples of life for himself and for future generations. Limited national interests always seem to prevail. And as population growth requires more food, water and fuel there seems to be only conflict, and not cooperation, over existing resources and their protection. If we can only think of what we are eating today, without provision for tomorrow, it is likely that there will be a tomorrow where many more will not eat at all.

We see many countries around the world today that are now well down the road to total ecological collapse. And even if they were able to freeze their population at today's figures, life and prosperity above a subsistence level will be difficult. But with continuing unplanned population growth, their economies appear doomed. Every new mouth to feed is a dangerous weapon pointed at mother earth, and every new birth is a mugging of the already born.

"If we were only concerned about sheer numbers of people added to the population, India's growth is far more alarming than that of the United States. But if we consider the impact of each person on the world's resources, we reach an entirely different conclusion. We Americans consume much more of the world's resources than do people in India. One American has the same impact on the earth's resources as 39 Indians. Two million additional Americans have the environmental impact of 78 million Indians. In this light, U.S. growth might be considered more alarming than India's growth."[4]

Demographics Unveiled,
Zero Population Growth

* * *

"Just consider. Every minute an average 44 hectares (108 acres) are now turned into barren desert. A thousand species of animals and about 25,000 plants are facing extinction. The area in forests is shrinking catastrophically. The earth's mineral resources are being depleted with 100 million tons extracted every year. Large parts of the world's ocean, not to speak of inland water, are turned into dumps. Some countries consume more oxygen than the plants on their territories are now capable of producing. The carbon dioxide concentration in the atmosphere has reached 16 per cent and is rising at an annual rate of 130 million tons. As a result, global climactic processes are disrupted. There is a shortage of drinking water in 75 countries of the world . . ."[5]

United Nations Bulletin

The experience of Ireland in the nineteenth century is a good example of the famous "utterly dismal theorem" of Malthus stating that: "If the only check on the growth of population is starvation and misery, then any technological improvement will have the ultimate effect of increasing the sum of human misery, as it permits a larger population to live in precisely the same state of misery and starvation as before the change." Is this our situation?

> "In the late seventeenth century, the population of Ireland was near two million people living in misery. Then came the introduction of the potato, a great new technological revolution of the first importance enabling the Irish to raise much more food per acre then ever before.

> "The result of this improvement was an increase in population from two million to eight million by 1845. The result of the technological improvement was to quadruple the amount of human misery on the unfortunate island. The failure of the potato crop in 1845 led to disastrous consequences. Two million Irish died of starvation, two million emigrated; and the remaining four million learned a sharp lesson which has not been forgotten.

> "The population of Ireland has been roughly stationary since that date, in spite of the fact that Ireland is a Roman Catholic country. The stability has been achieved by an extraordinary increase in the age at marriage."[6]

> Kenneth Boulding,
> The Utterly Dismal Theorem

Today, every woman around the world now has the fate of the earth in her hands. She simply must not give birth to more children than her family, and her planet, can provide for. She must not be frightened into childbirth. And women, as well as men, must seek and utilize contraception or remain abstinent. Or women may postpone marriage to a mature age like the women of Ireland. Birth control and abortion, if necessary, are part of her responsibility to our planet. We are now a global village, a small planet rapidly running out of room. What happened to Ireland can happen to the world. Only now there is no other earth to emigrate to in the event of disaster.

And in the realm of biological tinkering, nature does not always accept man's technological "progress." Take the case of Henry Ford and Daniel Ludwig, two titans of industry who assumed they could clear and tame the brazilian jungle, planting "miracle" seeds developed by science. Their plans envisioned the harvesting of fast growing trees and products from these new seeds.

Unfortunately, these "miracle" seeds, developed in the laboratory from a single genetic strain, or monoculture, did not ultimately have the strength of naturally developed strains of plant life. And within several years the weak genetic strains collapsed under nature's onslaught of pests that fed on these new seeds. Nearly a hundred years after a blight destroyed the highly uniform Irish potato crop, we saw the same experience in Brazil where man's miracle seeds were, in these cases, a colossal failure.

The growth of biotechnology today may also foreshadow more of these potentially disastrous encounters with Mother Nature's intelligence. The long term success of the new genetic experiments remains to be seen. Hopefully, their effects on resources and population will not reproduce the Irish experience in the future. As the world population explodes, and the time-tested survival methods of traditional agriculture are eclipsed by modern pesticide-based farming, we are increasingly out on a technological wing and a prayer.

Instead of using the traditional methods of food production, we can only hope that technological agriculture can provide, without interruptions and colossal crop failures due to the lack of genetic diversity and the coming of pesticide resistant bugs, the food for the many more millions of people on the earth each year. Shall we risk worldwide famine on such scientific hopes by putting all our farming eggs in one highly profit-motivated and technological basket? Shall we not consider population a problem because we know technology, a new potato, will bail us out? We should not forget the Irish experience. The biblical injunction - "Be fruitful and multiply" - cannot mean that we multiply to the point where the fruit runs out.

SHORT-TERM MORALITY -

With population pressures beginning to push against the fragile environment of planet earth, we can no longer wait for technology to provide the perfect morning-after pill. If women, or men, are still afraid to take birth control pills out of a false sense of religious guilt, and we then allow the world population to reach 12 or 25 billion frantic souls searching for food, water, shelter, jobs, and sex, we won't have to die to be in hell - our hell will be on earth.

The priests, and short-term moralists, in their myopic concern for the unborn instead of the living, most certainly are helping to create environmental problems, and perhaps a hell on earth. Our hell on earth, in the form of disastrous quantities of unwanted and unplanned people, is indirectly manufactured by their sincere and well-intentioned concern, but also utterly disastrous inability to examine the long-term consequences of their beliefs.

And religious beliefs are not necessarily "truth." Truth cannot fail to nurture the fragile environment that God created. Can we be so full of "compassion" that we drown in catastrophe, as billions of unwanted and unplanned people scrap the last of mother earth's precious resources, living and dying in agony like the poor wretched people in Ethiopia and other modern hells?

We can't deliver life faster than we can create air, water, food and shelter, or chaos is the result. But this is precisely what is happening today. We have reached the point where it is no longer just a matter of correcting allocations and economic injustice. We may be beyond simple political solutions. Our rising populations, and rising expectations, place unmeetable demands on the biosphere. In a limited world, we must begin to ask what is our fair share of the new crop of children that can be sustained by the earth and nurtured by society.

> "In over sixty developing countries, growth in agricultural production did not match population growth during the years 1970 to 1977. The world Food Council estimated that in 1979 the number of people who were severely undernourished had grown to 450 million and that of people with some degree of malnutrition to 1.3 billion. In 1978, according to UNICEF, thirty million children under age five starved to death. In 1978, 134 million were born and 22 percent of this number have died from starvation. The simple reality is that we are bringing more children into the world than we can provide for."[7]

> Stephen Mumford: Population,
> Global Growth and Security

And the figures are even worse today. This is not life as God, or man, intended it to be. And surely if present trends continue, we will witness the gradual elimination of many species of life on our green planet as we know it. Whole regions of the earth's surface are now desert and brutal testimony to the scourge of uncontrolled human and animal population in areas where once gardens bloomed. There are no more Cedars of Lebanon and there are no longer any forests in Greece even though the damage occurred centuries ago.

Ignorance is no longer an excuse, morality is no longer an excuse, and even God is no longer an excuse. We must act to control what is out of control. In the end, this is the only compassion. Morality cannot mean the inability to take action to prevent the desecration of the earth. Morality cannot mean failing to take action against an exploding human population to prevent starvation and ecological ruin.

"In 1982, more than 17 million children, or one every two seconds - died from disease and starvation."[8]

UNICEF, United Nations Report

* * *

"Ten times more children in the developed nations are dying because of the contaminated water, poor nutrition and common treatable diseases than have died in the african famine . . . without massive relief efforts, these problems will soon threaten half the world's children . . . More children die because their mothers did not space births apart than due to drought."[9]

World Watch Institute

And despite this tremendous number of unneccessary and tragic deaths, the unplanned and unwanted ones that now survive pile up faster and faster due to lack of any birth control. In past ages, when there was plenty of room on the earth and so many died so young, these religious ideas of non-interference with human reproduction were relatively harmless because Mother Nature was still in charge. Today, however, these inflexible notions of morality that discourage or prevent contraception and abortion are not only highly inappropriate, but ultimately lethal. However morally appealing, the old morality is simply dangerous in an era of overpopulation and over-exploitation of the earth's limited resources.

But truth and right, to be either true or right, must recognize and respond to, as well as change with our circumstances. Otherwise, we have only dead truths. Truth is living in the now, and old dead truth isn't true anymore. The religions and institutions of today must change and recognize the new revelations of impending ecological catastrophe. We must act according to the new realities of today and not the "truths" of yesterday, otherwise our religion, morality, and compassion, however defined, are doomed.

127

THE KILLING OF MOTHER EARTH -

Today, we are rapidly killing Mother Earth with our uncontrolled fertility and ecological devastation. And we can now begin to clearly see that forcing others to give birth to unwanted, unplanned, and uncared-for children can be the ultimate crime against the baby, the parents, our community, and our world.

Those who argue against contraception and abortion, leading to population control, are part of the problem and not part of the solution. The unfortunate reality is that so many of the mostly unwanted and unplanned children we "save" today breed more lives in need of saving tomorrow. Out of the penus and the womb are the ultimate weapons of earthly destruction fired - resulting in too many people on too little earth.

> "No matter how distracted we may be by the numbers of problems now facing us, one issue remains fundamental: overpopulation. The crowding of our cities, our nations, underlies all other problems."[10]

> Paul Ehrlich,
> The Population Bomb

In our modern scientific reality, we are now the gods in control of the fate of the earth. Would a just god have more children than he can reasonably provide for? Is it not human beings that have too many children, blame it on God, and then expect him to clean up the mess? God doesn't provide jobs, housing, food and clothing, only we can do that. One look around the world quickly illustrates that we are now failing miserably because we are swamped with political problems and more millions of humanity each year than can be provided for.

Our modern megalopolises, mega-cities, are being deluged with people seeking employment and refuge from rural poverty and ruined eco-regions. Our ability to provide for these millions is limited. And willingness to pay the taxes to support even more irresponsible and unplanned births has come to a halt. There are limits . . . and we have reached them. Lester Brown, whose World Watch Institute tracks a wide range of environmental problems occurring today, senses better than most the real magnitude of our problems today. He states:

> "I think we're reached the point where the Secretary General of the United Nations should urge national leaders everywhere to adopt the "Stop at Two Children" goal. It's clear the earth's life support systems are really beginning to stagger under the pressures of 5 billion of us, and 83 million more each year now."[11]

A two-child limit is our new reality. At this juncture we cannot afford more than a replacement level of population growth. However, the sad reality in many countries today is that their excessive population growth quickly cancels any real economic progress, as well as any chance to improve the human condition, meaning only more severe poverty. Consider that India alone adds a population the size of Austalia's every year! But they don't add any resources, it's always less available for more people. Human decency and our hopes for a better future are themselves aborted by our over-population. Today, tragically, the "Right to Life" in some countries means a right to be born and starve to death. How do we now define true "compassion" in an overcrowded world?

MACHO MEN AND MACHO CITIES -

"Our whole life's but a pile of kisses and babies"[12]
Lysistrata (Aristophanes)

Women have been beasts of burden for centuries. The hordes of poor and underfed children, in both developed and undeveloped coutries around the world, are testament to the slavery status of women. Today, it is imperative that more women rise up and rebel against their macho men and macho priests, who most often only advise them to obey their macho man. Sadly, these same macho men cannot possibly provide adequately for the many children they force upon their wives and society. The "macho" ethic itself must be aborted.

For thousands of years the lot of women has been to be constantly pregnant and unable to find time to explore their own creativity and being. This has been a tragic loss for mankind, resulting in an imbalance in our laws and social mores that reflect only a male ethos.

> "Women all over the world say they want fewer children, to be able to feed and educate them. But the husbands are the problem. The husbands have to prove to the village every two years that they can still get it up. It's as simple as that."[13]
>
> Perdita Huston, If Women
> Had a Foreign Policy

It's a vicious circle for young women forced into premature pregnancy. And we are now seeing children grow up in trash heaps outside the huge cities of San Paulo, Rio De Janeiro, Calcutta, Jakarta, Cairo, Mexico City and many other burgeoning shanty towns. And soon these unfortunate millions of street children will be giving birth to more and more street children, not because they want to, but because it happens when they explore their sexuality for the first time.

And yet in the face of this worsening reality the Church continues to prevent the secular forces of planned and responsible parenthood from reaching these poor children. Currently, their efforts only *prevent* proper sex education and thwart what could be the easy availability of contraception and, where necessary, abortion. This is morality turned on its head, and a sure death sentence for a decent life. A 1984 World Council on Population report stated:

> "There are 20 metropolises today with total populations of more than 5 million. By the end of the century, there will be 25 metropolises with populations of more than 10 million." This phenomenal growth will be

mostly in the impoverished third world countries. Unless we institute some curb on our growing numbers, the mathematics that point to catastrophe are inescapable."[14]

Consider that the population of Mexico City in 1950 was only 3.1 million people. But by the year 2000 it is now estimated that the population will be 26.3 miilion, making it the world's largest city. In only fifty years the city's population will have multiplied almost nine times! What will the next fifty years bring? It is evident that catastrophe is inescapable unless common sense prevails over Church dogma.

In many so-called third-world (we only have one world amongst us) countries, the fundamentalist religious forces actively prevent the education of people on matters relating to birth control. "Murder" from their perspective is always on the microcosmic scale - they fail to consider the macrocosm - the whole world which we share and the condition in which it it exists today. Indeed, their tactics and dogma only scare their adherents into believing in some future hell while they are inadvertently creating a hell in our here and now. Too many "pro-life" believers clothe themselves in the words of mercy and compassion when it comes to protecting the rights of the unborn. But when it comes down to protecting the life of the earth as a whole there is no compassion left.

MORE PEOPLE AND MORE POWER -

"The more people we have, the more powerful we are."[15]

Mao Tse-tung

This was the disastrous logic of Mao Tse-tung, one of the world's great butchers - a fanatic murderer of millions of people who opposed his sadistic brand of commmunism and an uncontrolled population growth. Today, China has had to institute a very severe policy of birth control because of the past policies of men in power like Mao Tse-tung. Population pressures have forced the state to take drastic measures to curb childbirth and limit the rights of Chinese citizens. But they have seen the folly of unlimited population growth and thus had the wisdom to act and protect the future stability of their culture, economy and resources. As of now, China is the only country that has taken overpopulation seriously. And as draconian as their measures may seem to some, other nations are only beginning to wake up to the necessity of similar proposals of limited childbirth privileges.

> "Could we in the Church learn something from China before it is too late?"[16]

> Father Arthur McCormack

Japan's post-war population boom threatened the security of a nation with limited land, resources and a war-torn economy. Realizing their future predicament, in 1948 they passed the "Eugenic Protection Act" authorizing and encouraging abortion by licensed physicians. The nation rose to the task and halved their birth rate. Today, many more island nations, with their neatly proscribed resource regions, must begin such a program to balance their populations with their limited island bioregions.

Unlike China and Japan, the logical conclusion, barring any sudden changes, is that most Catholic countries will, at their present fertility rates, continue to grow in population well beyond their ability to care for their people. Indeed, out-of-control emigration is evidence of the reality of their problems. But while a totalitarian country can quickly impose severe penalties on irresponsible parenthood, a "free" country must rely on persuasion and the good sense of its citizens. And in the absence of the necessary exercise of responsibility and good ecological sense, more countries will ultimately see their resources being outrun and their green landscapes coming to resemble the deserts of the middle east.

The degradation of the earth, and the decline of human living standards, will continue until we recognize that contraception, abstinence, and abortion are essential to stop the crush of people. The birthrates of many Latin American and African countries, among others, are out of control. The general welfare of the people cannot be increased as long as population continues to outpace economic output. They are on the road to ruin, and their misguided policies will be a major cause of their downfall and perhaps bloody destruction.

In the past, one might have accused the Church of a hidden agenda in encouraging population growth to increase the sheer number of believers and their income. Today, such a policy, couched in terms of morality, is no less repugnant if its ultimate effects are to smother the earth with people. Excess population is now the real sin, and the unrestrained production of more believers, for its own sake, is immoral.

We are fast approaching the crisis time when the governments of many countries will be forced to pass laws that penalize, or prevent, couples from having more than one or two children. And due to our own, and previous generation's irresponsible behavior, all the future generations may well pay the price of reduced living standards and the sight of ravaged environments. The secular governments of countries, where population growth is beyond replacement, will soon have to divorce their policies from the stranglehold of the Church, and other fundamentalist religious doctrines that prevent the the solution to their problems.

In the very near future it is highly probable that many governments, particularly in developing countries, will be forced to encourage and support both contraception and abortion and perhaps to tax births, beyond replacement, until they stop. This loss of freedom tomorrow will be the direct result of our abuse of freedom today.

If we can give women the freedom, and the means to regulate and curtail their reproduction, we can solve our population problems. But more countries need to emulate the policies of Hungary, for example, where a 1956 law authorizes a woman to "make a conscious determination of desired family size and . . . to interrupt an undesired pregnancy by means of an induced abortion." However, religious influence over the secular institutions still prevents many countries from acting in their own best interests in this fashion.

> "Control of the laity through exploitation of their sexuality was probably initially related to the desire of the (church) heirarchy to out-reproduce non-christians Since maximum reproductive output was the goal, anything that inhibited the maximum output was then made "immoral." Masturbation, sex among the unmarried, homosexuality, contraception, abortion, divorce, sex education, prostitution . . . nearly all sex-related acts that are considered immoral by the Church can be traced to the reduction of reproduction."

> "Since virtually everyone is guilty of at least one of these "sins," and since forgiveness of sins has to be sought and only the priest can give forgiveness, he retains considerable power over his flock. The great tragedy in all this is the tremendous social injustice caused by the Church because of these "immoralities" which seem to have at their root a lust for power. The untold mental anguish caused by production of guilt feelings, as well as the physical harm brought about by these "immoralities" is unconscionable."[17]

> Stephen Mumford, American
> Democracy And The Vatican

* * *

"Never think that wars are not irrational catastrophes: They happen when wrong ways of thinking and living then bring about more intolerable conditions"[18]

> Dorothy L. Sayers,
> Creed or Chaos

CARRYING-CAPACITY AND THE LIMITS OF MANKIND -

It is inevitable that the the morality of unlimited human reproduction will ultimately lead to war and violence, especially in resource-poor regions? Survival knows no morality. Have we now reached a natural carrying-capacity limit of the planet earth?

"Thanks to modern medical, agricultural and industrial technology, humankind is expanding its numbers at a rate that threatens the carrying capacity of our planet. We are using up finite resources of soil, fresh water, fossil fuels, and readily extracted minerals at an ever increasing rate. We are exploiting our renewable resources, such as forests and underground water faster than they can regenerate."

"We are creating wastes, toxic or otherwise, at an increasing rate and faster than we can suitably dispose of them. We are degrading our environment, killing our forests with acid rain, and contaminating soil and aquifers and lakes with harmful chemicals, fouling our air with noxious gases, and extinguishing animal and plant species at an accelerating rate . . ."

"Expanding population and upgrading our living standards both worsen the problem. And the population problem is not confined to the Third World. It is affecting our own country (U.S.A.) because, even though our own birth rate has slowed in recent years, immigration, both legal and illegal, from countries suffering from rampant population growth is spreading the population problem from the third world to our own country."[19]

Edward Doerr

What was once a beautiful and abundant earth with plenty of space for mankind is now rapidly turning into a killing machine. Man is the direct cause of the extinction of thousands of species of animals, up to several hundred a day, because of his failure to control his own numbers. Referring to the almost total extinction of that magnificient bird, the condor, a leading environmentalist aptly remarked:

> "When the vultures watching your own civilzation begin dropping dead . . . It is time to pause and wonder."[20]

> Ken Brower

TRAGEDY OF THE COMMONS -

In a classic essay on the evils of overpopulation, Garrett Hardin neatly states the problem and how it leads to an inevitable ecological disaster. Simply stated, at some point in the cycle of adding more animals to a pasture, the point is soon reached where the land is overgrazed and is now unable to replenish itself because of frequent overgrazing. With the increasing population of the herds, the common land and pasture does not regenerate and is now no longer able to support all the animals. Thus, starvation occurs.

As people pursue their own self-interest, increasing their herds, and competing for the limited supply of grass to graze their animals, they eventually exhaust the resource and everybody loses from ecological collapse. This is the tragedy of the commons. And this is the state of our world with its population growth out of control. It is also a parable of mankind, not just animals. It is indeed tragic that we are still ruining our own commons - the planet earth.

> "The people in poor nations are increasing faster than those in the rich: about twelve times as fast in absolute numbers. If people in poor countries persist in producing larger families than people in rich countries, and if poor nations are unable to feed all their citizens,

and if we hold that the right to food means that the rich must ship food to the poor, then we are setting up a one-way siphon that moves the food from slowly-growing rich countries to rapidly-growing poor countries . . .

"Charity then finances suicidal growth. If the world's resources are indeed finite, and few doubt this any more, then at some time in the future the right to food will produce disaster. And now considering the real magnitude of the malnutrition in the world, we can say the future is already here. But the new limit to growth, sheer want, created by substantially eliminating the old limits (disease, principally) turns the right to food and the right to breed into a suicidal combination . . .

"If these two rights now have a translegal existence - if, to use the language of earlier days, they are god-given rights - then we must bitterly conclude that god is bent on the utter destruction of civilization."[21]

> Garrett Hardin,
> Limited World, Limited Rights

Indeed, without birth control and abortion, where necessary, we are stuck in a tragic and ultimately destructive compassion trap in which we must send food to feed the hungry, who in turn will produce more hungry, who will in turn will likely reduce more landscape to ruin. The cycle is truly vicious and our moral dilemma is profound. But we must act.

And there *is* a limit to the growth of population, whether it be animals or man, in relation to the renewable and self-regenerating capacity of the local environment - the carrying capacity. The deserts in the middle east, described as green in biblical times, are now void of vegetation due to the contant grazing of animals and the inability of the environment to replenish itself. Eventually, the top soil is lost and the land is unable to sustain life. Anywhere from 150 to 1000 years are necessary to replenish land damaged by slash-and-burn agriculture and bulldozers. Today, the nomads, mankind itself, continues to move onto other green pastures that are in turn destroyed by the process of overpopulation. Only now we are now running out of *both* pastures and topsoil.

Today, with our current population growth rates, we are talking about the possible destruction of the entire earth - the death, or dormancy for centuries, of the planet due to overpopulation. We are playing a game of ecological roulette due to ignorance, irresponsibility, self-interest, and blind outdated religious doctrines. Mankind, and womankind, must simply change their habits, for we are all citizens of one small and fragile earth. Each birth today has more direct environmental consequences than in the past. As responsible citizens and parents, we must all consider these consequences prior to bringing children into the world. Consider the following riddle illustrating the dangers of unchecked growth:

"Suppose you own a pond on which a water lily is growing. The lily plant doubles in size each day. If the lily plant is allowed to grow unchecked, it would commpletely cover the water in 30 days, choking off the other forms of life in the water. For a long time the lily plant seems small, and so you decide not to worry about cutting it back until it covers half the pond. On what day will that be? On the twenty-ninth day, of course. You have one day to save your pond.[22]"

A French Riddle

The riddle, of course, is how many "days" do we have to save the earth from choking on its own population? We have surely reached the point where we must persuade people to cut back on their birth rate, giving them the freedom and the means to do so. When one considers that we are looking at adding another billion people, a thousand cities of one million beings each, in less than fifteen years, our impact, despite lower birth rates in some areas, is accelerating enormously. If we don't act responsibly as individuals, then we will be forced to cut back by the dictates of the state. Freedom will then be a luxury and not a right. A World Conservation Strategy report aptly stated:

> "We have not inherited the Earth from our parents, we have borrowed it from our children."[23]

BIG FAMILIES AND BIG TROUBLE -

In 1958, a Swedish newspaper ran a competition of sorts to locate the largest family in the country. A family of 265 living members turned up, headed by a 92 year-old woman. Soon after that, a Mormon couple in the State of Utah, in the United States, claimed 334 living descendents. But shortly thereafter, the largest family in America was then discovered to be the 400 Amish descendants of 95 year-old John Eli Miller. The effects of rapid population growth on this family, in a very short span of years, give us an idea of the environmental burden imposed by large families over time.

Early in the twentieth-century when modern medicine began to reduce infant mortality, the Miller family began from just seven children which led to 63 grandchildren and to 341 great-grandchildren of the 55 married grandchildren. So great was the rate of uncontrolled birth that had old John Miller lived another decade he would have seen his family grow to 1000 descendants!

> "John Miller had seen with his own eyes a population explosion in his own lifetime. His data were not statistics on a chart, but the scores of children at every family gathering who ran up to kiss Grandpa, so many that it confused the old man. His confusion can be forgiven for there were among them no less than 15 John Millers, all named in his honor."[24]

> Glenn D. Everett

WHERE WILL THEY ALL FIND GOOD FARMS? -

John Eli Miller had lived long enough to see the effects of uncontrolled population growth in his own family. The potential tragedy of this rapid growth was best expressed by the old man himself: "Where will they all find good farms?"

The obvious answer is that most of the descendants of such large families will wind up land-poor and possibly impoverished as the original family farm is cut into smaller pieces until it cannot support and feed all the new family members. And this is just the destructive procreative power of *one* couple and their descendants over one hundred years! The earth and mankind can no longer afford large families, and the arithmetic of disaster. This is especially true when we consider that the vast majority of today's poor families start with little or nothing to provide their own descendants. Many disenfranchised poor now wind up in the streets of today's huge urban cities. These are desperate people . . . and this is now a desperate world.

> "People of present think that five sons are not too many and each son has five sons also, before the death of the grandfather there are already 25 descendants. So therefore people are more and wealth is less; they work hard and receive little."[25]

> Han Fei-Tzu (circa 500 B.C.)

A POOR MAN'S SOCIAL SECURITY? -

The time when men and women would have as many children as possible to provide for their welfare in old age can no longer be tolerated. These children do not always come from love but from a sense of necessity, desperation, and despair as well as a lack of contraception. And aren't these selfish motives for giving birth to children? Today, the real burden of these excess births is thrown upon society and other more developed countries as these "redundant" children leave their homes to seek a better life elsewhere. Emigration to other fertile regions is a virtual certainty where one's native environment has already been stripped of its regenerative capacity. Thus the destruction of still another stable bio-region will begin.

Children born from selfishness, into a world of no inheritance and limited opportunities, will most likely be a burden to the parents today and society tomorrow. The old economic strategy of large families is now self-defeating. The macho motives of irresponsible fathers, who force their mates into continual childbirth for purely economic reasons, is still the primary engine of destruction leading to the devastation of many poor countries today.

And disguising these economic motives in "moral" and religious terms doesn't justify irresponsible behavior and the selfish birth. It is now up to the women of the world to refuse to become beasts of burden for man's ego and surplus offspring. With available contraception, and abortion if necessary, women can now be released from continual pregnancy and motherhood to seek their own identity and creativity. The world so desperately needs to unharness women from the life-sentence of mandatory childbearing. Unbridled patriarchy is proving suicidal for our planet.

NO BRAKES ON POPULATION -

We might say that the Catholic Church is like the General Motors of religion. But their theological product is desperately in need of a recall because the brakes (on the population explosion) simply don't work. Given today's trends and policies, it may be said that many countries, under the influence of the Catholic Church's pro-life policies, are most certainly heading towards a catastrophe - one in which many millions are destined for less than human lives.

But if the Church doesn't issue the recall, nature will. The truth is that there are millions of "accidents" every day involving unintended and unwanted pregnancies of mostly poor people prevented from obtaining contraception and basic sex education. And Mother Nature is being made to pay the price for our lack of control and unwillingness to examine the effects of our beliefs.

"It cannot be the task of a pluralistic state to protect the religious teaching of a church where this does not coincide with the generallly acknowledged common good of that society."[26]

Bernard Haring, Medical Ethics

If the effects of the Church's policies are to breed starvation, unemployment, and environmental degradation statistics one digit at a time, then their current beliefs are a success. But Mother Nature cannot tolerate this kind of success for very long. The Church itself is now caught in a population trap of their own making. The dogma trap ensnares poor people all over the world and offers them little hope for escaping. Intelligent Catholics, however, realize there is something wrong, and ultimately disastrous, about the Church's population and birth prevention policies.

Other religious groups have already acknowledged the problem and the need for contraception and abortion. The 1958 Lambeth conference of Protestant denominations acknowledged that responsible parenthood "requires a wise stewardship of the resources and abilities of the family, as well as a thoughtful consideration of the varying population needs and problems of society and the claims of future generations."

There wasn't a single law regulating abortion in the United States until 1821. Only in modern times has our society, under pressure from fundamentalist churches, sought to legislate control of the womb and exert total control over women's reproductive rights.

Before that time the Catholic Church found nothing wrong with the act of abortion as long as the procedure was performed prior to the event of "quickening," defined as the first fetal movement experienced by the pregnant woman. This event might take place anywhere between the second and sixth month of pregnancy. Quickening, or the early reflexive movement of the fetus, was thus considered synonymous with the first sign of "life." Ironically, the position of the Church on abortion has never been more dogmatic than it is today as any abortion after conception, regardless of quickening, is now prohibited in the latest change of canon law.

Given the fierce debates on the truth of reincarnation between the opposing christian camps in the early centuries after Christ, we might conclude that the meaning of quickening may also have been used, and confused with, the act of inhabiting the womb by the soul. From our review of hypnosis research on pre-natal life, it is apparent that quickening and ensoulment are most likely *two* different and distinct events. However, fetal movement prior to ensoulment cannot be said to represent conclusive evidence of the "presence" of human life anymore than the reflexive response of a severed frog leg to a current of electricity represents the presence of a living frog. It is safe to say this debate will not end soon.

But there is no doubt over the fact that what is now quickening within the body of the planet earth is an over-abundance of human population.

THE POPE'S CHILDREN -

Eventually, if present trends continue, all nations may well experience the tragedy of population overwhelming resources. And whether the people control themselves, or the state is forced to control the population, as China has attempted to do, remains to be seen. The world cannot support the millions of unfortunate and untimely children - the Pope's children - delivered by dogma, fear, and ignorance into an already overcrowded world. As Stephen Mumford stated:

> "The Pope is leading the world on an international suicide course. By the end of four decades with a population of nine billion, the living hell projected by the Global 2000 study will be upon us. Whole nations are likely to rise up in anger and physically destroy their national church. In the end, the church is certain to lose all its power."[27]

And what might the Pope say today to the desperate millions living in poverty in the major cities of Central and

South America? Can they love this man, this institution, for their predicament?

In Mexico City, over 4 million people out of over 17 million (and predicted to be 31 million by the year 2000) must sleep in the streets - a burgeoning Calcutta west. As of 1987, there are now estimated to be over one million young men who belong to gangs with names like "Born to Lose" that have become an "army of the unoccupied." More than half of the city's population are under 20. And this is in spite of the fact that approximately 60% of the hospital beds in Mexico City are reportedly used by women suffering complications from illegal abortions. Women are desperate for release from their continual pregnancy. Meanwhile, many children are desperate for survival.

In our burgeoning metropolises around the world, the fuse of social dynamite is now burning, and will continue to burn or explode unless sane population policies prevail. All nations in which population growth is out of control are wars waiting to happen.

Do the "right-to-life" moralists and fundamentalist churches really wish to continue to bring more wretched poor children into existence without first trying to better the conditions of those that exist? Will the Pope's Children some day storm the Vatican demanding their share of the wealth and property of the church? Will the deprived continue forever to give birth to more deprived and not wake up to the vicious cycle they are creating? Is this the sacredness of life they speak of? Is this our compassion? Is this our future? Or will a White Knight of contraception save us from ourselves?

At this point, it seems inevitable that one day the poor and underprivileged Catholic masses of the world, among others, will seriously question the dynamic, and dogma, of their own deplorable circumstances and turn their frustration upon the Church. Frustration, anger, envy, and the appealing slogans of communism will pose a serious challenge to democracy under these conditions.

Generation after short generation, hundreds of millions of unfortunate people attempt to earn a "living" in the slums of South and Central America, India, the Phillipines, and wherever religious dogma prevents people from improving their own circumstances by preventing unwanted births. Year by year the struggle gets worse and the slice of the eco-pie gets thinner and thinner. And unless we bring our population and resources into balance, the unwanted unfortunates of the world may have their day . . . and it will not be pretty.

"Living by their wits and petty crime, millions of abandoned children run wild in the nation's (Brazil) cities. In San Paulo these youths - who live under bridges - sniff glue and scuffle over small change. Few escape the urban slums, where family planning is virtually nonexistent and the infant mortality rate is now a national scandal."[28]

National Geographic Magazine

Just as Rome once collapsed under the weight of overpopulation with hungry people teeming in from the often over-grazed countryside demanding support, so it will happen again and again unless drastic measures are taken. But, today, there are mega-Romes all over the world.

The Catholic Church has an effective monopoly on morals in many countries. These countries, and other nations with "moral" beliefs that fail to see the harm in uncontrolled population growth, may soon self-destruct. Is this the only "compassionate" course for the fate of the earth and the fate of today's children in desparate conditions of poverty? This simply cannot be the case. The doctrine of an unlimited "natural" reproduction surely cannot continue in our crowded world. The dogma must change, for economic growth alone, burdened by its own eco-implications, cannot carry the whole burden of transforming the habits of centuries.

"Today the Church finds itself in a new and devastating Catch-22 situation. To revise its teachings on birth control, including abortion and sterilization, would now seriously undermine its claim of papal infallibility. Such a changed philosophy would also be admission of guilt for the untold human suffering, death, and misery inflicted upon hundreds of millions of men, women and children attributable to excesses in reproduction promoted by the church."[29]

Stephen Mumford

10,000 MOTHER TERESA'S? -

No one can argue with the wonderful work performed by Mother Teresa and others like her committed to alleviating the suffering of the poor in countries around the world. But in India too, old religions and dogma keep the faithful, and in many cases the state or local authorities, from helping to control the tremendous problem of overpopulation. A faith that refuses birth control and abortion is destined to drown in desperate and hungry people. In this situation, one might ask, what is the point of helping to create future suffering? In such cases, how do we define compassion and responsibility?

If we don't act soon to control overpopulation, we will need thousands more Mother Teresa's to feed the starving and dying. While Mother Teresa, obedient to her faith and her Pope, believes that abortion and birth control are somehow wrong, there are others of her faith who see it differently.

"As long as women in the church confine themselves to picking up the debris of failed social systems and don't analyze and criticize those systems, they are loved and respected."[30]

Daniel C. Maguire,
Catholic Theologian

PAY-AS-YOU-GO BABIES? -

In our increasingly crowded world, we are fast reaching the point where some nations and communities must resort to legislating fines against the parents of children, under a minimum responsible age, who bring babies to term. As it stands now, there is every financial incentive to have a baby and absolutely no penalties for the decision, the birth mistake, that we know tends to ruin the productive lives of literally millions of teenage parents today. Study after study has demonstrated that the vast majority of the young premature parents never complete their schooling, or have the chance to pursue their dreams once they are shot down by childbirth and its overwhelming responsibilities. Is it then compassionate that we watch this process continue, and pay for it besides?

> "Given policies of voluntarism, non-cooperators will outbreed cooperators."

> Garrett Hardin

All other consideration aside, we are now at the point in many urban locations around the world where taxpayers will simply revolt and refuse to pay the costs of "compassion" in the form of medical, social services, police, for this irresponsible population growth beyond the economic abilities of the community and the often immature parents. This will be especially necessary where legal and illegal immigration add substantially to the host community's social costs.

This sounds cruel, but consider the cruelty of Catholic and fundamentalist churches who, in effect, force the birth of a child on teenage parents, and then force the costs of parenting these unwanted children on other people, and other nations, all in the name of their particular ideology to which you may not subscribe. In these circumstances, freedom of religion must also mean freedom *from* religion, and its most undesirable side effects.

The desperate immigrants that so many developing nations export, because their population is out of control and they cannot provide for their economic or social well-being, are now invading the developed nations out of a perfectly understandable drive for a better life. But how long can the developed nations accept these immigrants? It is obvious that

147

there is a limit. And we are now seeing the limits of this compassion in the form of anti-immigrant legislation? How long can we afford to be charitable toward those countries and institutions whose actions and beliefs continue to aggravate the problem of overpopulation and ecological ruin.

> "It has to be one of the most macabre contradictions of all time that our government (United States) rushes more than $100 million worth of food into Ethiopia in a too-late effort to save the starving, even as that same government snatches away 17 million dollars from the International Planned Parenthood Federation. The people of Ethiopia and other food-short countries need food desperately - just as desperately as they need to understand that this is a time to avoid pregnancies."[32]

> Carl Rowan

Indeed, in a new self-righteous fit of moral myopia we continue to cut off aid to the United Nations and Planned Parenthood groups then our problems will only be made worse and more misery will be created. We have an unbalanced "people budget" on the earth. It simply must be brought into balance, hopefully by individuals making responsible decisions and not by states and nations forced to act with the power of the law. Balance is imperative . . . and moral.

A CASE OF BELIEF -

If it were only a case of belief, without any side effects on our world, the decisions about childbirth would be benign. With certain "moral" beliefs, it is the result of the effects over time, of those beliefs, that prove so dangerous. The inevitable result is the gradual breakdown in society due to the creation of millions of people unable to provide for themselves, and the inability and unwillingness of society, or private charity, to pay the cost. And what could be more dangerous? This is the population bomb - and we are now witnessing the explosion.

> "The explosion of overpopulation can be far more
> dangerous to the maintenance of international peace
> and security than the atom, hydrogen or cobalt
> bomb."[33]

Benjamin A. Cohen

Ironically, it was Dr. John Rock, a Roman Catholic physician, who developed the first birth control pill. He was strong enough to pursue the dictates of his conscience rather than the precepts of the Church. As reported in an article in the Los Angeles times upon his death in 1984, he attributes his independent streak to a buggy ride he took in 1904 as a lad of fourteen.

A Roman Catholic priest of unusual independence took him along on a weekly visit to a poor farm. The old clergyman advised the 14 year-old Rock to "always stick to your conscience . . . never let anyone else keep it for you . . . and I mean anyone else." His independence never flagged, even after the publication of his popular book on contraception, "The Time has Come." Predictably, the publication of his book soon resulted in an editorial denunciation from the Pilot, Boston's Archdiocesan paper, which cautioned him to "watch his step or else."

It is surely a scandal that many dissidents in the Church have had these mafia-like warnings about exerting their independence of thought, especially in a public forum where they might embarrass the Church. But it only illustrates that intolerance is a characteristic of true believers. Too often the moralist ego demands that it be right, and you be wrong, and that the flock keep in lockstep.

It may be that people will still be arguing the morality of abortion, and whether man has a soul, or how many angels can fit on the head of a pin, long after the last fish has been fished from the sea, the last tree burned for heat, the last animal slaughtered for food, and the last river run dry upon a parched earth. But by then it won't matter anyway. Under those circumstances there will be no room for morality or freedom, only survival.

And if the result of our myopic morality and compassion for the unborn is to create a vast wasteland of mother earth, like the surface of the planet Venus, then something is very seriously wrong with our "morality" and our ability to act with nothing other than the shortest term consequences in mind. In a badly overpopulated world, instead of terminating unwanted pregnancies in the womb, the unwanted children may look forward to a slow death in a world devoid of space, food, water, shelter, comfort or compassion. This sounds bleak, but it is happening in many locations around the world as you read this very page. Is this the type of world we intend to pass onto our children? Is this the state of our morality and our compassion?

PAY-AS-YOU-GO BELIEFS -

"The Vatican has unlimited financial muscle with which to influence political campaigns in America. Attesting to this fact are the Fonzo study of the Vatican, which shows assets of 50-60 billion, including stock it controls in major American corporations, and the Foster Report which shows that the Catholic Church has assets of more than 100 billion (more than ten times the total combined wealth of IBM, Exxon, General Motors and U.S. Steel)."[34]

Stephen Mumford

Will the religious organizations, whose doctrines are largely responsible for the creation of overpopulation problems, open their coffers to the many mouths who are in desperate need at this very moment? Or will they prefer to finance political campaigns to insure that their limited resources and compassion are misdirected toward the legal protection of the unborn and the removal of reproductive liberties for unbelievers?

150

Is it primarily necessary that church money, the accumulated savings of believers, be spent to protect their dogma in legislation? Or should the first concern be for the feeding and sheltering of those who have come into existence because of pregnant women's abject fear of abortion due to a Church defined other-wordly retribution?

It is readily apparent that there is a tremendous amount of Church energy and money now mis-directed toward influencing the morality of others. Why is there not more effort directed toward the immediate here-and-now needs of those whose unfortunate lives are due in large part to Church doctrine? Rather than dogmatically prying open the flood gates of the womb, we need to open our front doors and face the already hungry and homeless. The need to clean up the mess of untidy theology is already staring us in the face. Just how long will the many innocent victims of unconscious reproduction stare back at a world of plenty, and docilely accept the facile truths of plump men in robes who have never experienced the travails of parenthood?

Our theologies must nurture our environment and not threaten its very existence thru the over-production of the human species. We are our own shepherds. And when we don't control our numbers, and disregard the needs of our bioregions upon which we rely for our sustenance, nature will take its course. Nature will be forced to abort mankind.

Some suggest that humanity itself is a cancer upon the earth. Out of balance, we are the disease. And so now Mother Nature is fighting this burgeoning disease, excess mankind, with its own immunity cells . . . call them cancer and AIDS. Perhaps planet earth's (Gaia's) own immunity and defense systems have begun working to limit our numbers and restore balance. By assuming responsibility for the balance of population of our species, we can avoid the tragedies that nature, and mankind, must resort to in order to achieve the stability and long-term health of the environment that is our real moral duty.

* CHAPTER FOUR *

- Religious Second Opinions -

THE CHURCH AND YOU -

> "Remember that never is it right to snuff out a human
> life with abortion or euthanasia."[1]

Pope John Paul II

This pronouncement by Pope John Paul II may seem morally appealing until one is personally faced with the very real and agonizing dilemmas of unwanted pregnancies in our lives. In our continuing irreverence, we might ask, how many unwanted lives are now effectively "snuffed out" by the very fact of their having been born into the most miserable of human circumstances. How many "heretics" were burned at the stake? Are we now aborting our eco-system thru overpopulation?

And will the Catholic Church assume more responsibility for the poverty around the world that it breeds in the name of compassion? Presently, it ignores any such direct connection and responsibility, choosing instead to say it is the moral duty of developed countries to accept and provide for the overflow of humanity from countries where population, and often environmental degradation, is out of control. Without any moral apologies the Church in turn looks to secular society to provide the goods and services required, but then denies that same society's right to attempt to curb excess human births thru contraception and abortion services.

It is easy to be compassionate, in absencia, when you remove yourself from responsibility for the misery created by

153

your doctrine, as well as from the very sight of poverty, starvation, and the countless women condemned to childbirth under the worst of circumstances.

"Idealism increases in direct proportion to one's distance from the problem."[2]

John Galsworthy

So many priests and nuns who have had to deal with the everyday realities created by the Church's reproductive policies are the ones who have first come to question its validity. Is it any wonder that today we see many new forms of "liberation" theology, whose adherents are reaching for desperate solutions to the poverty and problems created, in large part, by overpopulation.

Historically, compassion has taken many forms. For example, if a horse breaks its leg, and is now unable to lead a normal life and will most certainly die a slow and agonizing death, what do we do? For centuries, farmers and pet-owners alike have had the compassion to put the animals out of their misery. They did not consider it compassionate to let the animal howl in pain, unable to walk and function normally, because they choose not to take a life? On the contrary, ending the life was the compassionate act.

What can we say about the many cases of young girls, child-women, who are now pregnant and riddled with fear, guilt, and anxiety. Unquestionably, they are in a state of pain and misery as a result of their one unfortunate sexual indulgence that now threatens not only their own lives but also those of the children born in these circumstances? And it is evident these child-women are simply not capable of providing the mature mothering environment we would wish upon a newborn.

Shall we let these young girls, who are nowhere near the age of responsible motherhood, stew in their mental and physical pain and misery rather than removing the unwanted fetal tissue? Where is our compassion? Upon whom shall it fall? Can we not say that there are instances where we put new souls *into* misery by mandating their life under the worst of circumstances? And even if we assume the soul had only one life, by then allowing that one life to occur under the worst of circumstances could be called more cruel than the postponement of that one life thru abortion!

But all these arguments simply ignore the primary rights of the mother to determine the timing of her own motherhood. Is it moral that a birth be made to happen, when it was not only not intended, but only because the mother did not have access to the means of prevention, or the psychological fortitude to control her reproductive life and future family welfare?

> "It is a man and a woman who must decide whether or not they wish their union to lead to the birth of a child, not the church or the synagogue, and certainly not the state."[3]

Rabbi Israel R. Margolies

Are humans less than animal? Are there not times when we can end life, or not begin life, in the name of mercy and compassion? To say never is to remove yourself from compassion and the circumstances of the moment. To say never is to make yourself hard against realities and the wishes of others. To say never is to condemm other people for their different definitions of compassion, religion and morality. To say never is to ignore the changes going on around you. To say never is to close your eyes to the needs of the mothers whose unwanted new children are dying in the tragic famines we now see occuring in Africa.

Only dogmatic true-believers and fanatics can say never. But the rest of us must live and deal with the tragic realities of premature motherhood. Premature motherhood, as well as *too much* motherhood, are the dire consequences of fanaticism regarding birth control and abortion.

IGNORE-THE-SITUATION ETHICS -

"For evil cannot produce good fruit"[4]

Luke 6:43

Imagine for a moment that you are a fifteen year-old girl who has just been brutally raped. The Church's "moral" prohibition of abortion, in effect, condemms you into carrying the child of a rapist! The child, of course, would have no father as such, and the rape would be a constant reminder to the woman of the injustice committed upon her. Is god not "screwing" the woman thru the agency of the rapist?

So how would we feel if we were that child? Or the mother? Can we assume that any good can come out of this rape? And just what would the Church really do under these circumstances? Their actions speak louder than their words.

> "Sister Marianna is 35 years old. As a teenager, she pledged her life to Christ and entered a nunnery. She became an English teacher, and was working in the 1960's in the Belgium Congo at the time of the uprisings and revolutions. As a part of these uprisings, Sister Marianna and other nuns were raped repeatedly by the natives. She finally escaped to Belgium, where it was found that as a result of these rapes, she was pregnant. The Church quietly condoned the interruption of this and other pregnancies created under these circumstances. This is the same church which is subsidizing the opposition to compassionate laws concerning abortion for women who are not nuns."[5]

> We Are The Women,
> Takey Crist, M.D.

In this case it appears that Church dogma is only for others. When rape hits close to home situation ethics will do, thank you.

Consider the widespread occurrence of incest. In 1982, 65,000 cases of sexual abuse were reported (many surely go unreported) by the National Center on Child Abuse and Neglect (NCCAN) of the U.S. Department of Health and Human Services. In one 1963 study, 19% of the child victims became pregnant - raped by relatives. Preventing abortion is these cases would be absolutely immoral and unjustifiable whatever your doctrine of personhood implied. Who will hold down the sub-teen mother on the birthing table? Forced pregnancy is but a second rape.

Is conception here a consequence of an act of God? This presumption certainly qualifies as blasphemy against god!

> "Fundamentalists portray people as passive victims of whatever may befall them. In effect, God is responsible for rape . . . God gives only the strength to bear tragedy . . . it is unthinkable for the fundamentalist to consider that people, made in the image of God, may have to make some god-like decisions regarding stewardship of procreative powers."[6]
>
> Dr. Paul D. Simmons, Ph.D.
> Professor of Christian Ethics

Surely we cannot say that God intends women to be victims, allowing any man to brutalize her and then justify the result, the child, on "moral" and religious grounds? And what are we to say of the morality of the soul who might use this "opportunity" for incarnation, assuming as some might that there is some form of conscious karmic intention (or is it punishment?) in this conception?

If there is any morality in heaven then not one single soul would step forward to take up residence in a raped woman's womb.

In the case of rape, we can safely say that the only "good" that comes out of these deplorable situations are the self-righteous feelings accruing to those interested in exercising "moral" authority over other people. Their moral supremacy would be achieved as a direct result of condemning the mother for acting in her own best interests and aborting the child.

The rapist may enjoy seeing the victim forced to produce his child! Now we have two crimes, first the rape, and then the birth. This will be the merciless consequence of dogma, not compassion. Only fanatics say never and attempt to deny other human beings the moral freedom to decide what is best for them within their own unique set of circumstances.

All women caught in the unfortunate dilemma of an unwanted pregnancy, become prey to the rigid fundamentalist's stance of not wanting to bend their dogma to allow abortion, even after a crime such as rape. It is more important that the dogma be upheld at all costs, the mother and child can suffer. This is the sad logic of absolutist morality, never bending in judgment for the particular situation of each individual. One's compassion for doctrine may not allow any mercy for the mother and her situation.

> "What if Beethoven's mother had an abortion? What indeed? With equal justice we can ask, What if Hitler's mother had had an abortion?"[7]

> Garrett Hardin, Biological
> Insights into Abortion

And what are we to say in the case of older people dying of terrible and painful disease who beg for release from life? Can we ignore their rights, and their control over their bodies, their lives? Do we now, as supposedly "free" citizens, have to obtain permission to die? Who owns us? How can we avoid the long arm of the state, it's lawyers, the private morality decisions of courts and legislatures, and the steely grip of defensive medical practitioners?

If a woman can decide to pull the plug and die, by taking her own life in hopeless medical situations, why do we not conclude that she also has the right to "unplug" a fetus to "save" her reproductive life. When pregnancy is unintended and unwanted, why do pro-life moralists insist that they have the right to plug the fetus into her life? Does the fact of pregnancy now obliterate the mother's rights and mystically transfer them to the fetus, now represented by self-anointed moralists?

Women are unique in nature in that they have both the ability to give life, and the ability to take or postpone life, as the case may be. And this is the case whether it be their own life, as in the case of euthanasia, or that of a fetus in an unwanted pregnancy. The real problem is that the male of the species has never forgiven her for having this unique and extraordinary power. But every few decades, century after century, it seems that men are unconsciously moved to rehash the same tired ideas about removing the rights of women to control their creativity and reproduction.

> "We affirm the right of the woman to make her own decision regarding the continuation or termination of problem pregnancies."[8]
>
> Reorganized Church of Jesus
> Christ of Latter Day Saints

> "We believe the path of mature Christian judgement may indicate the advisability of abortion. We encourage women in counsel with husbands, doctors and pastors to make their own responsible decisions."[9]
>
> United Methodist Church,
> General Conference 1984

> "In our Baptist tradition the integrity of each person's conscience must be respected; therefore we believe that abortion must be a matter of responsible, personal decision."[10]
>
> American Baptist Churches, 1981

It seems that at many junctures in our lives there are those who want to reduce us to the status of children, and eliminate the intrinsic right to decide our own fates. In the case of euthanasia, who is to say that the choice of a pill to save us excruciating pain and to take us into the next world is murder? Who has the right to deny it, if freely chosen? The answer is clearly no one, and particularly in a society that is ostensibly dedicated to the preservation and defense of the rights of the living, and extant, individual.

However, there is little respect for the living and breathing individual, the pregnant woman, in our current trend toward morality legislation. Can we say that those who can shove their ideology down people's throats, in the face of such pain and suffering, are somehow acting in a religious and compassionate manner? Or might we also conclude that they are zealots who use religion, and another woman's fetus, as an excuse to be "right" and feel morally superior?

Condemming women to give life via forced motherhood is a type of slavery. The problem is in the condemming, not in the choice between birth or termination of a pregnancy for those faced with such a decision. Others, outside a woman's personal situation, have taken it upon themselves to condemm to death her individuality, her person, and her right to control her life. They deliver a wilted morality bouquet of unnecessary traumatic guilt and recrimination. Whose life is it anyway?

> "If a woman grows weary and at last, dies from childbearing, it matters not. Let her die from bearing: she is there to do it."[11]

Martin Luther (1483-1546)

The greatest abortion in the world is the removal of the woman's own freedom by those assuming they have moral control over her body. What, and whose, morality is that? It is not the mother's. It is quite simply the morality of slavery and the unholy domination of one human being over another. And how can male priests, who may have had no sexual experience whatsoever, condemn women for solving their own sexual and reproductive problems? If there is no base of life experience to temper one's judgement and compassion for the problems of others, the dogma can cut with a knife edge.

Also, we might ask, what would the current Pope's moral position be if the present day situation were reversed and "Secular Humanists" were breeding at a rate two or three times that of Catholics? A guess is that a perceived threat to the

Church's religious dominance might result in a whole new ecclesiastical brand of situation-ethics.

GUILT AND THE BIG STICK -

In our recent history, the Catholic church, along with other fundamentalist Christian churches, has made it very difficult for women to control their reproductive destiny. Guilt has been the big weapon of their enslavement. The technique is very subtle and very old. And once coded into law by self-righteous politicians, and into heavy-duty moral suasion by priests, the club of guilt is brought down on the pregnant woman's head. It's a miracle if a woman ever has enough self-confidence and inner strength to survive the blow, when people around her suggest that by not giving birth and terminating her pregnancy she is committing "murder" and will now, without dispensation, automatically go to someone else's imaginary conception of "hell." To those women on the receiving end of this kind of dogmatic reception, they won't have to wait, they experience a private hell here and now.

"I fear men, not God. He understands and forgives, they
do not."[12]

Nikos Kazantzakis,
Report To Greco

And this mental anguish can only be extinguished by vaporizing the dogma in one's mind. For those whose religous education began at a very early age, the programming is often so deep that we do not fully appreciate the conditioning power of guilt and its effect on our adult lives.

For many people deprived of education and religious choice from a young age, such guilt is powerfullly persuasive medicine. Fear and guilt are the strategies of control, and they have no relation with compassion and morality. By making women fear for their very lives, and the damnation of their souls to some eternal hell, the priests are committing their own sin and only aggravating the very serious problem of overpopulation in our

161

world. In effect, the Church has little respect for the individuality of its members. Compassion and empathy must, by definition, require attention to individuals and their circumstances.

"Should one feel guilt? No. Concern? Yes. Responsibility? Absolutely, as well as the compassion and willingness to see the need that speaks behind that unfortunate act." Why has this pregnancy been allowed to take place? For what are you really longing? Why have you placed yourself in the posture of conceiving without being able, or allowing yourself, to receive the fruits of that conception?

"Yet, if this act (abortion) is used for growth if it opens the way for you to find your own meaning, your own needs, your own truth and beingness, then it is a gift." The most destructive, the most useless, the most stagnant energy of all is guilt. It is the denial of the God light within you. Not only is there no punishment in God, but there is no punishment in the universe."[13]

Emmanuel

Even dis-embodied spirits like Emmanuel tell us that guilt does not solve our problems. The truth is that we are capable of manufacturing punishment in our own minds, most probably in relation to the understanding we have of our own cosmic integrity and individuality, or lack thereof. But all too often religious fundamentalists harbor a suspicious and pervasive urge to punish young people for engaging in sex.

Given a deep-seated suspicion and instinctive fear of pleasure, the moralist's only solution to the problem of unintended pregnancies is to punish the sexual offenders with children. This is not the solution, but the birth of more problems! By preventing contraception and abortion, where necessary or desired by the mother, religious fundamentalists will ultimately punish everyone, and unneccessarily burden the earth's resources as well. This is the real moral problem.

162

In effect, we are all punished by the results of most fundamentalist doctrines in the form of unwanted children. So how can this type of forced motherhood be a part of a truly "compassionate" religious approach? The punishment of women reeks of the "sex is dirty" doctrine of past repressive eras peopled by persons of questionable mental stability. Needless to say, in most cases, it only punishes the women and not the men involved. This is male justice, or half-justice, at best, and total injustice at its worst.

In essence, if abortion is outlawed, those women whose religions teach that abortion may be a legitimate and moral solution to problem pregnancies would thus be denied the freedom to practice the tenets of their religion - the ultimate violation of our civil liberties.

Obviously, people can differ on the question of abortion in their own lives. But unless your life is free of coercion and control, however subtle, then there is no freedom to decide, there is only obedience. And intelligent Catholics are now increasingly aware of this problem. Our forefathers had good reason to mandate the separation of Church and State. They had seen the abuses, and if we again aren't vigilant in protecting our historic freedoms, we will see a return to such abuses . . . all in the name of morality, of course.

> "Within my own tradition, the power of the Pope definitely will shrink. Today we are now experiencing the last gasp of a dying order, and in 20 years most of it will be gone . . . Women will remake religion - both its institutions and theology. This will improve the church because it has been deprived of the emotional concern and the tenderness that women, performing at their best, bring to any environment . . . There are many ways of being catholic."[14]

> Andrew Greeley, Priest,
> Professor of Sociology

Indeed, there are many ways of being Catholic. But the unreasonableness of the Church theology toward women, and their unique problems in life, has forced many women to either leave the church or ignore that portion of Church doctrine. And for good reason, it can hardly be called compassion for the mother. The obsession with the unborn tends to treat the mother as if she weren't even there. The practitioners of one-dimensional religion and morality can look right past the mother's interests. Dogma makes the mother invisible.

A RELIGIOUS SECOND OPINION? -

When confronted with the reality of tough life-or-death medical questions, a responsible and concerned professional will normally seek a second opinion from another source to confirm or deny his diagnosis. He or she welcomes the other opinion knowing that two heads are always better, and in our legalistic environment, safer than one.

Whose standards of morality shall we choose in judging the reality of abortion? Whose Religion, Church, or State shall take precedence over all others in judging the morality of abortion? Obviously, there are many standards, but only one answer for the reluctant mother.

"Not only is there no one world-wide standard of right and wrong under which mankind lives, but much of the greater part of mankind are subject to two standards of right and wrong, that of the church and that of their nation."

"Throughout Christendom itself there are three standards: The secular state, the churches, and that of the Sermon on the Mount and the Golden Rule of the New Testament. In India, for instance, there is even greater disagreement as to what is right and wrong . . . conflicting standards of Hinduism, Islam, Buddhism, Parseeism, Judaism and primitive Animism."

> "Without taking into account the motive that initiates
> an act and the social environment in which the act
> is done, no right judgment can be reached as to
> whether any act is good or bad."[15]

W.Y. Evans-Wentz

Precisely. A moral decision does not take place in a vacuum.
If our motherhood decisions fail to consider the circumstances
and consequences of our acts, not only for ourselves and our
progeny but our communities as well, then how can they be
deemed moral?

Does your church allow a second religious opinion? Or
are they only interested in pushing their own particular
scriptures? Are you dammed if you listen to other views of
morality, life, religion and compassion? Is the search for a wider
truth a sin? The tragedy of many of the adherents of
fundamentalist doctrines is precisely that they always feel they
have a monopoly on truth, a direct line to god that no one
else could possibly have. It seems so many today are attracted
to the ego-gratifying "I'm saved, and you're not" school of
religion.

> "The Church has the power to define dogmatically the
> religion of the Catholic Church to be the only true
> religion."[16]

Syllabus of Pope Pius IX

Certainly "true" religion, like a compassionate God himself,
must embrace the all. God does not have a reason to give one
group a monopoly on truth. There are many paths to god,
and the road of life has many twists and turns. And what
might one God have to say to another? Are we also not talking
or, better yet, listening to the same diety? Or are *we* the deities
to whom we are speaking?

THE LOST GOSPELS -

As mentioned previously, it was several centuries after the birth of Christ when clerics and mystics were clashing mightily over the meaning of his words and the validity of many of the extant gospels. As the Church became more organized, the urge for uniformity caused certain gospels and doctrines to be shunned or eliminated. And the concepts concerning when the soul may inhabit the womb, along with references to reincarnation and all other "Gnostic" gospels indicating Christ's own references to other lives, were systematically expurgated by the end of the fifth century.

In 1945, however, the new discoveries of ancient Christian texts at the Nag Hammadi site in Egypt opened new vistas on the past.

> "The focus of this library (Nag Hammadi texts) has much in common with primitive Christianity, with eastern religions, and with holy men of all times, as well as with the more secular equivalents of today."[17]

> James M. Robinson,
> The Nag Hammadi Library

These "lost gospels" give us new insight into the dialogue between Jesus and his disciples. And just as with the earlier discovery of the Dead Sea Scrolls, we learned, in retrospect, that we can't take the word of man, in the form of today's bible, for the complete "word of god." The "orthodox" bible today represents only a portion of the inspired books of the early christian era and, at best, a partial explanation of Christ's teachings. For example, an interesting reference to reincarnation occurs in the Secret Book of John, where Christ is reportedly queried about the nature of life by his disciple, John:

"I said, 'Lord, how can the soul become youthful again, and return into her mother's womb, or into humanity?' He was glad when I asked about this and he said to me . . .

'Truly blessed are you, for you understand this soul needs to follow another soul in whom the Spirit of Life dwells, because she is saved thru the spirit. Then she will never be thrust into flesh again.'"[18]

The Secret Book of John

The advanced souls and enlightened masters such as Jesus, can be the source of our understanding of death and rebirth. Unfortunately, some of the well-meaning people who have invested their lives in the Church, and whose ego is bound up with a particular belief, and perhaps an "infallible" Pope's pronouncements, seem willing to go to any lengths to discourage independent thought, proclaim the heresy of certain "lost" gospels, and certify the infallible truth of their own translation of biblical documents.

Today, the adherents to this bureaucratic priestly mentality make up the patriarchal truth-squad seeking to prevent women from exercising control over both the contents of their minds and their bodies. Recently, Holland's Cardinal Simonis was quoted as stating that feminists were "overvaluing their sex" by feminizing god and deifying women, thus breaking the "correct" ties of dependency between men and women. In Jesus's own words, he describes the people who have turned his gospel into "infallible" dogma:

"They do business in my word . . . And there shall be others of those who are outside our number who name themselves bishop and also deacon, as if they have received their authority from God. They bend themselves under the judgement of the leaders. These people are dry canals."[19]

> Jesus Christ,
> The Apocalypse of Peter

INFALLIBILITY? -

"The doctrine of papal infallibility dates only from the nineteenth century. It was declared to be dogma in 1870 by the First Vatican Council, and it can also act retrospectively."[20]

> Edwin Kenyon

Moral opinion is one thing, but the Doctrine of "infallibility" is quite another. By suddenly declaring this new Doctrine just over one hundred years ago, the Church then decided to retroactively declare everything they believe, or annnounce thru the office of the Pope, as perfect truth! But this is especially embarrassing in view of the fact that it only took three hundred years to apologize to Galileo for imprisoning him after he informed the Church that the sun didn't revolve around the earth.

But Galileo, who chose not to continue a wrong world-view, and the many women who decide not to continue a pregnancy, are realists. They let their own truth enter and define their lives. The "Infallibility" of Church doctrine represents a closed-loop belief system leaving no room for new imput, new truth, or new compassion. If we don't learn from our mistakes and see the world with new eyes every day, then we are truly blind to new realities and may then arrogantly mistake the earth, or the Vatican, for the center of the universe.

"I do not feel obliged to believe that the same God who has endowed us with sense, reason, and intellect has intended for us to forego their use."[21]

Galileo Galilei (1564-1642)

Even today, it appears many fundamentalist church leaders are deathly afraid of dissent as well as the contrary opinions of the members of their congregations. Doubts are discouraged in that they tend to rock the boat of frozen theology that never leaves the dock to explore the real world. Thus, there is no living and vital exploration, discovery, refinement, change, or even validation of their beliefs as the case may be.

When the flock, or individual women, begin to think for themselves the Church gets worried. But, in the case of the Catholic Church, there have been so many Popes and so many redefinitions of "Infallibility" in the past century it would make any god dizzy. Are human beings infallible? Is the Pope a human being? Is the Pope infallible? Does it even matter? Or is it that the doctrine of Infallibility is the last refuge of a dying or dead religion?

To many others the posture of fallibility, of a socratic unknowing, of a zen style let-go, is infinitely more religious than the idea of infallibility. Infallibility is the religion of bullies, of one-upmanship, of holier-than-thou prelates, of private lines to God, of a "do it our way or you will go to hell" school of thought. Many religions would come a long way in re-establishing their humanity by repudiating this nonsense and joining the world community of fallible humans.

In utilizing the not very subtle truncheon of Infallibility, the Catholic Church has, in effect, prevented its adherents from considering the opinions and beliefs of all other religions. This is tall dogma. And we might ask, if they are infallible, why are they so afraid of other opinions? The answer may be that, if you do become independent, as is the case with a growing number of women who simply do not follow church policy on contraception and reproductive decisions, they no longer have control over you. In effect, the doctrine of papal Infallibility is really about control - control of your body, your mind, and your life. And referring to the Pope's own birth control pronouncements, Conor Cruise O'Brien had these important words of advice:

> "A good man giving bad advice is more dangerous than a nasty man giving bad advice. A good man, whom you believe to be infallible, and who gives you bad advice, can hurt you a lot, and through you, others."[22]

Conor Cruise O'Brien

So true. When confronted with the real problems of overpopulation, unwanted pregnancies and abortion, the Church uses their "infallible" doctrine like a club against its believers. And to what end? Is happiness produced? When we look around the world at the misery being created now thru overpopulation, by the mind-numbing suasion of young women into premature motherhood, it is only Church control that is enhanced. The welfare of the people involved is almost always worsened. So when "religious" people tell you they possess infallibility, the one and only answer, perhaps it is time to look elsewhere for guidance.

In many "Catholic" countries where the Church is a powerful secular force, and where population problems continue to aggravate living conditions and create illegal immigration, we might conclude that the Church is guilty of informacide - the censoring and suppression of vital information about sex, motherhood, and birth control. Can we not say that access to birth control and related information and services is, or should now be, a human right? A right-not-to-give-life, as well as the information and means necessary to control our own individual reproductive lives, and the size of our families and communities, is now an environmental imperative as well as a basic human right.

If a woman is berated, pressured and excommunicated from a religion for being independent and seeking to better her circumstances, where is our nurture, our compassion and Christian charity? Apparently, there is no forgiveness for going against dogma, only excommunication. One has only to ask the hundreds of former priests and nuns who have left the Church after years of heartfelt service. Their reward for doubt, independent thought, and expressing compassion for their parishioners in abortion decisions, was excommunication.

And does God forgive us, or does he excommunicate us? Excommunication, or being out of touch, is not an attribute of god. Only infinite compassion and understanding of our human foibles befits a god worthy of our worship. If we ourselves are part of the godhead, the trinity, the triune self, then we have only ourselves to answer to in any afterlife judgment. But the use of excommunication can only be the tool of an an insecure and frightened institution, or individual, fearful of loss of power and status. It has nothing to do with religion. Excommunication only protects belief engendered by fear.

> "... For what principal reasons are people excommunicated, and priests and ministers defrocked? For pride, vain-glory and hypocrisy? For envy, hatred, malice and all uncharitableness? For gluttony or sloth? For ownership of slums or shares in shady loan companies? For coldness of heart or a cruel tongue? Not on your life. You can live openly in such sins and hold a bishopric . . ."

> " . . . But once it is discovered that you have an irregular marriage, that you consort with a mistress or lover, that you take pleasure in unconvention modes of intercourse, or, worse, that you are actively homosexual, you are in real trouble. This overwhelming preoccupation with the sins of sex is reflected in popular speech, where "immorality" almost always means sexual immorality."

" . . . Many theologians recognize that this is a serious distortion of Christian ethics, pointing out that Jesus was lenient and compassionate toward those who had "sinned in the flesh" as contrasted with his rage against hypocrisy and exploitation of the poor."[23]

> Alan Watts,
> Beyond Theology

ORIGINAL SIN? -

It is easier to comprehend the Church's inflexible position on abortion when we understand that the doctrine of Original Sin condemns the innocent aborted fetus, or anyone who has not been baptized by the Church, to an eternal punishment. This fundamental tenet of the Catholic Church states that every child is born with, or into, Original Sin, and that without the baptism of the Church they are now irretrievably consigned to hell. It seems that Original Sin is somehow transmitted by sexual acts. To the woman-hating christian ascetics of Christ's day sex was dirty, women were unclean, and babies were damned from the start until their baptism into the Church.

Aside from the sheer cultural effrontery of such ideas, Original Sin ranks as one of the truly great misunderstandings and one of the most macheivellian theological concepts in the history of mankind. This single supposition sets the stage for control of mankind. It is the perfect strategy to induce guilt. As soon as we come naked into the world, we then need the Church to remove the guilt and sin of our being born. Eternity is a long time for a supposedly compassionate and forgiving God to be angry at an immortal soul, or a pregnant woman attempting to control her own reproductive life and act responsibly in a crowded world.

> "When we actually look at the Gospels, however, we get a different picture of what contitutes sin. The New Testament word for sin (amartia in Greek) means literally to "miss the mark." It is the same word that

172

an archer would use who shot an arrow at a target and missed it.

"This seems like a surprisingly benign word to use to describe something as destructive to human life and relationship to God as sin, for, after all, can it be so very bad to miss the mark? But the seriousness of missing the mark is that it reflects back upon the archer. The archer missed the mark by failing to be on center and by shooting unconsciously without taking aim . . . sin is living unconsciously and therefore missing the mark."[24]

> John A. Sanford,
> The Kingdom Within

Unconscious procreation is missing the mark. And what of those who "miss the mark" and give birth to unplanned and unwanted children in a crowded world? Can we not say that there are times when the sin is the pregnancy and not the abortion? And do the motives of fear, selfishness, and economic gain, that so often combine to unconsciously produce new life, amount to righteousness or sin?

Adam simply used his innate and god-given curiosity to seek knowledge. But why did God put that big juicy tree of knowledge in the garden in the first place if not to find it? This "original sin" of Adam and Eve eating the fruit of the Tree of Knowledge is a twisted parable attempting to teach women fear rather than courage. If being born, or descending into our material plane on the push-pull power of our not yet digested desires, is sin, then we are all guilty . . . but guilty in our desire to learn and understand in order to achieve the final understanding that ends in our enlightenment.

But once we declare everyone a "sinner" simply for being born into this world, the priest and the confessional become a necessity, amounting to a make-work or W.P.A. program for priests. Now it becomes a necessity to pass thru the Church's portals and pay the bribe of obedience to walk out "saved" from the sin of curiosity. But might we not say that original sin, rightly understood, more aptly describes our common condition of unenlightenment, and not the "sinful" pursuit of knowledge and alternate truths, especially those not requiring the necessity of obeisance to a certain faith?

This may sound like a rather harsh denunciation of Papal doctrine, but just consider the harshness of the Church's own condemnations of other world-views and religions. What goes out comes back. And where our actions have such important consequences, as in the case of childbirth, we must try to look into the real meaning, consequences, and *effects* of Church beliefs and policies. The Church is still operating in the same fashion that it did a thousand years ago, when only the priests knew how to read and the western world only knew of one book, largely because so many others had been burned by previous Popes.

> "Man is forbidden to eat from the tree of knowledge of good and evil. But from the standpoint of the Church, which now represents authority, this is essentially sin. From the standpoint of man however, this is just the beginning of freedom."[25]

Erich Fromm

This story of original sin may have worked well for hundreds of years on uneducated people, schooled by the church from the time of infancy, but it can only be called a sorry anachronism today. Blaming everyone for something a mythical character named "Adam" committed, as soon as we exit the womb, is unfair in the extreme. And the induced guilt nags at the individual until he or she either succumbs to it and begs for mercy from the dark confines of the confessional, or simply stands up, declares the concept utter nonsense, and accepts personal responsibility for his or her actions.

This guilt, free-floating and unspecified, greatly affects a woman's decision to even consider terminating a pregnancy, even though it may be in her best interests. The powerful ideas of sin and guilt, inculcated from a young age, effectively work

174

to discourage free and independent moral choice and keep women powerless over their reproductive destiny.

> "It is utterly incomprehensible that one man's disobedience should have involved the entire race in the guilt for his sin and, what is more, made them liable to the penalty of everlasting damnation. This seems in flat opposition to all our ideas of personal responsibility and integrity."

> "Today, the churches are huge prosperous organizations ... their politicking and lobbying is largely preoccupied with the maintenance of idiotic sumptuary laws against gambling, drinking, whoring, selling contraceptives, procuring abortions, dancing on sundays, getting divorced, etc. My point is only that if Christians want to stick to all these irrelevancies, the Church will shortly become a museum."[26]

Alan Watts

Are our churchs, temples, and mosques now only museums of religious intolerance?

There are other explanations of "original" sin that we might touch upon briefly to illustrate the nature of our human fallibility and religious misunderstandings. For example, Dr. Juris Zarins, a scholar of the pre-biblical civilizations of the middle east, has come to the conclusion that "Eden" was once the fertile spot north of the Persian gulf area. There, prior to ecological devastation visited upon the land, four major rivers coincided in an ancient and fertile pre-biblical era, providing the ideal delta land for mankind's first major development of agriculture. But there occurred a significant clash of cultures between those tribes that first controlled, thru knowledge, the seeds of nature and thus settled into agricultural pursuits, and those nomadic tribes who were continuously roaming the environment and foraging for their existence. It was this cultural clash that became the flashpoint for the story of Eden.[27]

In the eyes of the pre-biblical and pre-agricultural nomadic tribes of the middle east it was a sin to plant a seed in the ground, a usurptation of god's power. Thus, the biblical story that comes down to us may only represent the point of view of the hunter-gatherers who, having seen much of the delta lands of "Eden" flooded by a worldwide rise in sea level about 5000 B.C., concluded that "God" didn't like agriculture or the people who, with a new found knowledge, "sinned" and planted seed for their existence as opposed to others nomadic life-style. Here, the nomads viewed the freak deluge as simple cause and effect - thus the story of the garden and man's encounter with a "knowledge" of the creative power of seeds.

But in the Church's version of the story, what did they blame Adam for? The Church blames Adam and Eve for educating themselves and, with their own god-given curiosity, tasting the fruit of the Tree of Knowledge. To the Church, knowledge, and even science itself, is apparently dangerous. But can we not say that God gave us curiosity in order to find wisdom, and better solutions to our problems? Today our entire civilization is built upon the bounty produced from the agricultural inventions of many ancient tribes who utilized the bounty of nature in new and different ways. We don't look upon agriculture as a sin today. But, in the past, this was apparently the dogmatic viewpoint of one culture whose story we seem to have inherited because it suits the needs of one particular religious organization.

Today, however, modern nomads sprinkle their excess children on the earth and forage for their existence to the detriment of our common environment. While those with a "knowledge" of their greater environmental responsibility are not only feeding the burgeoning and newly nomadic billions upon the earth but are also attempting to act to prevent another pestilence of biblical proportions . . . a plague of people.

> "I will greatly multiply thy sorrow and thy conception; in sorrow thou shalt bring forth children, and thy desire shall be subject to thy husband, and he shall rule over thee."[28]

Genesis 3:16

Patriarchal gods, thru their earthly agents, have certainly multiplied women's sorrow and conception. These lines from Genesis do not seem to be the words of a just god but the ravings of an acetic and women-fearing man (Moses?) helping to bring to fruition the judeo-christian patriarchal conspiracy against women. As Barbara Walker stated: "The Church interpreted the fable of Genesis as God's mandate to compel women to bear as many children as possible, even at the cost of the children's or the mother's physical health and welfare. Men refused to deal with the problem of over-population and women were forbidden to do so by the Church's tradition." In addition, the Christian canon even omits the "First Book of Adam and Eve" which contradicted much of the Genesis tale and notions of original sin.

Oddly enough, the Doctrine of Free Will was then invented by the Church in order to counteract the natural reasoning that caused one to feel that only a savage and evil "god" could create a fiery hell, allow his creatures to become entraped, and then not act to prevent it! But even man's free will does not release God from the ultimate responsibility for the very sins he punishes. Sterry said: "If sin is part of God's plan, then the sinner as much as the saint can claim to be fulfilling God's will."[29] If this is the case, where is the sin or moral transgression in a woman's choice of abortion?

And so the story of the garden itself, without the knowledge of the cultures and historical circumstances that produced it, became tabula rasa for the Church, millenniums later, to freely interpret and use as the basis to create their own meaning and declare it the word of God. And from this "word of God" women have been browbeaten into second-class citizenship. Beware of fables justifying patriarchy.

ORIGINAL ENLIGHTENMENT? -

Other ancient religions recognize our past-life sins in the form of "karma" - we reap what we sow. We are born into, and we also create, our circumstances. And we tend to behave in the present, under the influence of past tendencies and patterns, more or less according to our present level of consciousness and spiritual development. But "original sin" is not an act we committed at the very birth of time or inherited from a mythical character.

If original sin exists, we might say it is part of god's plan to play hide-and-seek with himself by dimming the awareness of our true natures. And this "sin" is more likely an on-going phenomenon in direct proportion to our failure to perceive our underlying unified reality, and perhaps our inability to understand the playing out of our accumulated karmic desires. The unawareness of our unity with the whole of existence, and our responsibility for its welfare, is our "sin." To the extent our irresponsible and ill-considered actions aggravate the problems of a fragile and sacred earth, we have truly missed the mark.

We might conclude that Original Sin, if it existed, would be the unconscious production of human life in the worst of circumstances, that may end up minimizing the necessary environmental conditions for the new soul's attempts at self-understanding and self-realization in a difficult world. The original problem, or sin, is giving birth when conditions do not justify our playing with our god-like ability to give life. Sin is forcing the original innocence of young girls to bear the responsibilities of motherhood before their time.

> "We need to go back to Original Blessing - not Original Sin. 98% of biblical scholars agree with me and don't believe in original sin. Fall-redemption theology has fostered political and psychological interests to keep people in line, allowing subjugation of women, destruction of the environment and oppression of the weak."[30]

> Father Matthew Fox,
> Dominican Priest

A growing band of independent and provocative priests, like Father Matthew Fox, realize the need for women today to understand the destructive implications of the entire "fall/ redemption" theology. The whole patriarchal, ascetic, and celibate christian tradition has been obsessed with guilt and sin and the complete subservence of women to a "male" god. Father Fox's concept of "Original Blessing" is exactly the starting point of a new "creation spirituality" capable of celebrating the equal role of women in the cosmos.

"For sin will have no dominion over you, since you are
not under law but under grace."[31]

Romans 6:14

And why should our religious perspective not assume a presumption of innocence and "Original Blessing" rather than sin? We are innocent and blameless until we fail to act responsibly, giving due consideration to the effects of our private decisions upon the larger interests of our community and our world. In today's crowded world, having an ungodly number of children because of one's selfish and childish fear of religious retribution is a sin against our neighbors.

Why should our definition of morality, in the birth of a new life, not include the necessity of parental intention and responsibility? If such parental intention and capacity are not present, such conceptions simply cannot acquire moral status. Surely this presumption must weigh in with at least as much moral force as the idea of "original sin" or the idea of the "immorality" of abortion.

"The Kingdom of God is within you."[32]

Luke 17:21

The over-populated and resource-torn Kingdom of God is within our power, if that is the kingdom we choose. We simply cannot, however, choose this lack of responsibility for the big picture and call ourselves moral at the same time. The new souls themselves will look to us to maintain the beauty of planet earth and provide a decent environment for their birth. *This* is our sacred moral duty to future generations, not the uncontrolled admission to life on earth leading to ruination of the environment thru unlimited population growth.

Each new incarnation may represent the possibility of the moment of a soul's enlightenment. Our final transcendence may await us from our very first breath. New life is thus born into original enlightenment, with a clean slate, and not into original sin, although perhaps carrying, or later attracting, the propensities of previous lifetimes.

Even our memories of previous lives are mercifully erased in a constant redemption at birth. But if we are then reborn, or "twice-born" into our enlightenment during our lives, the entire cycle of lives and existence is glimpsed and digested, and karmic pressure and desire for rebirth is broken. Short of an uplifting "rapture" of most of the world's population, however, we need to have a limit as to how many beings can pursue their enlightenment upon the earth at one time. Enlightened beings should be able to see the wisdom of such a proposal.

And whether mankind's innate human potential, our ultimate transformation, is realized in any one existence is always a possibility. And there are those who would say that a fortunate birth is a necessity for spawning the conditions of such a realization. Others might argue that any birth is fortunate, but this would imply a fatalism and sense of non-responsibility for the conditions of the real world in which we find ourselves. And can we not say that that same sense of original sin, and other-worldly karmic fatalism, is ultimately responsible for the human lethargy, and the gross irresponsibility, that has produced some of the worst living conditions on the planet . . . all in the name of religion?

Certainly most of us can lay claim to other "sins" we can rightly call our own and therefore must attempt to understand and correct. But only by widening our knowledge and understanding of life and death can we begin to eliminate our errors. God put the Tree of Knowledge in the garden for Adam and Eve. But was there a Tree of Ignorance in the garden that God would have preferred Eve taste from? One look around

180

the world and you might be forced to conclude that the fruit of the Tree of Ignorance has become a staple.

In the Church's hands, the tale of original sin or, perhaps, the real story of our descent from consciousness to unconsciousness, from spirit to matter, has been turned into a parable of power and obedience. Our disobedience to God then becomes the same as disobedience to the one and only Church.

> "Lady, Lady, I do not make up things. That is lies. Lies is not true. But the truth can be made up if you know how. And that's the truth."[33]

> "Edith Ann" (Lily Tomlin)

To those who argue against abortion, the avoidance of "sin" is the imperative that demands non-interference with our procreative powers. But to others of different religious persuasions, it is precisely this avoidance of our duty to control unintended and unwanted pregnancies that is the sin.

THEIR BELIEF OR YOUR REALITY? -

Only by freeing themselves from dogma and guilt, based on male-oriented mythology, will women around the world be able to control their lives and their reproductive cycles. If the fate of the earth depends on the passing into history of a particular dogma, we can live without it. The only real question is . . . can we, planet earth, continue to live with it?

In this day and age, to prevent the use of birth control devices is to produce more and more unfortunate young girls who will produce even more poor and deprived children, so that men in robes can act righteous and, in effect, force the birth of a child on unprepared and unwilling young women. This is the unfortunate reality. Women must be strong in the face of such opposition to their own self-determination from these obstinate macho men playing god with their bodies and our world. Women are goddesses too.

181

"The Catholic hierarchy is kind of nuts about sex. Almost all the issues of real controversy within the church deal with sex - women priests, divorce, birth control, priestly celibacy, and abortion."[34]

Leonard Swidler,
Catholic Theologian

However, these sincere and well-meaning, but often sexually inexperienced, people can persuade you to ruin your life thru premature pregnancy and act like they're doing you a favor! A woman must be determined to protect her reproductive rights. It's her decision, it's her body, and it's her life. Firstly, women must act in their own best interests, then in the interests of her born children and, finally, in the interests of any unborn children. The motherhood decision must be made in the context of the larger world in which we all live and experience, directly or indirectly, the effects of other's reproductive decisions. The real sin is not in taking control of your life, it is in losing it.

If we don't subscribe to any particular religious view, we might also ask why we should feel compelled to obey those restrictive laws implicitly confirming one particular religious concept and negating ours and others? Each person has their own understanding of "life" and their own religious "truth" to follow. Original and personal truth, coming from within, must be the basis of our decision. One-religion law may not be either our law, or our religion.

But if we have a secular religious dictatorship, in the form of outlawing abortion, we are denied control over our lives consistent with our religious outlook. At that point, we are justified in seeking our own way elsewhere, for the State and the Church have no business in enforcing a selective cosmology. And heaven doesn't have Republican and Democratic legislatures, or liberal or conservative justices, that change the rules every few years. Original truth is a man and a woman's conscious decision to bring, or not to bring, new life into being.

And no one else but the parents, as of now, are responsible for, or entitled to, such a decision.

"Believe and be saved or die a sinner." The important question is believe what? Are we supposed to believe that taking control of our lives to make a better world for our planned and loved children is a sin? Then why believe? What does belief do for us? Believing is not a knowing, it does not necessarily embody experience or truth, whatever that may be. Truth simply does not lay down and conform to our own beliefs. And in the absence of real knowledge and experience, belief is only covering our doubt with a creed or dogma. But belief alone often produces only a brief sensation of ego satisfaction, thereby creating a certain blindness that shuts the door on the real. No particular "religious" belief is a requirement for faith and trust in our own decision-making abilities and moral integrity.

Doubt itself, and the simple willingness to listen to the silence within ourselves is our greatest friend. So often we pretend to talk to god, begging "him" for forgiveness and imploring "him" to take responsibility for our actions. Must we not learn to listen to God, and/or the greater part of ourselves, instead? Can we not say that it is only thru an openness, a creative doubt, that we are available to wider knowledge, experience, and truth, as well as a compassion for others who may disagree with our own feelings and beliefs?

In effect, doubt is the real engine of discovery that propels us closer to the truth. Belief alone often just serves to paralyze or halt our exploration. But creative doubt can lead us finally to greater self-reliance and responsibility by forcing us to ask the questions that need to be asked. There is no reason to be afraid of our doubt, or a decision to terminate an unwanted pregnancy.

There is no need to rush into a particular truth. We can only see truth in the absence of blind faith. Otherwise, there is no room for it to enter our circumscribed mentality. Truth, our truth, can only emerge from a clear, open, calm, fearless, and unprejudiced mind quietly witnessing our own lives as well as the state of the world around us.

Our decisions about childbirth must take place in an atmosphere of love and understanding of the real needs of motherhood, the child, the family, and the world at large. If our beliefs cause us to ignore the realities of life then our belief will be our punishment.

The simple statement "I don't know" is one of the most religious declarations we can make. Fearful people do not want to live with doubt or ambiguity. They are almost incapable of saying "I don't know." There is all too often a definite answer, buttressed by the one "right" religion or morality, to give believers the feeling of being right. In effect, the ego satisfaction of being "right" is their religion.

But the subtle tricks of the human mind are legion. And if the self-righteous ever relax their certainty and admit doubt, they must then consider your circumstances and question the very rightness of their "truth" in your case. Few zealots of any persuasion are willing to do just that. Their very definition of "right-to-life" is that you, the mother, simply don't have a right to live your own life.

TRUTH AND CIRCUMSTANCES -

Unlike belief, truth and compassion will change with circumstances. Consider that in the sixth century a.d., Mohammmed suggested that it was all right for one man to have four wives. The reason was simple and was compassionate in its own way. Because so many men had been killed in bloody religious battles (not unlike today) it was compassionate for a man to bring love, and the chance for childbirth, to several women. Otherwise, thousands of young widows would, by other "religious" standards, be condemned to live empty and barren lives. In this manner, the lost population would be restored and the balance of men and women more equal in the next generation. This was intended to be a temporary measure, in response to the circumstances of the moment.

But times change and only the dogma remains the same. It is no longer compassionate for one man in moslem societies to monopolize four or more women, and leave the other men to celibacy or homosexuality. Yet this is what happens when the "Truth" of any age is force-fed to another generation living in completely different circumstances. People, and also our institutions, forget.

And so we are often ignorant of the original reasons for our beliefs and moral codes. But only the hard-core true believers will stick with yesterday's truths in the face of today's realities. Thus does belief become an end in itself, and blind to the suffering it may cause, when it wanders beyond that present moment and circumstance into time and territory where it is no longer true or appropriate.

We are not the people we were two thousand years ago, and we are not the world we were two thousand years ago. Truth is not necessarily words on old papyrus. Truth is our own response in the moment, to the circumstances of now, without resort to the past. The past may have no relation to our problems and solutions today. Truth is not static, but aware, alive, and probing the realities of the moment. Truth is so alive it can't be written down. Truth is, in the case of your pregnancy decision, your here-and-now reality as you see it.

Act on your own truth and not that of others.

Consider the case of Socrates, one of the greatest explorers of truth in history. Because of his passion for unflinching dialogue in the pursuit of truth, he was convicted of "corrupting the morals of youth." Sound familiar? And so Socrates was handed the cup of poison by the true believers of his time because he had a nasty habit of asking embarrassing questions and forcing people to examine their own particular prejudice or truth. If, by some miracle, Socrates could have been made pregnant, and punished with childbirth against his will, this might have been considered appropriate punishment by a male-dominated court of the day - much as it is today by those who now force birth on reluctant women.

Abortion Is Not a Sin

Consider Christ and the priests of his day. They also decided that he must be crucified to avoid the embarrassment of his penetrating questions. And what happened to Joan of Arc? She was burned at the stake for having her own opinion. They called it "heresy." They still call it heresy. Living your own life and making your own decisions will always be heresy in a world where so many think they have the right to control your very body, mind, and religious definitions.

"Religion, in the true sense of the word, does not bring about separation, does it? But what happens when you are a Moslem and I am a Christian, or when I believe in something and you do not believe in it? Our beliefs separate us; therefore our beliefs have nothing to do with religion."

"Whether we believe in God or do not believe in God has very little significance because what we believe or disbelieve is determined by our conditioning, is it not? The society around us, the culture in which we are brought up, imprints upon the mind certain beliefs, fears and superstitions which we call religion."

"The fact that you believe in one way and I another, largely depends on where we happen to have been born, whether in England, in India, in Russia or America. So belief is not religion, it is only the result of our conditioning. And is that religion? Surely, one's mind must be free of all those things to find out what true religion is. So to discover what is true religion, you must inquire deeply into all these things and be free of fear."[35]

J. Krishnamurti

Being free of fear and guilt, in our motherhood decisions, is sage advice for taking control of one's life. There is no need to imprison ourselves with any one version of life, morality and truth. Only by seeking the widest view of the problem can we come to a decision that will have real meaning - one's own

186

meaning. Our decisions about motherhood need our full attention and understanding. And that right decision may be your best creation in that moment of time. You have the right to create your own life, and you have the right to control your own creations. If not, who does?

JUDGING RELIGIONS -

"Judge not lest ye be judged." If our religions judge our actions, what is to be our criteria for judging religions? If religions attempt to "judge" man, should not men and women dare to judge religions? And if religions disagree on such major questions as the right to abortion, and the issues of overpopulation, then may we not judge them in how their ideas, in practice, affect humanity and the planet?

Under what religions are people better off? Under what "truths" do people prosper and nurture the earth? Where on the earth does religion, morality, economics, and ecology intermingle to produce the most elevated and sustainable culture? These are questions we must now begin to ask. We can no longer afford the luxury of doctrines that endanger humanity's survival. We are all in the same boat. And if religions don't bring us together, but only divide us, what good are they? How true are they? If they only bind us to doctrine, as in the latin meaning of the word, and not to understanding, then religions in the plural are a nuisance. Truth can only be one, just as the earth is one.

If beliefs, be they sacred or profane, religious or economic, "Scientism" or "growthism," produce a world in which mankind slashes and burns the environment into near extinction, then we will ultimately need to declare a voluntary international moratorium on our beliefs while we assess the damage and consider the long-run viability of these beliefs. In a sense, this is happening now. We are now becoming one people, on one planet, interdependent, and hopefully inter-responsible. But the old beliefs that still separate us, now seem obscene in their quaintness, and their ultimate effects dangerous in a world of limits.

Then are our nation-states, and their related religious cultures, a lasting phenomenon? Or are all nations just in different historical stages of decay, one no better that the other, because of their inability to arrive at a steady-state economy? History is littered with many bygone civilizations that failed to sustain their own natural environment. The reasons for their decline are often very similar; they depleted the resources in their region. They grew too large and were no longer "viable" as a community. Too often unviable communities simply turned on their neighbors to rape, pillage, and plunder in an attempt to maintain their unbalanced lifestyles.

One could even go so far as to say that persisting in dogma and tradition, in the face of ecological catastrophe and obscenely cruel conditions of life, directly caused by overpopulation, is a form of insanity. Should there really be no birth control in Africa, Latin America, China, the Phillipines, many island nations, or wherever people are in the midst of starvation and causing a serious depletion of their resources? Shall they borrow the very capital of life from generations to come with no intent to replace it or pay it back? Dogma then becomes selfishness in action.

Can we not say that God purposely gave men and women flexible, inquiring, and responsive minds in order to elevating our condition by responding to necessity, and preventing the desecration of his green earth? Or did he give us dogmatic beliefs so humans could persist in what some call "moral" behavior that succeeds in effectively destroying productive lives, as well as the environment, and at the same time feel self-righteous in the process?

A religion or culture whose precepts inevitably lead to economic disintegration cannot be said to be "viable" - they simply do not withstand the test of time. The practice of its precepts, especially in the case of unplanned and unwanted procreation leading to unlimited population growth, becomes dangerous to the long run health of its adherents and others of different faiths sharing the same small and precious environment - planet earth. Should we then require "warning labels" on unhealthy religions? And should they state that if we believe abortion and contraception are sins it may be dangerous to planetary health, affecting not just the believer but, ultimately, everyone on earth?

> "Americans are aware of the Church's highly successful efforts to undermine government support for family planning, abortion, and population growth control in most countries of the world. Americans are aware that during his October 1979 visit to New York, Pope John Paul II declared in a major address that all aliens have the right to freely immigrate to the United States. Americans are aware that the Catholic Church is the only significant promoter of illegal immigration in America and the only significant opposition to illegal immigration control. They are also aware that 90 percent of all illegal immigrants are Roman Catholic, making them suspicious of the Church's motives."[36]

> > Stephen Mumford, American
> > Democracy And The Vatican

Certainly no one country is obligated to provide for the excess population, created in other countries due to the influence of a particular religious doctrine. And no country, whether democratic or theocratic, is exempt from rational population growth, or better yet, in our late stages of planetary overpopulation and resource limitation, zero-population growth. At some point in the earth's saga, a steady-state, or no-growth, limit of mankind must be reached. Unless we want to continue to manufacture poverty and disaster for our children for generations to come, we must act to set our own limits of procreation. The moral act must consider the future.

THOU SHALT NOT KILL DEBATE -

> "When a book has been denounced by the official authorities it is a grave sin for a Catholic knowingly to buy, sell, borrow, own, read, or lend it to any other

189

person. The penalties apply to booksellers, publishers, readers, and reviewers unless they secure special permission to handle contraband goods."

"We believe that the rulers of a Catholic country have the right to restrict the activities of those who would lead their people away from allegiance to the Catholic Church ... they possess the right to prevent propaganda against the Church. This is merely a logical conclusion from the basic Catholic tenet that the Son of God established one religion and commanded all men to accept it under pain of eternal damnation."[37]

Published Teachings For Priests

Commanded? Pain? Sin? Restrict? Damnation? The Church's own words vividly portray the nature of the lopsided bureaucratic beast. Is it merely a "logical" conclusion, or a self-righteous blindness, that we conclude there is only one right religion and one true prophet? Is control and damnation the way? Or is it simply a total lack of respect for other traditions? And is this the only logic we have available in our motherhood morass?

And just where is the forgiveness of Christ in eternal damnation? In effect, control and damnation is the doctrine. And freedom of thought is forbidden, even a grave sin. It now appears as if the dark ages, in the form of dark teachings, are still with us.

Since when are ideas contraband goods? It is difficult to understand what benefit people can gain from an institution and belief system that so negates the individual and his or her own being. The real benefits of communion, fellowship, and prayer, that we derive from our religious beliefs and association, need not be attained at the expense of the dignity of the individual. And neither must the community be made to suffer the effects of the *sum* of many irresponsible motherhood choices as a result of particular beliefs.

We so often speak of "Human Rights" abuses by other countries and political systems around the world, but what about the human rights abuses of religious groups? What can we say about the human rights abuses against pregnant women who are denied an abortion, on "religious" and "moral" grounds, because of the power of a particular church doctrine? For almost two hundred years after Galileo had to recant his discovery that the earth revolves around the sun (to avoid being burned at the stake like his predecessor Giordano Bruno), the Catholic Church banned any book teaching that the sun, and not the earth, was the center of the solar system. Inevitably, the progress of science was thus stunted in Catholic countries, affecting them to this day.

Even book burning became a part of the auto-da-fe, or act-of faith, in Spain in the year 1502. It was against the law for a layman to read a book not approved by the local Bishop, and even possession of a vernacular copy of either Testament of the Bible was enough to allow the inquisition to burn you at the stake. It is not surprising then that the art of reading was nearly extinguished along with many of the fine classic texts of the day. Debate disappeared.

As Morton Kelsey relates in his book "Afterlife," the movement within the church to modernize its doctrine and recognize the truths of modern science was soon stopped dead in its tracks in 1907 by a decree from Pope Pius X. The real effect of this decree was such that . . . "By 1910 every cleric in the Catholic Church - including practically every professor at the beginning of each academic year - and each seminarian had to sign a statement agreeing to accept the faith as it was taught, as final, complete, and not subject to growth or change in any of the ways suggested by the modernists." And this in a university!

Apparently, even today, it is still a church rule that all Catholic publishers must submit, before publication, all books of a religious nature to a censor appointed by his or her bishop. The "Catholic Encyclopedia" states that "a Catholic publisher who issues a book on religion or morals without this Imprimatur risks immediate excommunication and nationwide boycott under Canon 2318."

Indeed, even non-catholic publishers have been pressured by the Church not to publish certain books critical of Church policy. What is sad is that publishers may have succumbed to such pressure against their better judgment. The obscenity of the Church's thought control is neatly outlined in Father Henry Davis's book, in which he states that, against the following classes of books, all Catholic Bishops must enforce a boycott:

> "1. Books by any writers which defend heresy or schism or attempt in any way to undermine the very foundations of religion; 2. All books . . . which affect to prove that true divorce is permissable in cases of adultery; 3. Books which attack or hold up to ridicule any Catholic dogma, such as the creation of man, original sin, the infallibility of the Pope; 4. Books which professedly treat of, narrate, or teach matters that are obscene, such as the defense of methods of birth control."[38]

> Father Henry Davis,
> Moral And Pastoral Theology

Is birth control obscene and indefensible? Must any book attempting to teach young women how to avoid ruining their lives with an unwanted pregnancy be considered obscene? Where is the compassion, faith, trust, respect, honor, liberty and freedom in these words? Where our freedom of thought, and a multiplicity of religious affiliation, is not treasured and protected by law, this book, and others like it, might never see the light of day.

Today, it appears that women are experiencing a theological tantrum from the "right-to-life" movement and fundamentalist churches. The impulse to control women's bodies and minds seems never to abate. And we have almost as many different laws as religions, but with the same objective, to remove control from the woman over her own creation.

Over a century ago, Josephine Henry, a suffragist and woman's rights pamphleteer, was asking the same relevant questions of the Church for which, even today, there are few answers.

> "Has the Church ever issued an edict that women must be equal with man before the canon or the civil law, that her thoughts should be incorporated in creed or code, that she should own her own body and property . . . No institution in modern civilization is so tyrannical and unjust to woman as is the Christian Church. It demands everything from her and gives her nothing in return. The history of the Church does not even contain a single suggestion for the equality of woman . . . Through tyranny and falsehood alone is Christianity able to hold women in subjection."[39]

> Josephine Henry

* CHAPTER FIVE *

- ABORTION AND THE LAW -

"THOU SHALT NOT KILL" -

Can we not say that this commandment also includes Mankind as a whole? And does it not apply to the ongoing "killing" of our planet's fragile and limited ecosystem? Does it only apply to one species? If we crush our own precious environment thru the many pressures created by overpopulation, we are then slowly killing the earth, birth by birth, as we procreate beyond our capacity to provide a humane existence for all human beings. We need to ask on what scale are we "saving" or "killing" life and existence itself.

In the light of the realities of modern motherhood and our emerging ecological crisis, we need to re-examine the biblical commandment, along with its origins and many various interpretations. We must remember that these scriptures emanate from rabidly patriarchal and mosaic times when "God" was smiting the "enemies" of "his people" left and right. We should also note that, unfortunately, we have few records of the scriptures and commandments from earlier matriarchal civilizations when man did not interfere in women's affairs - especially childbirth.

Is abortion a killing? Or murder? Did God prohibit killing, or murder, or mercy killing, or euthanasia? We must remember that there is no biblical commandment that states "Thou shalt not commit abortion." But in relation to the sixth commandment, we might ask if perhaps there a missing commandment saying "Thou shalt not go to war." Does God, or our various world-wide anthropomorphic forms of worshipped dieties, believe in self-defense? Or in the right of women to control their fertility, along with the sheer numbers of children and the environmental destiny of the planet?

"On the very next page of Exodus we have the command to kill those who break certain laws. It is nonsense to suggest God forbids what he also commands. The verb used ("Rasach") refers to "illegal killing inimical to the community" and is rightly rendered by the New English Bible "Thou Shalt Not Murder."[1]

R.F.R. Garner, Abortion - The Personal Dilemma

* * *

"There are many who would forbid abortion on the grounds that it violates the sixth commandment. This argument rests on error. In the King James version and the Douay versions of the Bible there is the commandment: "Thou shalt not kill." More recent translations, translations based on sounder scholarship, render this as "Thou shall not commit murder" The difference is significant. Murder, by definition, is unlawful killing: making this distinction implies that other forms of killing may be lawful (e.g. killing in self-defense) And the Bible does not forbid killing, only murder. Murder is a matter of definition."[2]

Garrett Hardin, The Case For Legalized Abortion

Nobody likes to think of themselves as "killing" anything. However unwitting and unconscious it may be, the fact is that we "kill" everyday. When we drink a glass of water we digest microscopic animals visible only when we peer thru an electron microscope and witness the hidden reality of millions of tiny microscopic dinosaur-like creatures in miniature. When we walk on the grass we crush small unseen animals. At many levels of existence we are "sinners" in the natural order of things - the way god planned his creation.

Like it or not, this is Mother Nature's grand scheme - one species feeds on another, thereby keeping the balance. Does one animal "sin" when it feeds on another? And who feeds on man? Only mankind itself, the community of planet earth, can act to decrease its numbers and not upset the balance of life. The act of balancing the human population is now the province of sacred and responsible motherhood and, where necessary, it may involve the termination of a pregnancy.

Is it murder when we sit down at the dinner table and eat animals that have been raised and "killed" for our food? Certainly we can disagree on the necessity and propriety of an animal-based diet. And it is plain that many "pro-life" politicians do not see the irony of their beefsteak meals, and support of saturation bombing, when they espouse concern for the rights of the unborn?

Even the Catholic Church has never taken a stand against wars and killing, as have the Quakers, and refused its adherents the right to bear arms and participate in wartime madness. With a "holy-war" and "god-is-on-our-side" mindset, the Church has often blessed the wartime efforts of many bloody regimes and become a great practitioner of situation politics. Today, the "holy-war" and moral crusade is against women and their reproductive rights.

If we look at the Jains in India, we see a most devout sect dedicated to "ahimsa" or non-injury of all living things. Joel Fisher relates the following story about the sometimes obsessive concerns of the Jains: "Their exaggerated regard for life is maintained to this very day and all devout Jains are expected to follow ahimsa to its minutest detail, with no concessions; for example, they may not kill any grubs found in vegetables. Western tourists in India are often puzzled by the tedious progress of white-garbed Jain monks who, wearing masks to prevent murderous inhalations, are careful to whisk away all possible insects from their path."

Thus, the most pious of Jains decline to travel by car because of the havoc wreaked on insect life. But they now arrange, when ascending mountains designated as shrines, to be carried aloft in sedan chairs by Hindu bearers who are not allowed the moral privilege of extending such courtesy and concern for the meticulous preservation of the local insect population. The "morality" of Jain priests requires sedan chairs, born by hindus who shall not have the same right to engage in such meticulous moral rectitude.

When carried to extremes, it appears that the pious Jain's main concern is with their own holiness and not whether their Hindu bearer accidentally steps on a grub or squashes a gnat - if this were the case they would never leave the house. Here, it seems rather obvious that such ego-laden piousness is nothing but an ego-laden self-righteouness, refusing the privilege of their "compassion" to those who must live in the real world and bear their burdens.

Like those who would prohibit abortion, they leave the believers and non-believers alike to deal with the realities of a messy world, while the priestly arbiters of truth clothe themselves in fine robes and remain cloistered in temples without windows. Such is often the attitude of many toward women who must deal with the real world of today and bear the heavy burdens of childbirth and nurture.

> "To revile and calumniate a worshipper of the Supreme
> Brahman is a sin ten million times worse than that
> of killing a woman."[3]

Mahanirvanatantra

> "Any woman who causes to fall what her womb holds
> shall be tried, convicted and impaled upon a stake
> and shall not be buried."[4]

Assyrian Code of Law

It is also apparent that women have often not even had the status of insects in some cultures. Given these extremes of piety, the Brahmins of ancient India, along with the rabid anti-feminist patriarchs of Assyria and other biblical cultures, eventually destroyed the Mother Goddess of earlier matriarchal religions and turned their ascetic vengeance upon women. Even killing women was better than insulting a Brahmin!

The fetus, a potential male warrior or economic slave, was considered more valuable than a woman in a male-dominated culture. The ancient counterparts of today's prelates, who consider themselves "pro-life," in some ages have often not even considered women to be worthy of moral protection. Only children, who were valuable property, beasts of burden, useful to a slave-like economy had value. And women produced this valuable crop of slave labor. Beasts of burden, of whatever species, apparently do not have legal standing.

But where dogma is threatened, the Church has not hesitated to recommend the death penalty, in fact, they lobbied for it. An incredible case in point occured in France, in 1942, when a woman "abortionist" was actually sent to the guillotine! In effect, she was then killed under the law instituted and pronounced "moral" by the Catholic Church at that time. The history of the Church is filled with these instances of the selective utilization or enforcement of their commandments. The legions of "witches" burned at the stake during the middle ages are brute testimony to the Church's hypocrisy regarding the sixth commandment. Do we abort unwanted fetuses or murder human rights?

Can we not say that true awareness must lead us to a compassion with which we can deal with the realities of the world, forcing us to face the responsibilities of our own existence, and our children's existence. Shades of gray, and not just black and white, are also part of the spectrum of light and morality in childbirth decisions. When childbirth may be "inimical to the community," or to our own welfare, it may then require the postponement of life.

In the west, throughout the centuries, the Church has also had its share of compassionate and reasonable men who wrestled with the problems of life in the womb. But all too often, their own compassion and reason, expressed in an independent and undogmatic manner, was simply suppressed outright by Church authorities thru the rigid dictates of doctrinal committees thousands of miles removed from the parish. For centuries the front line priests, dealing with the realities of parishioners, have done battle to bend the application of doctrine sent down from remote locations by more removed and doctrinaire Bishops and Popes.

NO SOUL - NO MURDER

Internal battles over Church doctrine have continued to this day. And in evidence of this ongoing re-interpretation of Church doctrine we find, in Gratian's Decretum, from the year 1140 A.D., one of the first efforts at compiling the Catholic Church's ecclesiastic legislation. Here, we discover the recognition of the vital importance of deciding when a soul entered the body, so crucial and important in determining whether or not "murder" is said to occur upon abortion.

"He is not a murderer who brings about abortion before the soul is in the body."[5]

Decretum, 1140 A.D.

Indeed, the very definition of "murder" rests on the definition of "life" and its whereabouts. In the biblical sense, it also rested upon whether an event was "inimical to the community." Circumstances were, and are, important. As we saw earlier in our discussion, we don't really have any proof of "life" "in" the fetus, in the form of an animating soul, at any particular point in time during pregnancy. And the results of numerous hypnosis studies we examined appear to validate the fact that souls do not attach to the fetus, or "quicken," until just prior to the birth event.

Thus any animation or movement of the fetus may not equate with "life" or soul being "in" the fetus. In addition, purely reflexive tissue responses do not, in and of themselves, imply the totality of animation or ensoulment as we have seen.

Questions of animation aside, most reasonable people now believe, as many laws recognize, that any abortion beyond the sixth month of gestation would not be considered appropriate. Once the fetus has reached a "viable" stage many feel that termination is no longer legitimate unless the mother's health is endangered, or that a fetus is so deformed that compassion dictates that such a tragic "life" not be allowed to begin.

However, one must wonder about the morality of cases, when the fetus may be on the cusp of viability, and where the intransigent and reluctant "mother" is going to be forced to give birth to "save" the life of the child against her own will and better judgment. Even if the mother has come that far, not necessarily by choice but from an early lack of available medical options and the untimely necessity of obtaining approvals, many would say she has now "forfeited" her right to determine her future. Can this be a "solution" to the problem of unwanted births? Must society now entitle the fetus to the right to crush the life of the mother? Can we "forfeit" our rights to a fetal "person" that is our own creation? If we can unplug our life, can we not unplug our own creation?

We must ask what sort of a relationship is being forged between the legions of immature and reluctant "mothers" and "fathers" and their unplanned children. It is all too evident that in the vast majority of these cases the father and mother may have no real interest in the child, or even the necessary emotional and financial capacity for parenthood. And even when the father's identity may be in doubt the state would be intervening to enforce birth against the mother's wishes. Is the state doing this child a favor? Can we not postpone the soul-cycle until the timing is better for both mother, father, and child? Or are we only interested in punishing the mother, with birth, for her sexual "sin" and "saving" the child into a disastrous "family" situation?

Would we not be more compassionate in sparing the new soul the pain of these negative life circumstances? On the other hand, if the soul, in relation with either the mother or the father, *creates* the conception event, with a karmic

201

foreknowledge of the abortion event, then we are now dealing with very different circumstances. We are denying the mother her instinct to terminate the abortion and thus interfering with the pre-ordained verdict of "nature." We may be interfering with the "will of god."

In a world of simultaneous reality events, structured in other dimensions by our greater beings, we are at a loss for words as to the "morality" of these events. Our limited "intelligence" is simply not up to the task. Some might say we are only sleepwalking thru the multiple events created in our "dreamtime" reality, of which our limited consciousness, in our waking reality, is only dimly aware. Aside from these otherwordly speculations, we can only judge the rightness of motherhood decisions by the outward and visible circumstances of our world and the needs of the mother.

The right to shape our lives, our parenthood, must be part of our freedom on the material plane. Our lack of knowledge of our deeper spiritual realities, along with the meaning and the shaping of life events, should give us pause in using terms like "killing" and "murder" where we are, in effect, both creator and destroyer.

Obviously, pregnancy terminations will always be difficult decisions. But the reality is that too many births are forced in too many cases, resulting only in the worst of situations for the newborn and the mother. Will time heal all wounds in these circumstances, or will the majority of these cases turn out to be filled with misfortune for the saved? Could the new soul have gotten a better life elsewhere?

To put the question of abortion and "murder" in a more timeless perspective let us consider the perrenial wisdom embodied in the familiar passage of Ecclesiates 3:2 in the Old Testament:

> "To every thing there is a season, and a time to every purpose under heaven; A time to be born, and a time to die; A time to plant, and a time to pluck up that which is planted; A time to kill and a time to heal."[6]

Ecclesiastes 3:2

In Ecclesiates we have a beautiful and yet unflinching expression of the ancient biblical and agrarian wisdom that reflects the realities of our human lives. Here, there is no question of Church authority, god's will, or other patriarchal religious precepts. The age-old wisdom of farmers, mothers, and of mankind, recognizes that there are no real absolutes. Instead there is a season, and a reason, for all of life's occurrences. Garrett Hardin aptly comments on this particular passage in one of his fine essays on the subject of abortion and overpopulation: "Ecclesiastes 3:2 is one example of the loss of commonsense which has followed the alienation of modern man from the realities of life that people close to the soil naturally and easily comprehend." Amen. Awomen.

In our role as stewards of mother earth, of being gardeners interested in the long term health of the garden, there are times when we must "pluck up what is planted." In Japan, for example, where they have approved of abortion for centuries, they refer to the practice as "mabiki" meaning "thinning seedlings." In this sense, there are no absolutes in life, there is only the condition of our garden; it is either green and lush and providing for everyone, or it is choking with weeds and dying from continuous raking. Our garden is the planet earth, and its condition affects the welfare of the totality of families and their well-being.

Wisdom and compassion must co-exist in truth. An old Zen expression says "the head must match the tail." And so the head of wisdom must match the tail of compassion or we have an unbalanced beast of tragic proportions. Both wisdom without compassion, and compassion without wisdom, may become a recipe for disaster. Where population is out of control, an unbalanced beast of tragic proportions is on the loose.

THE LAW - MORE MEN IN BLACK ROBES -

Everybody is "pro-life." The question is whose life are we considering. The problem for women arises when men sit in judgement and pontificate about the existence of "life" before its actual and earthly existence, with the intention of punishing women for not going along with their own, or society's, religious beliefs. On raised platforms, in black robes, male judges in too many courts have stared down at women and condemned them for following their own god-given instincts and controlling their reproductive lives.

From our explorations into metaphysics and the new hypnosis research, we have seen that the soul may not choose to "inhabit" the fetus until the birth event, or, at the earliest, near the six month of gestation or beyond when the brain and neuronal connections are fully formed. Presumably, this would be the point when a complete and "viable" being exists that may be capable of the full expression of human consciouness. As we noted, however, many insist that our incarnation and habitation of the fetus, does not take place until immediately prior to birth. From this we can conclude that the fetus is not synonymous with "life" itself, but only with the vessel that receives life.

And from the soul's point of view, we might presume that there is no point in taking up residence within a microscopic vessel that is not yet capable of expressing the fully human dimensions of consciousness. We might assume this would be the point when the raw fetal material is fully formed, the essential brain and neuronal connections are fully developed, and the fetus is capable of life outside the body.

If this is the case, the current state of the law as embodied in decisions such as Roe vs. Wade, forbidding an abortion in the third trimester appears to be a reasonable compromise. Reasonable, of course, to the extent that society sanctions any intervention in the women's body at all prior to birth. It is obvious that we are denying the mother's rights for the rights of the fetus whose "personhood" is now deemed to have priority over the mother, the only extant living person before the court. Is this reasonable? Whose "human" rights are being violated here? And just where is the other "person" deemed to have these special rights? Is that person in residence in the fetus? Can the court prove it? If we cannot how can we condemn or outlaw abortion?

Can we prove that even one single soul has ever been "killed" or annihilated by the act of abortion?

Our right-to-life logic goes from "This is a human fetus" to "This fetus is human" and finally to "This fetus is a human being." To the extent that the fetus becomes human in the eyes of the law, and gains the full rights of personhood before the court, the mother becomes correspondingly inhuman, losing her own human rights. Given the sheer vagueness and uncertainty in the concepts of personhood, ensoulment, and viability, the "forfeiture" of a mother's right to pregnancy termination and procreative freedom proceeds on the shakiest of legal, moral, and religious grounds.

> "Because there is no quantum leap into consciousness during fetal development, there is no clean and sharp boundary between sentient and nonsentient fetuses. There is therefore no precise point at which a fetus acquires moral standing. An early abortion belongs in the same moral category as contraception."[7]
>
> L.W. Sumner, Abortion
> And Moral Theory

The problem with legal intervention in private matters is precisely whether we should be allowing others to decide whether to allow an abortion for one woman whose conception date is subjectively pinned at 165 days and then disallow an abortion for one whose date is similarly guessed to be 166 days. Obviously, the fact that we allow such cases to get away from the mother and her physician, and into a court of law in the first place is more the problem than the solution. The decision must remain private. Any law in these private matters is destined to be a nightmare of injustice.

Recently courts in Georgia and Minnesota have struck down "parental-consent" laws requiring minors to obtain parental permission to have an abortion. The courts found that teen birth rates soared and more risky late-term abortions were performed when young girls were forced to deal with parents and bureaucrats during these extremely emotional times. And one might ask how a "mother," of whatever age, can be a "minor" in the eyes of the law? If an underage "mother" can be required to get permission to have an abortion, why is she not required to get permission to have a baby? Is not negligent conception, carried to term, an obvious societal crime that in all too many cases results in "damage" and punitive costs to taxpayers? Is it only the unborn who have rights?

Short of the wisdom of a Solomon or a Buddha, the 1973 landmark decision in the Roe vs. Wade case, by the United States Supreme court, was probably the only possible political compromise of the interests of the individual, the state and the unborn. The only real question remains on what basis are we justified in compromising the rights of the mother before the birth of a living person? The Supreme Court decided that the "viability" of the fetus was paramount in the decision - viability meaning the ability of the fetus to live outside the womb. In effect, the court decided that human life, in any legal form, did not exist before this point. Implicitly, they also decided that the mother's life did not exist *after* this point.

> "We need not resolve the question of when life begins, but when does the state acquire a legitimate interest in protecting potential life. For the stage prior to approximately the end of the first trimester, the abortion decision must be left to the medical judgement of the women's attending physician."[8]

> Chief Justice Blackmun,
> Roe vs. Wade, 1973

With typical male-defined reason, a woman's right to decide was, in effect, passed to the doctor within a very short time after a woman, or teenage girl, may have learned she is pregnant

206

- perhaps the same day! How reasonable and moral is this shift of parental responsibility away from the patient to the physician?

The court also completely bypassed the real essential question of when "life" begins, obviously, due to the fact that no one can supply the answer with any legal degree of certainty. And yet in deciding they could not reasonably answer that critical question, the court simply brushed it aside and proceeded to the issue of viability - a construct upon which they could compromise the rights of the mother and then justify the intervention of the state. Thus, pregnancy is sliced into three artificial periods, dating from a largely unknown point of conception, and then the rights of the mother and fetus are divided accordingly.

This is a perfectly "logical" outcome for a court made up of male judges. If there were five or more women on the court, my guess is the decision would be different. And just what court decisions can we point to that so fundamentally compromise the rights of the male body as Roe vs. Wade, among others, does to the integrity of the female body?

We might say that terminating a pregnancy, prior to the stage of viability, is the right to perform an operation on oneself, like euthanasia, where people want the right to control their own deaths and avoid becoming a victim of the medical and legal system at the end of their life. Especially in the absence of intent to become pregnant, the fetus becomes, in effect, a parasite - to be removed by operation. Here, a woman wants to prevent life forming in her body at that particular time. Normally, we are speaking of postponement only. But who can say that the same soul will not take up residence in the woman's womb upon the next conception? Will the judge in full possession of the spiritual and moral truth please step forward and cast the first stone?

The circus of intervention in women's lives that we see today is tragic and repugnant. There is a lot of talk about "ethics" and "morality" but there is little respect for the woman who is having her freedom aborted by the state. She, and the unwanted child, will be forced into a "wrongful life."

The irony of our legal decisions is that it is usually the more irresponsible "mother" who due to ignorance, poverty, fear and guilt, waits longer to have an abortion than good conscience would dictate. Unfortunately, these are often the very cases where having the baby would be the biggest mistake. Sadly, it is in these instances where the law is most likely to enforce motherhood against the wishes of the mother, and most likely only give birth to more societal problems.

So at these traumatic moments in our life, we are forced to deal with those uninvited people who, not only don't want to let you determine your own right to die, but they want to prevent your own "right-to-life" by denying your right to terminate an unwanted and unplanned pregnancy. The force of law, in forced motherhood, is no answer to these deeply personal questions of the postponement of life and the determination of the seasons of one's motherhood.

Should the state acquire an interest in "potential life" by robbing the woman of her legitimate right, title and interest to her own body and its issue? Certainly, there are cases of the abuse of motherhood that cause us concern for the unborn. Consider the recent case where an unwanted child was born to a drug-addicted prostitute. Her baby was afflicted with both AIDS and drug addiction at birth, the mother, even knowing of her affliction, believed that abortion was murder! Our current experience, without an effective AIDS vaccine, is that the odds are overwhelming that these babies will live in pain for several miserable years and then die, all at great costs to themselves, society, and the mother.

Can we really say this was a moral decision to have the child in these circumstances? In cases like this it is highly probable that the mother's reflexive antipathy for abortion, perhaps selfishly motivated by fear of religious retribution, prevented her from terminating a doomed and vicious pregnancy. Here, in this instance, giving birth will result in the slow and painful death of a child because of the "moral" decision of an irresponsible mother.

In these horrifying circumstances, will not our sense of compassion compel us to now counsel a termination of the pregnancy, the forfeiture of motherhood, in the interests of protecting the unborn from a wrongful life? Must our morality condemn the new soul to this tragic "life" at any costs? And is not society bearing the real costs of many pregnancies?

In most cases of pregnancy termination the essential question is that of the primacy of the individual rights of the mother, until the actual birth of a living being, versus the rights of society. The woman must retain her right to decide when her motherhood is going to begin. The failure of contraception and other circumstances that explain the unwanted pregnancy, are not justification for the suspension of the mother's rights of self-determination. Even this so-called "reasonable" Supreme Court decision crosses into dangerous philosophical territory when the state invades the mother's body to protect the fetus.

What Supreme Court Justice or Priest can stand up and say they know exactly what life is, and just when a soul takes up residence in the womb? Will the condemning judge or priest now agree to assume the full responsibilities of parenthood for the child of the woman, or woman-child, who wishes not to become a mother? And where are the expert witnesses in the life of the soul?

Irrespective of the particular stage of gestation, is a fetus "viable" when the mother doesn't want it and where the pregnancy was not intended? Is the mother viable? Must not a determination of viability, upon which the mother's rights may be removed and her jurisdiction over her body eliminated, include provision for a home and nurturing environment? Can third parties, via the state, force birth without also assuming responsibility for that child? If such responsibility is not transferred, then we have a form of involuntary servitude.

And where the *intent* to become pregnant cannot be shown, there is no reason a woman cannot cancel her own motherhood. The issue of fetal viability, while compassionate and real, nevertheless assumes that motherhood is viable, was intended, and that the state, without proving intent, can force the completion of a pregnancy by denying abortion. What kind of society will we breed where the notion of fetal viability, to the exclusion of all other concerns, mandates irresponsible parenthood?

There are far too many people in positions of power today eager to interfere in the mother's life on the basis of their personal religious assumptions about pre-natal "life." In effect, their own theological assumptions become the basis of their legal conviction, and their own personal metaphysical cage becomes the woman's prison. We enforce pregnancy . . . and we abort human rights. In effect, in all too many cases, we then sanction immaturity and sanctify irresponsibility . . . and we all too often produce heartbreak.

> "For by the works of the law shall no flesh be justified . . .
> But if, while we seek to be justified by Christ, we
> ourselves also are found sinners, is therefore Christ
> the minister of sin? God forbid."[9]

Galatians 3:16-17

If we decide the state can invade the body of the mother for the right of the fetus, why then stop at six months? On the basis of declaring a state interest in the unborn, the invasion of the woman's body can take place the first day, if the police are peering thru the bedroom window. Just where does the doctrine of "potential Life" or "viability" begin or end? Does it start in the scrotum or ovaries? And will women have to go into hiding when they get pregnant to avoid state interference and control over their lifestyle?

If we can set an age for the "viability" of the fetus, why can we not also set a minimum age for the viability of motherhood, below which the question of fetal viability has no standing? Are we are so concerned with fetal viability that we don't care about responsible motherhood?

And in our new age of medical wonders, will the many proponents of invasive medical technology insist that the pregnant women be chained to the table, from day one, to justify the use of new technology? Will the fact of pregnancy become the automatic justification for society and the court to establish jurisdiction over the woman's body? Could not masturbation become a "potential life" question? And just where does "potential" life begin? And where will this potential legal intervention end? What we have here is the potential for the complete loss of freedom during pregnancy and a virtually unlimited amount of legal nightmares.

DOES YOUR FETUS BELONG TO THE STATE? -

"The fetus is the socialist property of the entire society."[10]

Nicolae Ceausescu

Is the fetus the property of the mother or of the state? This is really the crux of the issue. In the backward communist dictatorship of Romania, the ruling party chief, Nicolae Ceausescu, has declared that the fetus belongs to the state. Obviously, in a communist country everybody belongs to the state! There is no such thing as an individual, or free agent, upon the earth without allegiance to a system or religion such as marxism. Ironically, this totalitarian position is in sharp contrast to Lenin's original ideas. After the 1917 revolution in Russia, Lenin expressed the belief that no woman in the new communist society should be forced to bear a child against her will! It is ironic that the Soviet Union was the first country in modern times to legalize abortion.

The moment we invade the mother's womb to "protect the fetus" we invade our own system of rights declaring the primacy of the individual. At this point, our philosophy is identical with that of communist and fascist dictatorships in which there is little freedom for the individual. Ironically, if the fetus is "saved" in this manner, by aborting the freedom of the mother, we have only given birth to another slave of society. Even Hitler was pro-aryan-life.

"I'll put an end to the idea that a woman's body belongs to her . . . Nazi ideals demand that the practice of abortion shall be exterminated with a strong hand."[11]

Adolph Hitler,
Mein Kampf

The issue of motherhood is simply not an issue for the courts. It must remain a matter between a mother and her physician, or midwife, or god, as she chooses. Otherwise we proceed from fuzzy religious and legal justifications toward increasingly fuzzy definitions of freedom. Who is free from whom, and for how long?

The human rights of life, liberty, and the pursuit of happiness, by definition, grant the women control over her body and her reproductive future. The mother is the only extant human able to exercise these freedoms. The fact that she may choose to exercise those freedoms in a manner contrary to our beliefs is not justification for the removal of her own liberties. We can counsel, but we cannot coerce or prosecute without aborting the freedom of the living individual along with the essential concept of the separation of church and state.

If motherhood must be forced, what good is it? The obvious answer is not very good. Where is our concern for the soul, or fetus, and their ultimate good? Should we force the bad trip, the wrongful life? If the state forces a baby out of the mother's womb, then the state becomes the father. And forcing mandatory pregnancy is the raping of a woman by the state. There is no overwhelming interest of the state that justifies denying the rights of the living mother. Does the state, in the form of the individual taxpayers, want the paternity, the obligation of child support, and the fatherhood where no willing or responsible motherhood exists?

Even the rights of the father are suspect. If we force a pregnancy against the mother's will for the benefit of the father, the state is just destroying the institution of marriage and motherhood. Nature has dictated to us that the mother is primary in this process. If she is not a willing participant, then

212

the result of forced parenthood cannot possibly lead to harmony or serve the interests of society, the family, or the unborn.

The era of male-controlled legislation regarding women's bodies must come to an end. In the interests of women everywhere, I pose this simple question: If men attempt to legislate control over women's womb's then, in turn, what part of man's anatomy might women now attempt to gain control of, assuming they were in the legislative majority?

Putting the shoe on the other foot, so to speak, if women were the majority in legislatures around the world, I venture to say we would see some drastic penalties for misuse of a loaded weapon, namely the male member. Will legislation to control and penalize the actions of the male penus be an inevitable part of the female backlash once women gain the majority in a court forum? After all, what is the legal and sexist corollary of womb control? If today's male-oriented court decisions are a precedent, women could safely make their way into the confines of the male scrotum using the doctrine of "potential life."

If life, or consciousness, as history's greatest sages have defined it, doesn't begin or end but endures thru the birth and death process in an evolutionary spiral to perfection and cessation of rebirth, then the destruction of an unborn body or "vehicle" in the mother's womb cannot be said to be the "taking of a life." At most, it is the postponement of a life, of a soul's incarnation thru the mother's body. And the mother's choice to postpone that incarnation, the making of that body, is not "murder" - it is her right. And for all we know it may be her role in a fore-ordained karmic drama, or even nature may dictate a miscarriage, perhaps reflecting the mother's own psychic disaffinity for the pregnancy! Does this possibility now make every miscarriage suspect?

The essential point is that we don't know nature's intention, or outcome, but we pretend we do and base our legal sanctions upon that guess. In typical male fashion, we play god by imprisoning our goddesses.

"Every man (woman) has a property in his (her) person"[12]

John Locke

Thus, the Roe vs. Wade decision, while reasonable on its face, sanctions the intrusion of the state into the woman's body prior to actual birth. This is a significant leap into dangerous philosophical territory giving the state powers over the individual that may portend even greater removal of liberties. The court was called upon to decide between the positions of those who want to control your body from conception and those who want to leave the decision to you until birth. They seem to have fallen right down the middle, as a legally hypothetical "reasonable man" might decide in this situation given the uncertainty of the "facts" about the creation of life.

But does this "reasonable man" (why don't we have "reasonable women" in legal matters?) come into court with a head cleared of religious admonitions, or is he able to embrace, rather than eschew, other notions of cosmology? Or should the real question be, just how might a jury of twelve "reasonable women" decide the issue? And what is to be our legal test of religious fairness in a secular court of law - swearing on the bible?

Rather than crush our freedoms, the real goal of society must be to educate its citizens to cherish the procreative act, as distinct from the pleasure derived from lovemaking. The act of love between two people is essential to their spiritual growth. But we don't breed sane and creative people by thwarting the natural and loving expression of their beings.

The real work is to raise the consciousness of all people, especially teenagers, about the act of procreation. Short of state control, we can only educate our young people regarding their duty to prevent procreation until such time as they are mature, able, and willing to truly devote their energies to the life-long tasks of parenting. And now, at this juncture of human affairs, we must educate our young women about the impact of large families upon the environment over time. We must see the future in our decisions. And the state must not become the temple of short-sightedness.

COURTROOM IN THE HOSPITAL -

There is a great tendency today to confuse the new ability of modern invasive medical technology to monitor and manipulate fetal "life" with the presence of what we have seen is the soul-consciousness of the fetus. Even if the "life" or soul-force is not yet "in" the fetus, or is now "out" of the cadaver, modern medicine is capable of controlling and prolonging basic life functions, before both birth and death. But all too often the real outcome of such efforts is only the prolongation of pain and suffering for the family.

Should we take this growing medical control as our rational for extending legal and philosophical control over our bodies and beings? If we do, the new medical technology is not liberating us, it is enslaving us. And to the extent that control in the hospital becomes control in the courtroom we are no longer free to control our lives. The rights of the patient, the spouse, and the family are replaced by the right of the machine - the medical machine and the legal machine.

And in the case of abortion, we might say that unless an "intervenor," whether in the form of another person or the state, is willing to step forward and post bond to assume all the responsibilities of the natural parent, they have no business, capacity or legal standing, for interfering in the decisions of birth reserved by nature to the mother and her physician or midwife. The concept of "viability" is much too imprecise and vague a legal construct to serve as the reason around which fundamental rights of living persons, the mother, are unconstitutionally removed.

Either we believe in freedom and responsibility or we don't. Either we are a free society, peopled by free individuals, or we are a totalitarian society. In denying women the right to control their reproductive lives, they may well experience the ultimate miscarriage of justice.

In a democracy, surely the state must protect the decisions of the mother, a living person, over the "potential" interests of a fetus. To do otherwise is to begin the long slide into the dangerous totalitarian status of the state as the Big Brother, or should we say the Big Father. The state will own the children and the men in black robes will play god, justifying their decisions on "precedent" that may only swear into evidence one religious viewpoint.

> "All sorts of substitutes for wisdom are used by the world. When the court doesn't know, it consults precedent. The court that made the precedent guessed at it. And yesterday's guess, grown gray and wearing a big wig, becomes today's justice."[13]

> Dr. Frank Crane

If our only reason for intervention in pregnancy is that someone may do something that you would not do, acting in accordance with your particular religious and moral code, then we simply have a difference of opinion about "life" and not the basis for imprisoning the mother in motherhood against her wishes.

Now, we might ask, do the rights of women stop when they are impregnated by man? If this is the case, women are then justified in keeping men out of the womb entirely and proceeding directly to the petrie dish. With modern genetic "baby-making" technology, man is now almost irrelevant. You can get a man in a bottle. Sperm can be bought and paid for. So if by screwing around with men, women are losing control over their reproductive rights, who can blame them if they do their own thing when it comes to babymaking. And what if a woman decides to "abort" her creation in the petrie dish? Is there a difference after "hatching" or conception?

Many women active in the feminist movement are still justifiably unhappy with the degree of state interference in the woman's body. After thousands of years of women helping women decide on these issues, without the interference of men, these court decisions, though reasonable and compassionate on their face, still reek of male domination over a women's body.

> "The bottom line is this: either every woman is to be her own moral agent and is to decide for herself whether to continue a problem pregnancy, or government — male-dominated government — will assume the power to force her to become a mother against her will."[14]

Edd Doerr

You are your own moral agent. But the courts are full of men deciding women's issues - *that* is the bottom line. Will these decisions be the same when the courts are full of women, if such an event ever takes place? Should a male judge disqualify himself in deciding on an issue dealing with pregnancy? Just what is the courtroom doing in the hospital anyway? And what is the priest doing at the supreme court? Shall we all sue to uphold our particular belief in god? Or shall we pick a womb to sue for the fun of it, or for legal training to prepare for the big leagues of big brotherhood? Sometimes only facetiousness and sarcasm can adequately convey the proper sense of absurdity and tragedy over our current religious, political, and legal situations where we attempt to control a mother's reproductive rights by using the courtroom to settle religious disputes.

The only reason abortion is even a political and legal question is because a woman currently needs the help of a third party to remove the fetus. If the woman alone were able to effect the termination, as she may well be capable of doing in the near future, the problem would simply disappear from public view and remain in the privacy of the woman's domain where it belongs.

In another sense what we're really talking about in restricting abortion is the "rights" of legislators, doctors, lawyers, and judges and not that of women! And unless we deputize morality-police by restricting abortion the "problem" of pregnancy termination is likely to disappear with the development of better contraception and morning-after pills.

But if we continue to intervene in other people's personal affairs, where will it end? There is no limit to the number of decisions that society, in the name of justice or morality, can steal from the individual. And with the right to abortion, it is expecially ironic that if courts were to remove that right today, they may be paving the way for more uncontrolled population growth and hastening the arrival of a future time when that very same uncontrolled growth must be curbed, ironically by more legal decisions, for the very survival of humanity and the planet! In this case, in our current efforts to restrict abortion we are accelerating the arrival of injustice - that time when the state is forced to intervene again, to prevent pregnancies, without any quaint and sentimental mention of personal rights.

Finally, it is as if the judges believe there is no one in the hospital, or the birthing room, with any compassion. But can the doctor, or midwife, remove the judge if they don't like his legal operation? Can the mother or the family remove the judge, or the doctor, and abort the legal decision? In today's world, legal appeals take more time than it takes to create an entire family. It seems our freedom is only as great as our power, and if we are powerless then we are not free.

> "Law and justice are not always the same. When they aren't, destroying the law may be the first step toward changing it."[15]

> Gloria Steinem

"NATURAL LAW" -

St. Thomas Aquinas, recognized today as one of the greatest of Catholic theologians, was originally deemed a heretic by the Church but later exonerated. His writings on natural law, and achieving the proper balance in a community, recognized society's vulnerability from overpopulation. Dr. Frederick Flynn, Professor of Ethics and Philosophy at the College of St. Thomas, writes, in his commentary on Natural Law and the problems of overpopulation, the following about Aquinas' teachings: "St. Thomas takes the view that in giving him reason God intended man to take care of his human problems by using his reason." Aquinas states:

> "The rational creature is subject to Divine Providence in the most excellent way, insofar as he partakes of a share of Providence, by being provident both for himself and for others. And finally what obligation do married persons have in regard to society? Certainly one of them is to beget and train sufficient citizens for the welfare of the body politic. And just as certainly the other is not to beget more citizens than they themselves or society can adequately take care of in a human way."

> "In short, the frustration of nature is often necessary for man's survival."[16]

St. Thomas Aquinas

Aquinas realized that any "Divine Providence" only comes to those who are provident! Indeed, the frustration of our nature, as this most eminent of Catholic philosophers states, is essential to the orderly conduct of human affairs. This was never so true as in today's crowded world.

The philosophy of non-frustration of nature, as in the stand against all forms of birth control which the Church has adamantly pursued in recent years, is itself the problem. In practice, this simply amounts to an abdication of our own community responsibility, especially when nature has already been prevented by man from exercising its cruel, but very effective, limitations on population.

Even the term "natural law" is at odds with itself. Can we not say that Nature is a process experienced, but largely unknown to man. And when man intervenes in nature's process, there is no natural law, only our own behavior. With man's modern medical technology compassionately intervening in the life processes, in essence, we now have unnatural law. So if we then follow "natural law" and our behavior results in the progressive destruction of nature, is this then natural or desirable? Should we then proceed to follow "natural law" to destroy ourselves and accelerate the ruination of our planet? Is this natural? Is this provident? Is this moral?

And speaking of mankind's destruction of nature, should not other species, presently being annihilated by the rapid growth of the human species, also have legal standing on a par with the human fetus? Must our legal system only be concerned with the preservation and rights of one species? Should our moral, ethical and legal concern only reflect and protect our human hubris and insensitivity to the point where we seek to enshrine the one species, mankind, whose presence is so threatening to the balance of other natural life forms on the planet? Are we "born free" to destroy nature?

We have poked a hole in nature's prophylactic and it is up to us, as individuals making conscious decisions, to stem the flow. If fetuses, small children, and old people are no longer subject to the death rates of the past due to our control of nature's diseases, then who is left to control the runaway growth in mankind, resulting in the pathetic shanty towns now surrounding the urban centers of the world. Our unnatural law, or man's merciful interventions to save life, counterbalanced by women's responsible motherhood decisions to prevent life, is now the only alternative.

We are part of nature and yet now responsible for the natural world. We are also partners in the creation and the destruction of life . . . and Mother Nature is now counting on us to keep the balance.

FETAL RIGHTS? - THE UNBORN AND YOUR LIFE -

New legal cases based on the idea of "fetal rights" have opened a whole new pandora's box of lawsuits for our litigious society to further complicate the emotional setting of motherhood by invading the family and destroying the right to privacy. Consider the case in a Michigan court where it was recently decided that a father can sue a mother because he claims the child's teeth are discolored due to her "prenatal" influence in taking a drug during pregnancy. Should one sue his spouse for fetal neglect if their child doesn't get into Harvard? There is no end to this nonsense.

Judith Jarvis Thompson artfully explored the real argument of fetal rights, in the case of rape, with her own "famous Violinist" analogy. It goes like this:

"You wake up in the morning and find yourself back to back in bed with an unconscious violinist. A famous unconscious violinist. He has been found to have a fatal kidney ailment, and the Society of Music Lovers has canvassed all the available medical records and found that you alone have the right blood type to help.

"They have therefore kidnapped you, and last night the vioinist's circulatory system was plugged into yours, so that your kidneys can be used to extract the poisons from his blood as well as your own. The Director of the hospital now tells you, "look, we're sorry the Society of Music Lovers did this to you - we would never have permitted it if we had known. But still, they did it, and the violinist now is plugged into you. To unplug now would be to kill him. But never mind, its only for nine months. By then he will have recovered from his ailment, and can safely be unplugged from you." Is it morally incumbent on you to accede to this situation?

"No doubt it would be nice of you if you did, a great kindness. But do you have to accede to it? What if it were not for nine months but nine years? Or longer still? What is the Director of the hospital says, "Tough luck, I agree, but you've now got to stay in bed, with the violinist plugged into you, for the rest of your life. Because remember this, all persons have a right to life, and violinists are persons. Granted you have a right to decide what happens in and to your body,

221

but a person's right to life outweighs your right to decide what happens in and to your body. So you cannot ever be unplugged from him." I imagine you would regard this as outrageous."[17]

Judith Jarvis Thompson,
A Defense of Abortion

The point is that women should not be hooked up to a fetus against their will, regardless of the circumstances. When we consider early teenage pregnancies, those caused by rape, as well as those births destined for deformity due to drugs or chemical exposure, what is our responsibility to the fetus? Are we to force the birth? What about the fetus's right not to be born, especially under the most tragic of circumstances? What do we know of the fetus's conscious or unconscious participation in the incarnation process? Is a blind desire propelling the unfortunate soul into these unfortunate circumstances? Did he/she choose to be aborted? Was it their Karma? Are we just actors in some preordained cosmic drama, already spelled out in a timeless spectrum of rebirths?

While these may be significant questions, they remain unanswerable, legally speaking. But because they may be empirically unanswerable is not to say they have no relevance, or standing, when other religious cosmologies are currently being used to explain away a mother's right to an abortion. But our only legitimate guide in motherhood decisions is our common sense and intuition as to what may be "right" in our particular circumstances, for ourselves, our child, and our world.

Our legal system is voracious in opening new vistas for potential litigation. But rather than encouraging our personal responsibility, the system currently works on the thesis that there is always someone else out there (preferably with money) who is responsible for any particular situation. Who can we sue? The current legal atmosphere in combination with a single religious "right-to-life" dogma can be a trap for women seeking help in public institutions.

If there is to be any discussion about fetal rights, it is solely a matter for the mother alone, who in prayerful communication with her God and any attendant soul-fetus "discusses" her willingness to give birth at that time. Even amongst this trinity, or oneness, as the case may be, the mother's conscious consent to birth must be primary.

> "The real question posed by this phenomenon has less to do with the rights of the fetus than with the status of women. And the issue is one of control: control over abortion, control over pregnancy, control over the birth process - in short, control over our bodies and our lives . . . There are enormous dangers in relying on criminal laws or court action instead of education and provision of adequate prenatal care for all pregnant women."[18]

> Janet Gallagher,
> The Fetus and the law

* * *

> "We do have a moral obligation to non-persons, to fetuses, animals, trees, and all the organic life . . . the problem is, of course, that the survival of these living things may conflict with some important rights and needs of actual persons, and that in the face of such conflict, we must give priority to actual, conscious human beings over other forms of life."[19]

> Rosalind Petchesky,
> Abortion and Women's Choice

In criminalizing a pregnant woman's behavior from the time of conception, she could be convicted of "prenatal neglect" for something that occurred even before she knew she was pregnant! When we consider that, in the United States, 900,000 women suffer miscarriages and stillbirths each year, it is conceivable that every one of them could be hauled into court to prove their innocence regarding prenatal treatment. The totalitarian implications of these proposed laws are just staggering. If courts and bureaucratic procedures are allowed to interfere with pregnancies they are bound to multiply the heartbreak and suffering involved.

NO WOMAN CAN CALL HERSELF FREE -

"No woman can call herself free who does not own and control her body. No woman can call herself free until she can choose consciously whether she will or will not be a mother."[20]

Margaret Sanger

Without choice there is no freedom. In the 1870's Margaret Sanger, a brave pioneer of women's rights, couldn't even speak the words relating to women's vital functions. The "obscenity" of this victorian morality was supposedly in the utterance of innocent descriptive words, obscenely branded "obscene" and not in the truly obscene denial of a woman's right and freedom to control her body.

Throughout history, we've seen recurrent waves of righteousness in scores of people motivated by "god" to take away the rights of other people. Of course, it is always in the name of morality - their morality, not yours. As long as people put their "morality" ahead of your freedom we're in trouble. We seem to be engaged in a societal game where people declare that "my morality is better than yours" and thus deserves to be exclusively enshrined in common law. All morality legislation has always led to disrepect for the law itself, and with good cause where privacy and personal choice has been eroded. Where the law itself does not respect the individual, the individual does not respect the law.

The difficult thing to understand is why so many politically "conservative" individuals, who should be the first to protect the liberties of the individual from the encroachments of the church and state, are the first to call for intervention and resort to courts to enforce their will on women's bodies. Here, they don't appear to understand their own political ideals. Emotions seem to overwhelm their credo when it comes to the ramifications of the state intervening in the bodies of individuals.

Are we wards of the state, or are we truly free individuals? The churches should be in the forefront of the ongoing battle to defend the rights and liberties of actual persons from encroachment by the state. Instead, many prefer that the state become the blunt instrument of theological enforcement and control over women's wombs.

> "Excess people, not acts of God, create poverty, famine and war . . . all society would gain . . . if birth control were allowed to shut off the spigot that floods the world with weaklings. When sick and unfit mothers were not forced to breed, there would be an end to unwanted children who grow up to fill our prisons and asylums."[21]

Margaret Sanger

In Margaret Sanger's day thousands of babies were left on doorsteps and deposited in trash heaps. In London's "Foundling" hospitals, between 1756 and 1760, the death rate for children was between 80 and 90 percent! As Barbara Walker relates, "Parish officers entrusted the care of newborns to women nicknamed "killing nurses" because they were expected to do the state's dirty work, and see to it that the unwanted children did not long survive." Rather than allow the more humane approach of abortion and birth control the Church and state, in effect, created the environment where babies were left to die, *after* their birth and desertion by their mothers. Such was the mandate of dogma and victorian "morality."

But those who would ask that the state invade your body, based on their personal moral or religious perceptions, are denying you the right to your own definition of life and morality. This is just pure soviet-style politics, where the state, in effect, owns your body and controls all the little children. It is a classic example of good intentions breeding bad policy, especially in a "free" country.

And if others can control the womb, they may soon control the brain or any other part of our anatomy. The same principles of "morality" and "compassion" that paralyze our critical faculties and lead us to conclude that an amorphous "we" have rights superior to the women responsible for giving birth can easily remove our individuality and control over other regions of the body. In all too many cases it amounts to saying simply that, I am more moral than you, therefore I can now make your decision. Legislation and judicial rulings removing one's right to control one's own body are nothing more than a game of "moral" one-upsmanship - a game where the loser becomes a slave to the state and the "moral majority."

> "I am appalled at the ethical bankruptcy of those who preach a "right to life" that means a bare existence in utter misery for so many poor women and their children."[22]

> Justice Thurgood Marshall
> Beal vs. Doe, 1977

The so-called conservative "right-to-life" moralists, with their politically self-contradictory desire to control your life and your womb, seem to be a recurring phenomenoa in American politics. Women have been fighting for centuries to maintain control over their own bodies. But there seems to be no end to the battle. The seasons of the self-righteous rise and ebb like the tide.

> "America, despite the guarantees of our constitution, has periodically succumbed to religious zealot pressure. In 1873, spiritual ancestors of our modern Moral Majority bullied a timid congress into a federal law forbidding the dissemination of any information regarding contraception and birth control. Most state legislatures followed suit.

> "Anthony Comstock, an American Protestant zealot, organized a Society for the Suppression of Vice. A moral crusader, Comstock and his organization sought out

226

violators of the 1873 law. Margaret Sanger, one of the first organizers of the birth control movement in America, was persecuted, prosecuted and jailed by Comstock and the courts. Thru her literature, she had committed a crime by using words legally designated as "lewd" and "obscene." The proscribed words included: uterus, ovary, womb, pregnant and spermatoza."[23]

Anthony Hiller

A return to the era of the Comstock laws is what some are seeking today. They are perfectly able to live their lives within their own personal set of Comstock laws, but the real obscenity rises when they seek to require, by force of law, that others be controlled by their opinions and beliefs.

WHAT ABOUT SOCIAL VIABILITY? -

Many opponents of abortion use the construct of "viability," defined as the ability of the fetus to live independent of the mother, as the dividing line between when an abortion should, or should not, take place. The question not asked in so many difficult situations is . . . what is the viability of a reasonable life after birth? What are the chances of starvation, of real opportunity in life, or of coming into circumstances in which the baby is not wanted? Can we blind ourselves to all other circumstances surrounding the birth in defining the viability of a fetus?

Can we not have a duty to protect a fourteen year old girl *from* a baby? From another perspective, just what sort of morality is it that justifies, on the basis of one sexual experience of a minor girl, the right of the fetus or incarnating soul to rape/impregnate an underage minor to gain access to the world? Regardless of what mystic dimensions we are dealing with in such an argument, do we consider the fourteen year-old mother capable of consent to motherhood?

Should we force a young girl to go thru with the birth, only to encourage her to give the baby up for adoption because we already know she is not capable of providing an independent and mature motherhood? Do we then sentence the newborn to eternal bastardization, or the bleak future of institutional life and the uncertain prospects of adoption in a world where babies are made to order in test tubes? And when the soul is born, because an abortion may have been effectively prevented, do we arrest the soul/baby for being an accessory to rape and unwanted motherhood?

But is it not now a mother's duty to protect life from tragic and inferior circumstances in an already seriously overcrowded world? The often glibly assumed presumption is that we are, in effect, protecting the defenseless and saving life by protecting the fetus. And, in some cases, motherhood itself is defenseless. We must act to protect motherhood, and not "life" per se. Otherwise, as in the many cases of teenage pregnancy, life will strangle real and honest motherhood.

So if the outside world of the fetus is not viable, or nurturing, protective and responsible, then can we say that a new baby is viable? Is sheer fetal viability, and the ability to pack even more people on the planet, even against the will of many reluctant mothers, to be our only guidepost in dismissing a mother's rights? Is there not also to be a duty to provide or guarantee a social viability, in the form of food, shelter, education, or even employment prior to qualifying for a right to life? If there is a right to life, is there not also a duty, a responsibility to exhibit the capacity to properly care for that life?

If our courts play god with such a limited concept of viability, and go against the wishes of the mother, or the dictates of the environment, then we sanction life at its worst. If, in our rigid pro-life stance, we cannot face the problem of unwanted pregnancies and attempt to hide the worsening realities of our world in vague hopes that things will get better, then we are simply abetting the very process of human decay and environmental desecration.

And how "viable" is the fetus if the community must support the child? How viable is it if there is a great chance of it being retarded or severely handicapped? What is the viability of the child where the mother doesn't want it and plans to "give it away" because she won't terminate the pregnancy out of fear based on questionable religious ideas? Does an unwanted baby give an irresponsible mother the right to make the community responsible for her child? Of course, once it comes we will have no choice. How long will many communities accept this notion of viability?

And what is the social and economic viability of a fetus when it must take food from the mouths of the already born and barely living? The moralists avoid these questions like the plague. Obviously, the thought of forcing abortions on women is just as repugnant as that of forcing motherhood. Where there is no choice, one is just as bad as the other. Short of draconian legislation that effects a woman only after the fact of an unplanned and unwanted pregnancy, all we can really do is to counsel responsible motherhood and give women the choice, as well as the means, to terminate a pregnancy or give birth as they see fit.

> "There is no such thing as the viability of states or of nations, there is only viability of people: people, actual persons like you or me, are viable when they can stand on their own feet and earn their keep. You do not make non-viable people viable by putting large numbers of them into one huge community."[24]

> E.F. Schumacher,
> Small is Beautiful

When does life become profane? We might say that life is sacred, but only when we do not create a hell on earth by creating more life then we can provide for. When does the creation of life become sacreligious? Is unconsciousness and irresponsibility, and it's issue, sacred?

Once the courts and churches attempt to take away the decision from the mother, our legal questions of "viability" and "life" descend into a wild netherland of unknowables, to be decided by the unknowledgeable, for the disenfranchised. And society, the innocent bystanders, must then pick up the inevitable public costs of the poor and unfortunate children resulting, directly or indirectly, from the moralist's crusade against birth control and abortion.

Consider the current famine in Africa. Can we deny birth control or abortion to a starving mother, whose living children are now dying of hunger, and whom she wishes she could now transport to a world of plenty for their survivial? Can the Pope or other self-righteous moralists stand amidst these people, looking into the eyes of the pathetic and starving stick-thin children, and tell them they are sinning if they do not let nature take its course? Here, the Church's birth control dogma is plainly cruel. It simply has no place in today's crowded and imperfect world. And yet this is the future of mankind if we continue to prevent contraception, birth control, and abortion.

* Chapter Six *

- The Viability of Motherhood -

WHERE ARE THE MOTHER'S RIGHTS? -

When we speak of the rights of the unborn, those who would interfere in pregnancy decisions are impliciting denying the rights of the already born, specifically the mother. And propelled by a lopsided religious argument, they urge the state to declare that society has the right to invade your body, intervene in your pregnancy, and supercede your natural rights as a mother. Thus, they would now control a pregnancy, in the interests of a child that you, the mother, may not wish to carry to term. At the very least, the moralists might be happy with a lifetime of recrimination and guilt experienced by the mother who decides to abort an unwanted pregnancy.

It is as if the woman, the mother in question, has become invisible. Those who speak of the prevailing rights of the unborn seem to look thru the flesh and blood mother as though she were not even alive. The mother's own definition of viability does not even enter the legal equation.

With the courtroom now invading the womb, there are now more and more extremely anguishing situations in premature births and miscarriages. Where the fetus is on the cusp of life, and may or may not survive, the mother is suddenly removed from control over her life and that of her baby.

And speaking of Big Brother, now, in the United States, if anyone outside of the family and the personal physician involved does disagree, for whatever reason, with the medical decisions in these agonizing situations, they are now urged to call a government official, or attorney, who will then obtain a court order to forbid the physician or mother from making any further decisions about neonatal care. Why would a women want to opt for a hospital birth under these conditions?

At this point, mother, doctor, *and* the fetus have become prisoners of the system. The legal doctors will now operate on the mother's freedom. These "Baby Doe" guidelines require a hotline in all hospitals enabling anyone to intevene in the decisions of the mother and her physician. This is the direct line to Big Brother.

There will always be heart-breaking situations in pre-natal affairs for the mother, family, and physician, but widening the circle of judgement, by mandating intervention and trying to make doctors out of lawyers, and gods out of judges, is nonsense and produces only more anguish for all involved.

The conflict between the medical and legal worlds has gotten so bad that we now see cases where obstetricians, because of skyrocketing malpractice costs and threats of suits, are refusing to treat or even attend to the needs of pregnant female attorneys or clerks from law firms that have sued them - all's fair in love and lawsuits! Today, any problem in pregnancy and birth (despite nature's ultimate hand in the scheme of things) may turn into a vendetta against the doctors and their flush insurance companies. The twin spectres of "malpractice" and "morality" stalk the corridors of the hospitals and clinics serving women. At any moment one or the other may strike and sever the natural rights of motherhood.

Even the very production of birth control devices is now threatened due to the huge liability insurance costs involved. Many companies have simply withdrawn from the market in the United States because they are unable to meet the tremendous liability insurance costs. Now the law itself *creates* the need for more abortions! Once again, women are the losers and there are even fewer choices for women in need. We have the audacity to create the need for abortions and then attempt to outlaw them. One might conclude that the torture of women is still in vogue.

MOTHERHOOD AS IMPRISONMENT -

Today, in the worst of moments, a pregnant woman isolated in a hospital birthing ward, can easily become a prisoner of the state and subject to the decisions of other people about her life, her abortion, or premature infant. The mother's will is now no longer of any legal import and the fetus, whether viable or not, becomes a prisoner and a ward of the state. Whatever the circumstances, the mother and fetus will now be forced to undergo a third party's view of "compassion." The baby, and the parents, may be forced to live a deformed life, a retarded life. The mother, and often the community, are also sentenced to a lifetime of expensive care in the case of many unwanted children.

Take the case of Sherri Finkbine as related in Kristin Luker's "Abortion - The Politics of Motherhood." A mother of four children under seven years of age, Sherri, in 1962, discovered she had been taking Thalidomide while pregnant. Hearing the first reports of its dangers to the fetus, she immediately contacted her physician who informed her that due to the large doses she had ingested the chances were extremely high that her baby would be born deformed. An abortion was agreed to and scheduled within several days.

The state of the law in California at that time required that she write a letter to the hospital's three-member therapeutic abortion board. Concerned about other pregnant mother's possible exposure to the drug, she called a friend, who worked for a newspaper, to give an interview to get the word out about the real dangers of Thalidimide. A story appeared the next day - "Baby-Deforming Drug May Cost Woman Her Child Here." Within hours of publication of the story, her scheduled abortion was cancelled by the hospital board. Thus, in a reaction to the publicity, they terrorized the mother with their sudden self-serving policy switch.

The next day her physician asked for a court order to go ahead with the abortion. At this point, Sherri and her husband had become unwitting media figures. Luker relates that: "The reaction was instantaneous and almost overwhelming. Wire services picked up the story, and now Finkbine and her husband were deluged with reporters. Thousands of letters, cards and phone calls came in. A few of these made death threats against her and her children, and the FBI was called in to protect her."

Under siege at home, Sherri and her husband applied for visas to Japan, were turned down, and subsequently they went to Sweden where her request for an abortion was granted. But Luker notes that as Sherri came out of the anesthetic, the obstetrician told her the embryo was so seriously deformed that it would never have survived.

"Christianity might be a good thing if anyone ever tried it."[1]

George Bernard Shaw

Upon returning home, Sherri lost her job and then suffered the fate of a public figure whose predicament aroused the hate and ire of those who chose to condemm her. Here, the Finkbine case illustrates how once we allow others to exercise their version of "compassion" in our affairs, there is no drawing the line. Your life is not yours, and your baby is not yours. What is yours? Are we free individuals when we allow the state, a judge, to now make our god-given life and death decisions? The self-righteous "intervenors" who press these cases seem to have no compassion or respect for the rights and decision of the family and physician involved.

Mostly these difficult situations of motherhood have only led to painful prolongation of life for the preemie and unconscionable costs inflicted upon the family. This intervention in the name of the unborn, or the prematurely born, is a very serious legal step toward totalitarianism. Intervention, and the removal of the rights of the people involved, is always in the name of "compassion" and "saving lives" but never in the name of preserving freedom.

The real question is do others have the right to exercise their version of compassion in these intensely personal affairs of our lives? Who does the baby belong to? Does it belong to society? Do *you* belong to society? In a democracy, can we sanction rights in the unborn, or the prematurely born and dependent individual, over the rights of the responsible and independent mother and father? Also, we might ask, just what principle of societal determination has undermined our self-determination?

> "With spiritual maturity one recognizes that no one else's God has any jurisdiction over your own mind, or heart."[2]

> Buyer's Guide to Gods

For thousands of years these decisions have rested with the mother, father, midwife and physician. What is the need of any change in this time-honored relationship? If our medical technology only serves to undermine our rights as free individuals and family units, then what good is it? Dare we risk utilizing it, and exposing ourselves to injustice, if the outcome can be so tragic and expensive? Those who undermine these rights also undermine the family and a free society. Good intentions and bad law, it's the same old story.

Just as many old people, and their families, suffer needlessly because hospitals are able to prolong life in many terminal illnesses, suddenly you may find yourself not in control of your own life or that of your loved ones. The State is now your family, via court order, on the basis of a third party's idea of their religious obligation, or an institution's fears of its legal obligations. And in these difficult and emotional situations surrounding birth and death, we find unrelated people very willing to inflict their unrequested religious opinions upon your life.

This is completely contrary to the principle of the separation of Church and State, as well as a neighborly sense of non-interference in family affairs. There is no compelling reason why the mother, her unborn or newborn, and her chosen physician should be subject to the dictates of the unwanted, the unrelated, and the uninvited. If we cannot respect the decisions of others in these private matters, no matter how repugnant to our particular value systems, then as a society "we" as individuals have no rights if we are able to force our religious and moral views upon others.

ECONOMIC SURVIVAL - THE NEW ECONOMY -

In more and more countries today, the vast majority of women no longer have the luxury of staying at home with the children. Women must work in a marketplace where her salary and contribution are critical to the family. Or, if she is single, it is *all* there is. The prospect of a pregnancy in this situation may imperil her family, the children as well as the mother. Times have changed and most women no longer sit on the back porch and watch the corn grow while the kids play. When a pregnancy occurs that threatens the livelihood of the working woman, she has a difficult choice to make. It is now obvious that yesterday's morality and social order are not necessarily relevant to the situation of many women today.

> "Lots of women understand that it is still too economically difficult for a young, unmarried, working mother to support herself and a child alone at the wages most women make. And that is exactly who gets 64% of all abortions. Most women are between the ages of 15 and 24, while 81% of all women who have abortions are single.

> "For many of these women, contraception has failed. Francis Kissling, Executive director of Catholics for a Free Choice, put it well when she told me, "It's not the woman who's made the moral choice about abortion. Society has made the choice for her and then put the blame on women."[3]

> Amanda Spake, Propaganda
> War Over Abortion

Indeed, society has made the choice for the single woman. And when she finally decides not to have the baby, due in large measure to her lack of economic freedom, she is met at the doors to the abortion clinic by "pro-life" protestors shouting slogans and calling her names. She is subject to discrimination at work for the very fact of being a woman and vulnerable to pregnancy. And she must learn to suppress her maternal instincts in the marketplace and world of work. But, still, she must make a difficult decision about aborting an unplanned baby. And, to make matters worse, she must then face the self-righteous wrath of mostly male doctors, judges, priests and preachers telling her how to run, or ruin, her life.

It seems that everywhere a woman turns, when she needs understanding in her preproductive affairs, she is likely to encounter others who are all to eager to enforce their version of truth and compassion. At the door to the clinic they shout epithets, insult her intelligence and right to choose, and assault her rights as a free human being.

We can contrast the modern woman's plight with that of the teenage unplanned pregnancy, where children are having children. Here, everyone, thru the taxes of the federal, state, and city governments, must pay year after year for this tragic and preventable folly. And not just in the millions of dollar for the medical and psychiatric services, but millions more in welfare, social workers, and all too often, court, crime, and incarceration costs at a later date. We've seen the pattern and the results in city after city, country after country. Young women must simply learn to come to grips with their unpreparedness and not expect society, or their families, to bail them out of the heavy responsibilities of proper sexual conduct, abortion, and/or motherhood.

We owe the responsible woman, concerned with planning and shaping her own motherhood amidst the powerful societal forces around her, the compassion and respect due one who gives considerable forethought to the creation, and even the prevention, of new life. We owe her the right to control her own body *and* her reproduction, period.

* Chapter Seven *

- Toughlove and Free Choice -

"TOUGHLOVE" - THE NEW APPROACH?

When parents are faced with teenage drug abuse, as is the case with so many uncontrollable children raised in ghettoes of poverty and neglect, as well as ghettoes of parental distance with too much material satisfaction and permissiveness, a new hard line approach had to be developed to deal with the most intransigent of these kids. "ToughLove" is the name given to this powerful parental backlash that enabled parents to regain respect from, and control over, their errant children. Drugs as a problem are bad enough, but compared to the ultimate effects of teenage pregnancy and mushrooming overpopulation, they are secondary. We have to stop breeding future addicts, *and* premature mothers, and begin to treat the problems that already exist.

We need to seriously consider the idea of using a ToughLove approach with irresponsible teenagers who are foisting the product of their failure to prevent pregnancy upon society-at-large. But teenage mothers are victims as well, especially when one considers the lack of information and contraception available in some locals. Due to this failure of society to provide the means of prevention, and the moral support, both the underage mother and the baby are victims.

If there are no mores or sanctions for behavior that we know from the statistics is detrimental, not only to the unfortunate baby and "parents" but to the community and the long-term health of our society, then we send a message

239

condoning this irresponsible behavior and we will continue to pay for it. The signals given out by our current welfare system convey the message to "go ahead and have another child, it just means more money from the state each month." The County of Los Angeles, for example, has over 900,000 people on welfare, of which the majority of recipients are said to be the direct result of unwanted teen pregnancies. The cost for one community alone is over two billion dollars per year!

Our current sociology uniformly indicates that these unfortunate babies, of grossly underage mothers, will most likely pay the price of their "parents" irresponsible behavior for the rest of their lives. A "viable" community cannot go on paying, in never ending support, for the "mistakes" that are directly, and indirectly, the result of the political actions of certain "pro-life" religious leaders in preventing sex education, contraception, and access to abortion.

> "Do they want people to be born just so they can starve in Somalia and have 29 year-old grandmothers in Brooklyn."[1]

> Jimmy Breslin

There are those who dislike paying taxes to fund family planning and abortion facilities. But mandatory motherhood is a life sentence. There are also many who dislike funding the open-ended welfare demands resulting from the yearly crop of unplanned pregnancies, as well as the ideas propagated in state-supported parochial schools that, in effect, only aggravates our present situation. The sword cuts both ways.

THEY PRAY FOR DEATH -

The opponents of abortion, sex education, and a woman's right to choose can often go to extreme lengths in their self-righteousness. Several fanatic fundamentalist preachers have condemned the U.S. Supreme Court Justices who, after affirming the Roe vs. Wade decision, voted to uphold the right

of a woman to choose. One such "minister" said that members
of his congregation . . .

> "Will pray that God takes the lives of Hitler-like men
> from the face of the earth."[2]

> > Robert L. Hymers, Pastor,
> > Fundamentalist Tabernacle

This is the mindset of someone who doesn't really believe
in the freedom of the individual. The more rabid opponents
of choice want to control your life and then condemm to death
others who disagree with their opinions. Their zeal to "save"
your unwanted fetus overrides any niceties of mature
civilization. They feel perfectly comfortable in asking the state
to force you into giving birth against your wishes. And some
are willing to go to any length to save the life of a fetus, but
when it comes to the mother saving and planning her own
life, they are very much opposed to any such independence.

> "He mated with the mindlessness that is in him and
> produced his own authorities."[3]

> > The Secret Book of John,
> > The Secret Teaching of Jesus

* * *

> "One who is spiritually mature is not a follower of
> dualistic religion. He does not become a slave to any
> type of religious or social movement. All of a person's
> viewpoints, and concepts about life and religious
> convictions are a manifestation of his (her) energy.
> When the nervous system is restored and refined, one
> becomes calm and objective. Then one can see clearly.
> The undeveloped human mind may be impressed with
> a domineering image which is like a tyrannical, invisible
> ruler. This image enhances the aggressive and
> destructive tendency of the undeveloped human
> mind."[4]

> > Lao-Tzu, Hua Hu Ching

241

Five thousand years ago, Lao-Tzu, one of the great taoist sages of all time, understood the state of mind of the "true-believer" and those who claim to know what is good for you and "speak for God." Often, they are unsettled people driven to enter into the personal affairs of others without invitation, and solely to exercise their particular viewpoint. Do they ever ask you what *you* believe or don't believe? Will they even listen? Do they respect it? A young women seeking an abortion today needs guts to face the onslaught of self- righteous people willing to interfere in her private affairs.

"The minds of those clinging to right and wrong are
obstructed."[5]

The Zen Teachings of Hui Hai

Consider, Joseph Scheidler, a "pro-lifer" who has led a "holy war" against doctors and abortion clinics serving young women. His book "CLOSED - 99 Ways to Stop Abortion" is essentially a terrorist manual giving misguided true believers the rational and methods to intimidate and harass those who may disagree with their beliefs - namely, women seeking the termination of their unwanted pregnancy.

"When you save someone, that's when you get hooked.
Direct action gets in your blood."[6]

Joseph Scheidler

"Saving" someone, the unwanted fetus, even against the wishes of the mother, is apparently like a drug to some of these "pro-life" activists. But who saves the mother's life?

The real tragedy is that these sincere and well-meaning people cause more problems than they solve. The fact that abortion opponents not only prevent people from having the means to prevent conception, but then go on to prohibit abortion is almost diabolical in its logic. "Mothers" giving birth to unplanned and unwanted children are not "going" to hell but are, in sorrowful fact, creating hell for themselves and society. Is this a compassionate hell we are currently creating?

The efforts and energy behind this "moral" intolerance would be so much better expended in the search for a decent home environment for the already born and needy. Terrorist tactics against the rights of women can only serve to increase the problem, and slow our search for solutions to the urgent problems of overpopulation and unwanted children. Beliefs that engender intolerance endanger both the believer, and the non-believer, and result only in more misunderstanding and violence.

> "He who regards his knowledge as ignorance has deep insight . . . He who regards his ignorance as definite truth is deeply sick . . . only when one is sick of this sickness can one cease to be sick."[7]

> Lao-Tzu, Tao Teh Ching

Some of the "pro-life" activists do not, for the most part, seem to be the compassionate and considerate men that one could talk to about one's problem and leave with any feeling of self-dignity. And here again we see it is mostly men who are crusading against the rights of women. They are armed with their "compassion" and "morality." Some of the more radical extremists seem willing to go to any length in their moral crusades, much like the witch-burners and book-burners of past centuries. But we cannot let our courts and institutions fall prey to such ill-tempered and intolerant viewpoints.

> "What passes for Christianity today is the tendency to see the devil in the other person but not in ourselves. Many people project evil into everything they do not understand. They see people who espouse contrary points of view as evil and therefore as belonging to Satan."

> "They see themselves, on the other hand, as God's children and therefore in total posession of the truth. Such a combination of projection and self-righteousness only alienates people from each other

and often leads to truly demonic consequences because it encourages such a low level of consciousness."[8]

John A. Sanford,
Episcopal Priest

Consider the mentality and *morality* behind several "counseling centers" in the United States, where young women had gone seeking counseling and abortion services. Instead, they were met with a barrage of pro-life pressure from the people at these "clinics" who even went so far as to advertise their "abortion services" in the telephone book. And once the distraught young women were in their grasps, one can imagine the one-sided and one-religion-based psychological pressure and guilt exerted upon their "clients."

"This city has several "crisis pregnancy centers" advertised in the Yellow Pages. They are small offices staffed by volunteers, and they offer free pregnancy testing, glossy photos of dead fetuses, and movies. I had a client recently whose mother is active in the anti-abortion movement. The young woman went to the local crisis center and was told that the doctor would make her touch her dismembered baby, that the pain would be the most horrible she could imagine, and that she might, after an abortion, never be able to have children. All lies. They called her at home and at work, over and over and over, but she had been wise enough to give a false name. She came to us a fugitive."[9]

Sallie Tisdale, Clinic Nurse

Terrorism of women's clinics is still a relatively infrequent occurence, but it points up the problems women may encounter in attempting to take control of their lives in a difficult situation such as an unwanted pregnancy. The tactics employed by the people who staffed these bogus clinics speak volumes about the mentality of abortion opponents. We can differ on the question of the propriety of abortion in our lives, but is it any wonder that we now see organizations such as "Fundamentalists Anonymous" helping people to begin to understand the nature of their own addiction to an egoistic religious self-righteousness?

However, this type of anti-abortion effort is in no way to be compared with the wonderful work done by many legitimate adoption services run by people who care for the many unwanted and abandoned children produced by irresponsible "parents." Without the efforts of these truly compassionate people, the unwanted and abandoned child would truly be lost.

"That view involves both a right and a wrong and this view involves both a right and a wrong: are there two views, or is there actually one?"[10]

Chuang-Tzu, 5th century B.C.

The righteousness of belief is a powerful force. Today and throughout history, many true believers have been willing to go to just about any length to force their opinions on other people. The difference between war and peace is often just the process of keeping the true believers of all countries from killing themselves and others. But those who want to "save" you, or your fetus, always comfort themselves with their feelings of moral superiority and the knowledge that god is safely on their side.

Consider the fact that Jehovah's witnesses are now being told that they must violate confidentiality if a member is discovered to have committed a "sin." And speaking of Christian ethics, if a fellow Witness is now discovered to have had an abortion, for instance, her spiritual sisters and brothers must then report her to the "elders" - presumably to be spanked, or sent straight to hell. There is no area of life that is spared from the intrustion of the self-righteous moralists under the guise of "religion." Even your friends may be forced to turn on you under this sort of dogma. God has now been turned into Big Brother - the ultimate fall.

Certainly no one questions or doubts the sincerity of people who are passionately involved in the "pro-life" movement. But some of these same people, armed with their belief in the sanctity of all life (all except the mothers) are willing to invade

245

your body to prove they are right. Once the fetus is saved, the mother will be discarded. But why is only one of the lives involved sacred?

"God made me do it"[11]

> Pro-life activist, after
> bombing a clinic

* * *

"Minds are like parachutes . . . they only work when they're open"[12]

> Anonymous

In recent years, there have been numerous bombings of abortion clinics, where desperate women go for counseling and the termination of unwanted pregnancies. Terrorism has become a weapon used against women making a free choice. And who are these terrorists? Men, of course. When it comes to what goes on between women's thighs, no one gets hotter than men. The combination of religious zeal, chauvinism, and moral certitude turns into lethal politics and physical violence against their "enemies" attending to women's needs.

And why is it that our "religions" divide people, rather than uniting those that disagree? We might ask what of what value are these "religions" if discord is their product? And why do so many people derive a sense of moral superiority from that division? Another fundamentalist minister had this to say:

> "God does not look on all his children the same way. He sees us divided into categories, the Jews and the Gentiles. God has one plan, an earthly plan, for the Jews. And he has a second plan, a heavenly plan for the born-again Christians. The other peoples of the world - Muslims, Buddhists, and those of other faiths as well as those of Christians not born again - do not concern him. As for destroying planet earth, we can do nothing. Peace, for us, is not in God's book."[13]

> Dr. John Walvoord, Southwestern
> School Of the Bible

So god is only a christian? This doctrine of division, of god is on our side, is giving God a bum rap. And the fundamentalists of other religions around the world respond with the same type of self-righteous answer - only they are saved. For centuries these religious zealots have been fighting one another, and much to heaven's dismay. But can we not say that we can only commune with one another, understand and forgive one another, when we drop our claims of being special and "saved" by our various and sundry limited understandings of "God" called religion?

Religions are many but truth is one. And if we look into our holy books and find no compassion or understanding for the predicaments of others, but see only hate and division, then holy wars will continue. We should be embarrassed to blame God for our human foibles, the conditions of our existence, and then assume God is willing to destroy the world to protect our personal version of morality and religion. Intolerance is dynamite enough.

"The bible is something like a mirror. If an ass peers in, you can't expect an apostle to peer out."[14]

Rev. William Sloane Coffin

Given the energies activated by the question of abortion it would be helpful if this same zealotry could be turned toward more positive functions, such as adoption and support of the poor and unfortunate children in the world that already exist. Many religious groups do wonderful work around the world in this regard. But it is easy to get the feeling that the self-righteousness of the more radical moralists will be more apt to delight in its own self-declared sanctity and avoid involvement in the dirty work. One is forced to the conclusion that many of these militant pro-lifer's would rather scream epithets at defenseless and emotionally-wrought women seeking the services of their local physician or clinic, than tackle the real problems of adoption, contraception and sex-education, resource depletion, and over-population.

How many men who vehemently oppose abortion, we might ask, would have the capacity, or willingness, to care for a single child brought into the world by uncaring and incapable parents? When it comes to dealing with the reality of raising and caring for young children, most zealots appear to have little time or money for such details. They'll leave it to the poor women whom they want to force to carry the burden, even if they were raped, or the "father" has deserted the mother, or the baby is deformed, or the mother is insane, or any number of legitimate reasons to seek an abortion.

These self-anointed men, in radical groups such as the "Army of God" want only to continue to "save lives" by preventing a pregnant woman's access to abortion. But let them adopt one unwanted child before they come forward to speak against abortion. Let them stop preventing education regarding contraception in the schools so that fewer innocent young women will have to resort to terminating unwanted pregnancies. Too many arrogant men who disapprove of women's reproductive rights appear to be incapable of giving birth to anything but intolerance, indignation, and self-righteousness.

> "In the shelters for poor women, we see many who are pregnant, raped, deserted, abused. They don't have the skills to provide for themselves or the children they may already have. And we force incredible deprivation and suffering on these women. If the men who make these decisions stuggled with some of the hardships, there might be more latitude in (the church's) moral teaching."[15]

> Rhonda Meister, Coordinator,
> House of Ruth Shelter

In our modern world men no longer have the tribal hunt for the release of their primal instinctual energy. And much of today's unsatisfying economic activity thwarts man's need for physical and emotional release. Now it seems much of manhood is squeezed into the mind, where distorted and often unreleased, it often works havoc on their prey, the weaker sex. We are not many years removed from the age of women as property and possessions, if at all. But the spears of dogma, from our male-dominated religions, continue to pierce the very source of life - the mother.

"CATHOLICS FOR A FREE CHOICE" -

The issue of sexuality and freedom has now indeed splintered the Church and caused the exodus of many members, priests, and nuns who could no longer abide the infallible doctrine. An organization called Catholics For a Free Choice (CFFC) has become a national voice for the 77 per cent of American Catholics who believe in the right of abortion.

"Catholics For a Free Choice is a growing organization that offers an important presence in the pro-choice movement. The Catholic pro-choice position needs to be explained to dispel the myth that all Catholics are anti-abortion. All Catholics are not anti-abortion. The reality is this: 77 percent of all Catholics now support the right to choose abortion in most circumstances."

"Catholics for a Free Choice is looking for Catholics who are willing to be community contacts for us in their towns and cities across the country. What is important for us is to get the word out now, to counter the rapidly accelerating push by the Catholic Church to end safe abortions for women in this country."[16]

Donna Ruscavage, Catholics
For Free Choice (CFCC)

* * *

"Are we asking government to make criminal what we believe to be sinful because we ourselves can't stop committing the sin? The price of seeking to force our belief on others is that they might some day force their belief on us."[17]

Mario Cuomo, Gov. of New York

Recently the Vatican has declared it immoral for childless couples seeking to have a baby to utilize the new "baby-making" techniques made possible by new advances in medicine. An official Catholic Church pronouncement entitled "Instruction on Respect for Human Life in its Origins and on The Dignity of Procreation" condemms artificial insemination and in-vitro fertilizations even when the married couple may provide their own sperm and ova. Here, they deny a child to a childless couple, and elsewhere they force pregnancy on those who don't want a baby and are incapable of providing for new life! Again, the dogma of celibate priests seems to triumph over compassion and common sense.

Why is the Church opposed to the "creation" of a wanted child by a childless couple, thru artificial means, and not opposed to the unconscious, careless, and unplanned human procreation that threatens the very fabric of society and the resources of our planet? How can the Church oppose the creation, by whatever means, of the one and only child of an infertile couple, and not oppose on moral grounds the careless creation of a fifth, sixth, or tenth child by a couple unable to provide a decent environment?

Is God only interested in the sheer numbers of beings conceived by flesh pounding away in the missionary position? Or might we conclude that He/She is really interested in the quality of life, the intention in procreation, and the state of the earth? The question is not how, it really is what do we end up with? What is the effect of our religious beliefs on our children and our environment? Certainly God must care about the end result.

After this latest Vatican pronouncement, one Catholic woman, who had remained infertile and opted for in vitro fertilization, replied to this condemnation of her only option for child-bearing: "I simply will not remain a Roman Catholic.

Children are the number one priority of my husband and me, and we're willing to sacrifice a lot for it." Here, the shedding of compassionless dogma, that makes an infertile woman feel guilty for having a baby thru the only route open to her, is not a sacrifice but a release, a deliverance.

Whether women are attempting to have a baby, or not have a baby, the Church offers not compassion but guilt, and even excommunication, for the sin of making a conscious and free choice. Such a church may not exist for long where it seems to maintain so little compassion and respect for its adherents, their individual and unique problems, and the precarious state of the earth and its limited resources.

What are the chances that we might see a pronouncement from the Catholic Church entitled: "Instruction on Respect for Motherhood in its origins and on the dignity of pregnancy prevention?"

* Chapter Eight *

- A Woman's Church -

NUNS IN REVOLT - "THE VATICAN 24" -

In recent decades the Church has lost over thirty percent of its nuns because of their archaic treatment and outlook on women. And many who remain within the church fight an uphill battle against centuries of male chauvinism. In 1985, 96 catholics, including 24 nuns and three priests signed a statement for the "Catholic Committee on Pluralism and Abortion." Their concern was that there could be differences of opinion about abortion within the church - that Catholics can legitimately believe that Church teaching on abortion is not binding. Their mistake was that they believed the church would allow independence of thought, free choice and diversity amongst catholics. They were wrong.

> "Statements of recent Popes and of the Catholic hierachy have condemmed the direct termination of prenatal life as morally wrong in all instances. There is the mistaken belief in American society that this is the only legitimate Catholic position. In fact, a diversity of opinion regarding abortion exists among committed Catholics."[1]

> Statement, "Vatican 24"

The response to these dissidents from the Committee on Doctrine of the National Conference of Catholic Bishops was essentially - "believe or leave." Members of the Vatican 24, as the rebellious nuns and priests were called, soon felt the wrath of an endangered dogma, a cornered ideology. This is the beginning of a confrontation that could easily escalate into a watershed for American Catholics, especially women.

> "We are appalled by the recent action of the Vatican against women who are members of religious orders (nuns). We believe that this Vatican action is a cause for scandal to Catholics everywhere. It seeks to stifle freedom of speech and public discussion in the Roman Catholic Church and create the appearance of a consensus where none exists."[2]

> Statement, "Vatican 24"

I am certain that many people find solace and fellowship within the confines of an organized church. But it is curious that so many women will continue to patronize (or should we say matronize) Catholic and other fundamentalist churches given the doctrinal abuse they are subjected to by male clerics. Therein, the scriptures of doubtful divinity, written and re-written by men, centuries after the death of Christ, purport to define women's subservience to men. Even today they appear to be trying to put women back in a place that no longer exists in our society. Unfortunately, there has been an utter lack of respect and upward mobility for women within the Church, based largely on the questionable authority of scriptures from an era that is no more.

> "Let your women keep silence in the churches: for it is not permitted unto them to speak."[3]

> I Corinthians 14:34
> * * *

> "No bishop, no priest, no deacon in the Catholic Church has been a woman for almost 2000 years."[4]

> Marvin Cetron,
> Religions of the Future
> * * *

"Women are not called to the priesthood."[5]

Pope John Paul II

The Church apparently still believes that women cannot get a call from God, or from the spark of deity within our own beings. Only the Pope answers the phone calls from heaven - women cannot pick up the receiver. And, the Pope continues, "the Church is irrevocably committed to this truth." Heaven is apparently still segregated. Whose heaven is this anyway?

But in dealing with our earthly realities, the very nuns on the front lines of parenthood problems, who must encounter and nurture the women facing difficult decisions, are given no leeway to use their hearts and minds and exercise their own judgment and compassion as they see fit. Instead, they must simply tow the vatican line or quit the Church. So their own feelings, instincts, and decisions to console the members of their congregation must be aborted to make way for dogma - the judgment of men thousands of miles removed from the gripping anguish of the situation.

> "The sexual ethics of the church are now developed by male, celibate clerics. We women need to be part of that decision-making process too. This ultimatum is a way of putting us in our place, keeping us submissive, and treating us as children."[6]

Sister Judith Vaughn

* * *

"God put me on this earth to give the Pope a hard time."[7]

Frances Kissling,
Catholics For Free Choice

But change is in the air. Either the Church will change or the women will leave. Pope John Paul's recent insistence on towing the line is certain to hasten the end of the Church, at least for independently minded people. We don't need agents to handle our communications with our god. If he or she exists, or is other than us, we can go direct . . . and more women are finding this out.

> "He thinks of Nuns as a servant class, he brought nuns with him to Rome to cook his sausage. All his statements about women have only one thing to say: motherhood."[8]

Dr. Rosemary Ruether,
Prof. of Theology

* * *

> "The joke went around that he (Pope John Paul II) should step on the ground and kiss the women, and instead he kissed the ground and stepped on the women."[9]

Suzanne Hiatt,
Episcopal Priest

We now live in an information age where more people have access to all religious viewpoints and can begin to make comparisons, evaluating the religious ideas and doctrines they have grown up with. As internationally-oriented planetary citizens we now have access to more information, and more wisdom, and thus more of a choice. Even just decades ago, and most certainly two thousand years ago, people only knew what was in their immediate culture and village. They believed and obeyed mostly out of fear.

And raised from childhood with terrifying images of burning in hell, the very thought of disagreeing with the Church produced too much stress for the average person. And so their belief was most often just a function of fear. But, unlike today, Mother Nature was not thwarted and she took care of the effects of that belief (unlimited reproduction) in a cruel fashion. But habits, pardon the expression, die hard.

"WOMEN-CHURCH" - A NEW LITURGY? -

The entrenched male priesthood has steadfastly refused to allow women priests, owing to the biblical idea of man's dominion over women. So to obtain freedom, along with their reproductive rights, many women have had to leave the Church. The history of religion is not pretty when it comes to the treatment of women. Just ask Joan of Arc or any of the other "witches" burned at the stake for defying the male edicts of their time.

Today, because the Church continues to interfere in a women's maternal affairs, many are leaving traditional institutions to form their own "communities of nurture" and re-write the dogma of the past, written by men, in the name of god, to exclude and dominate women. The emerging feminist religious revolution will likely restore the imbalance of centuries of male domination of all churches.

Male prelates are so certain god is a male, it's taken for granted. The thought that god incorporates both he/she has not penetrated into the power structures and chambers of the western religious mind. The thought that we may live many lives as both male and female is even further from view. In effect, for centuries, we have all been brainwashed by the military-like organizations, titles, and semantics of "holy" religious power. Lord, Master, Kingdom, Cardinal, Bishop, Pope, etc. These have become the position headings of corporate, grey-flannel, and male-oriented religions. It has required mighty organizational strength, and at times tortuous doctrinal hoopla to maintain the centuries-old, and often irrelevant and questionable, beliefs that remain frozen in time against changing circumstances.

"Traditionally, women were the primary healers in society. Modern elite male medicine . . . systematically deprived women of the right to practice healing arts, culminating in the male medical takeover of midwifery. People (women) are made to feel that they are incapable of healing themselves and each other and must depend on specialists. Women have sought to take back control over their own bodies, particularly in sexual and reproduction matters, and to relearn traditions of holistic medicine."[10]

Dr. Rosemary Reuther

Dr. Rosemary Reuther's landmark book on liberating women from the hopelessly male-dominated church is indeed a new "manifesto" for religious revolution. "Woman-Church" neatly covers the sorry history of female persecution, and exclusion from the priesthood. Reuther has also given form to many new litanies and rites of healing for women. These liturgies form the basis for a new communal church, free from the domination of dogma where god is always a man. And it's about time, when one considers that the old churches started with the myth of women being fashioned from Adam's rib. It's been an uphill battle for women ever since.

"Being she is responsible for the fall, woman is in a state of subjugation."[11]

Martin Luther

* * *

"The woman is in a state of subjugation in the original order of things. For this reason she cannot represent headship in society or in the church. Only the male can represent Christ. For this reason it was necessary that Christ be incarnated as a male. It follows, therefore, that she cannot receive the sign of Holy Orders."[12]

Thomas Aquinas

* * *

"Her very name, fe-mina means "absence of faith." She is insatiable lust by nature. Because of this lust she consorts even with devils. It is for this reason that women are prone to the crime of witchcraft."[13]

> Malleua Maleficarum, (15th
> Cent.) Manual of Dominican
> Inquisitors against Witches
>
> * * *

"In the year 584, in Lyons, France, forty three Catholic bishops and twenty men representing other Bishops held a most peculiar debate: "Are Women Human?" After many lengthy arguments, a vote was taken. The results were: thirty-two, yes; thirty-one, no. Women were declared human by one vote."[14]

> Meg Bowman, Why We Burn:
> Sexism Exorcised

But even during the centuries of persecution of women, throughout the bloody history of the church, customs from earlier times managed to survive. The wisdom of earlier matriarchal societies is evident in the following gypsy prayer addressed to the Goddess in all women:

"Thou destroyest and dost make everything on earth; thou canst see nothing old, for death lives in thee, thou givest birth to all upon the earth for thou thyself are life . . . Thou are the mother of every living creature and the distributor of good; thou doest according to thy wisdom in destroying what is useless or what has lived its destined time; by thy wisdom thou makest the earth to regenerate all that is new . . . Thou art the benefactress of mankind."[15]

It is a testament to woman's forgiving nature that she could hang around institutions that treated her like the devil. The realization of a "women-church" is badly needed to salve the wounds of women who have had an abortion and need to get on with their lives. The following rite of this unique church, a sanctuary for women, is an excellent step in that direction. It addresses the wounds of women who proceed to control their reproductive destiny in a largely unsympathetic, and male-dominated, culture.

A RITE OF HEALING FROM AN ABORTION -

In Dr. Reuther's vision of a "Women-Church" women today require healing and bonding litanies for many rites of passage in their lives, and especially for abortion. These new-era prayers, and communal ritual, give women the chance to redefine themselves and their spirituality free from the male-dominated rituals of the past. But even when women act in their own best interests, the residual guilt from centuries of doctrine acts upon their psyche. For this reason, these new prayers, from a woman's perspective, are so important and effective. These are the powerful words from the healing rite for one of life's most troubling decisions:

" . . . And the new church shall heal and nurture women:"

" . . . Community Prayer: O great Mother and Father, power of all life and new life, we are sorrowful this day. We are saddened by the conflicts we often experience between life and life, between the affirmation of a potential new life which was barely begun and the ongoing life that we must nurture and sustain. We are more than sad, we are also angry that we are faced with such choices, for these are choices in which there is no wholly good way; these are choices between two bad things, choices against a potential life or against existing life . . .

" . . . We don't like to have to make these choices. We would like to arrange our lives so that we don't have to make these choices, but this is not always possible.

We are surrounded by fragmentation and insufficiency, mistakes of judgment, and sometimes by coercion in these choices we would like to make freely. We are surrounded by a world of coercion and violence and stifling of the kind of knowledge and self-understanding that would allow us to make better choices, to think and plan in advance . . ."

" . . . We are surrounded by a world in which vast numbers of people go to bed hungry and where many children come into the world unwanted and without the most minimal opportunities for love and development . . ."

" . . . We don't want to create life in that way. We want to create life that is chosen, wanted, and can be sustained and nourished. Our sister has made her hard choice. We don't want to pretend that this choice was easy or simple, without pain or hurt, but we also trust that she has made the best choice that she could make . . ."

" . . . We affirm her and uphold her in her ongoing life, as she gathers her life together and centers her energies on how she is going to continue to sustain her own life and the lives around her which it nourishes . . ."

"(The Woman who has had an abortion now speaks. She reflects as long as she wishes on what the decision means to her and her ongoing plans for her life.)

"(A group of women now surrounds the woman seated in the center and lays hands on her saying:)

"Be Healed sister, be whole!"

"(Then one of the women brings a flower pot with new soil in front of her and scatters seeds in it, saying;)

"Life is broken, life dies, but life is reborn, life continues. We do not look back to the past, but to the new futures

261

that arise each day with the new rising of the sun, with the fresh dews on the grass and the sunshine of our new possibilities. Let these seeds symbolize the new possibilities of life that open up before us, even as we mourn the flickers of life that are not to be."

"(The woman in the center takes a watering can and waters the seeds, and the flower pot is presented to her.)[16]

Where would we find such a ceremony in an orthodox church today? In the unplanned pregnancy situation, women of all ages are beset with male-dominated churches, hospitals, and clinics all too quick to condemm and control motherhood. It is precisely this lack of a supportive environment that is part of the unneccessary mental torture of the young girl or woman terminating a pregnancy. The communal aspects of a new "Women-Church" approach appears to be the only sensible alternative for women escaping from the aged and rotten dogma of sin and slavery cast upon women for two thousand years.

The idea of a new healing rite goes a long way in restoring the ancient power of the Priestess and the Goddess in all women. Long before the Christian era, the panoply of mythological gods included both powerful and vulnerable women attending to their problems on an equal footing with men. And all of the most ancient myths tell of a Creatress, rather than a Creator, due to the natural fact that living things were only made by women . . . the female of the species. Women had the magic and men had none. Motherhood was the only bond of relationship in times when the concept of fatherhood did not even exist.

Because of the harsh facts of life in older "primitive" cultures, tribal men and women recognized the need to commune with the spirit world, thanking them for their sustenance and, at the same time, apologizing for taking life so that they might live. It was evident to our ancestors that our very bodies are made of material that once was resident in other humans, plants and animals. We are them and they are us in a very real sense. The Shamans of these ancient cultures played a role in mediating between the world of the living and the dead, the seen and the unseen. Joan Halifax, in her book "Shaman: The Wounded Healer," relates these words of wisdom from an Eskimo Shaman to an arctic explorer:

> "The greatest peril of life lies in the fact that human food consists entirely of souls. All the creatures that we have to kill and eat, all those that we have to strike down and destroy to make clothes for ourselves, have souls, souls that do not perish and which must therefore be pacified lest they should revenge themselves on us for taking away their bodies."[17]

In the untold millenniums of tribal culture, the very act of hunting, the killing of the here-and-now living animals for food and clothing, necessitated both thanks and apologies to the spirit world. Today, our termination of a pregnancy, or the postponement of an incarnation of a potential being not yet living, should also involve both a thanks, for the remembrance of our fertility, as well as an apology for the postponement of life. This is the ancient way, the prayer of thanks and forgiveness that heals and strengthens the bond between this world and the next, the known and the unknown.

Jesus, and all other sages of the past, have said essentially the same thing about the nature of our intrinsic powers: "The Kingdom of God is within you." Would not the true sage of today also tell us that what is within the power of women is the calamity of god, in the force of uncontrolled fertility and childbirth. The ordered and peaceful Kingdom, or Queendom, is not within an organization, or any charismatic figure other than oneself.

Pregnancy is a serious event. It necessitiates a new re-evaluation of the direction of our lives. By looking within ourselves, into the core of our being, as well as outside to the realities of our world, we will arrive at our own "right" solution to the decision to enter or postpone motherhood. The solutions of others are not necessarily our solutions, and their revelations are not our discovery. All people are free to define their own version of "natural law" but they are not free to define ours unless we let them. Your motherhood is yours, period.

RIGHT MOTHERHOOD -

Perhaps within the Buddhist definition of the great Middle Way, or Right Doing, we might place the definition of "Right Motherhood." In today's world, Right Motherhood will recognize the sacredness of all life, and necessarily that of the mother above that of the unborn. It will recognize her primary obligation to the here and now, the living and existing children, as well as any potential life. But the notion of Right Motherhood in our age is perhaps simply wrong if it does not include a global sense of responsibility to our planet, our community, our village, our family, and our living children before that of the unborn. Right motherhood must include a sense of every woman's responsibility for ecological balance.

In motherhood choices, our communication with potential souls is reverent and respectful. But it is only the mother's decision to bring life into the earth plane. Every soul must borrow a woman's body to enter life, and be thankful for the privilege given. But it cannot be "god's will" that we surrender our intelligence and capacity to properly order our existence, and pass on a peaceful and plentiful world to our children. Indeed, we can now say it is essential, in an already overcrowded world, to assume even more god-like responsibilities and make mature choices in motherhood. Buddha understood very well the prisons of guilt we so often create for ourselves:

> "Seek nought from the helpless gods by gift and hymm, nor bribe with blood, nor feed with fruit and cakes: Within yourselves deliverance must be sought, each one his prison makes."

> "I, Buddha, who wept with all my brother's tears, whose heart was broken by a whole world's woe, laugh and

am glad, for there is liberty! Know you suffer! Know you suffer from yourselves."[18]

Buddha, The Dhammapada

If it is necessary to terminate a pregnancy to bring order into our lives and our world, then so be it. If we fail to act, when our deepest feelings and circumstances argue against the timing of a particular act of conception, then the stage is set for a lifetime of potential regret, ongoing recrimination, and antipathy toward the child and the father. If, as sexual beings, we cannot control or neatly order our sexuality then we must surely control our conception of new life.

Our attitudes and consciousness preceeding and during the deliberate and loving act of conception are most important. Motherhood, and fatherhood, is serious business. In pursuing our own Right Motherhood, there is no substitute for a spiritual and loving intention, where a mature and responsible man and woman come together for the sole purpose of conception. We are woefully ignorant of the nature of the energies involved in conception and birth - so much depends on the mother.

"What type of soul enters you depends on where you are. When you are in a deep meditative state and the energy is flowing, you conceive a higher quality soul. This almost always happens - that people make love when they are sexual. Sexuality is a lower center. It happens sometimes that when people are angry and fighting, they make love."

"That too is very low, very low. You open your door to a much lower soul. Or people make love as a routine, a mechanical habit, something that has to be done every day or twice a week or whatever. They do it just as a mechanical routine or as part of a physical hygiene, but then it is very mechanical. It has nothing of your heart in it, and then you allow very low souls to enter you . . ."

" . . . Love should be almost like a prayer. Love is sacred. It is the holiest thing that exists in man. So first one should prepare oneself to move into love. Pray, meditate, and when you are full of a different kind of energy which has nothing to do with the physical, in fact nothing to do with the sexual, then you are vulnerable to a higher quality soul. So, much depends on the mother . . ."

" . . . You can become a mother - you are ready - but if you are not very alert about it, you will get entangled with a very ordinary soul. People are almost unaware of what they are doing. If you go to purchase a car, even then you think much about it. If you go to purchase furniture for your room, you have a thousand and one alternatives and you think about this and that, which one will suit. But as far as children are concerned, you never think about what type of children you would like, what type of soul you are going to invoke, invite . . ."

" . . . And millions are the alternatives . . . from Judas to Jesus, from the darkest soul to the holiest. Millions are the alternatives and your attitude will decide. Whatsoever your attitude, you become available to that sort of soul. If you go higher, you become available to higher souls. You go lower, you become available to lower souls. So remember this much."[19]

Bhagwan Shree Rajneesh

THE FUTURE -

There is no reason or rationale, however lofty, to require the vast majority of women around the world to return to the horrible and backward past of illegal abortions, where women on the run from authorities seek any help they can get, whether qualified or not. We have seen the past, and it does not work. Unless women are vigilant in protecting the basic human rights of motherhood from the recurrent threat of morality legislation, defining the state as father of your baby, then women will lose their right of privacy and control over their reproductive futures and their children.

The way we think about the nature of life, and our relationship to a god or creator, as well as the condition of our personal circumstances or relationship, is the framework within which most women make their decisions about pregnancy termination. The mechanisms of entrapment and control that sway us from our better instincts are both subtle and gross, psychic and physical, imaginary and real. Often, the more we look outside ourselves for solutions to our problems the more confused we become. But since motherhood creates the world, mothers must look at the world to see what kind of a world it is they are creating.

And even worse than the problems surrounding the choice of a pregnancy termination is the exposure and risk of women giving birth in modern hospitals that become mired in questionable legal and ethical procedures to take control away from the mother and protect the interests of the hospital and physician. Many women today are still unaware, as we saw in the case with Sherri Finkbine, of the frightening and tragic consequences of other people's legalistic interests in your body and womb. For too many women and young girls childbirth is a nightmare that brings us suddenly into the cold light of reality with regard to our loss of personal freedom and autonomy in hospital situations. Too often we are operated on in more ways than one. Like the analogy of the "unconscious violinist" we may find ourselves suddenly plugged into the interests of medical and legal practitioners without our understanding and consent.

As we look around the world today, we've only just begun to see the tragic future in store for humanity destined to ruin their environment and struggle over scarce resources. Surely we cannot turn the earth into a "zero-sum society" where every additional human lives at the expense of another, and where quantity crushes the quality of life in the ongoing degradation of our environment. But population control is still an individual issue until the day that that power is taken from free people by the state. And our freedoms always seem to disappear in the name of "compassion" or "morality." But the next removal of our freedom could well be in the name of survival itself.

On the other hand, we can manage our families and populations rationally to prevent poverty and starvation. At the present time, economic growth is seen as the savior to stave off excess population growth. Still the problem for many countries is simply that population continually grows faster than the economy. And humanity has now arrived at a point in our earthly saga where even the religion of "Growthism" must ultimately give way to a steady-state environment, otherwise continuous population growth will lead to our eventual demise.

Unfortunately, both politics and religion continue to play havoc with solutions such as education, contraception and abortion. Is war, famine, and disease to be our only birth control? Must we resort to "Life-boat Ethics" that require saving only certain portions of the burgeoning population because there is simply not enough for everyone? Will more technological marvels only lead to more population straining the natural limits of the planet? It remains to be seen what the ultimate effects of our technology will be.

But given the new world of medical technology, and the advent of the morning-after pill, we may soon bypass the religious debates and legislative wars by putting control over procreation back in the privacy of a woman's bedroom where it belongs. Will such a pill be available to the people who need it most? Or will its distribution be prevented by the same moralists who now argue against abortion? Some opponents of abortion even go so far as to state that there is no such thing as a "right to privacy" allowing a woman the freedom to control her own body. But how can totalitarian control of your reproductive freedom ever be considered "pro-life?" The only life it protects is that of the state and the morality police.

And might not the new experimental anti-aging pills lengthen our life spans even further so that we now have four or five generations of each family living at the same time? Will living great-grandparents soon become commonplace? Technology creates new miracles and new problems. If man is going to do the miracles, then man must control the side effects. If the "miracle drugs" end up producing more population and misery, due to lack of individual responsibility and control, then our future is certain to be filled with government control.

On the other hand, if new and safe contraception is developed in the near future, men and women can once again experience the joys of love without the fear of unplanned pregnancies. A world of wanted and loved children, born to mature and responsible parents, will be the basis of a new and better world.

Abortion, where necessary, is simply another form of human rights and self-determination for the mother. But can we not also say that abortion is really a basic and necessary form of life-control — a mother's final decision to control her own life and that of any children she may bear? And in some circumstances it may be the only choice and the last form of birth control that is available. We cannot deny a mother her basic human right of life-control and self-determination. So fetal rights must remain secondary to mother's rights or we invite chaos, repression, and environmental degradation into our world. We degrade life by letting it happen in the worst of circumstances against our better judgment.

Even today there are those who say we have a "birth dearth" and that people in the "west" are not multiplying fast enough (as if mother earth knew east from west). The fact that some races or nations are multiplying faster than others is not occasion to speed up the birth rate of industrialized nations. Surely the time has come to slow the real rate of increase in developing nations currently slaughtering their futures with excessive birth rates. We simply cannot sink into rascist games involving some kind of sum-of-the-people competition. This type of logic is tantamount to saying that because the west has

269

only 60,000 nuclear warheads to the east's 120,000, we better start rapidly increasing the number of our warheads! Both sheer numbers of people, and their outmoded ideas, can ultimately have the same effects as a rain of nuclear warheads upon the earth.

Today, the new vision of "Ecofeminism" being forged by independent women around the world is helping to heal the old separation between man and nature. Women must play a new role in ending the lopsided patriachal domination of women and nature that has existed for centuries. Women, by their very nature, will likely be better and more efficient housekeepers of a precious planet, and its human and natural resources, if given the chance to co-create our destiny on an equal footing with the male of the species.

The future of our planet and the conditions of life for all the children to come will be the result of millions of individual decisions and, unfortunately, non-decisions about new life being made today. It is essential today that all women, in every country of the world, have freedom of choice in reproductive decisions, and the chance to make these choices according to our own understanding of the deeper meanings of life, in the best interests of our own families, and our rapidly shrinking planet. It is now extremely important for future planetary balance that women all over the world make their motherhood "right motherhood." We are the problem . . . and we must be the solution.

A CREDO FOR ABORTION RIGHTS -

In summary, I can do no better than to relate the proposed credo, for all women of the world, suggested by S. Chandrasekhar, a man with years of experience as Minister of Health and Family Planning in India, a country beset with the realities of family planning issues. Worldwide, this credo setting forth the inalienable rights of motherhood must soon become the foundation for sane population policies. A new enlightened attitude towards the freedom of women to control their own reproductive futures upon our crowded and fragile environment - planet earth - is now imperative. In his insightful book, "Abortion In a Crowded World," Chandrasekhar states: "The role of abortion in our society, whether it is for demographic, eugenic, economic, legal, medical or humanitarian purposes, must encompass in the near future the following credo:"

"1. The fundamental right to choose whether to bear children or not is a right of privacy which no law of any country, no matter what its religious affiliation or political ideology, should curtail.

2. Abortion must be made available on demand while gynaecologists, psychiatrists and social workers might be permitted to counsel the pregnant woman to the contrary. But the pregnant woman's decision must be final, subject only to the safety of her person

3. Abortion in the last analysis must be a matter left entirely to the pregnant woman and her physician. (Of course, there are millions of sick and suffering women in the world who have no physician to consult at all.)

4. No distinction should be made between married and unmarried women, unless the pregnant woman is less than sixteen years of age, when the consent of the parents should be obtained.

5. A woman must be able to obtain an abortion, if necessary, free of charge in an approved, tax-supported clinic or hospital. But if any fee is to be charged in such an institution it must be based on the principal of ability to pay, without impairing in any way the quality of service.

6. The woman must be thoroughly informed of all the available and effective methods of family planning so that she can avoid the need for further abortions.

7. The hospital and other relevant agencies must keep the identity of the woman undergoing abortion confidential for it is the woman's private concern."[20]

271

* APPENDIX A *

In 1973, Garrett Hardin, one of this century's great essayists, wrote this satirical courtroom scene in reply to the advocates of a proposed Twenty-Eight amendment to the Constitution outlawing abortion. The amendment never passed.

"A Truth's Day in Court"

"Your Honor. My client has been accused of murder under the Twenty-Eighth amendment (a proposed anti-abortion amendment) of the constitution of the United Sates. There is no argument as to the facts, so I ask the court to look deeper into the meaning of those facts."

"My client, Dr. Samaritan, is a profoundly compassionate man. His behavior on the witness stand, I am sure, convinced everyone of this. As Margaret's physician, he was deeply touched when this unfortunate woman came to him with her problem. Six children already; and now impregnated with a seventh by a husband who had left home to live with another woman - whom he also made pregnant. No financial reserves. A job that barely supported her family; and that job would be lost if she went through with the pregnancy and childbirth."

"What man of compassion and imagination could fail to be touched by the poor woman's plight? Dr. Samaritan is rich in both compassion and imagination. And courage. So he performed the single operation the woman desired, and a family was saved from disaster."

"I will not base my argument on a peculiarity found in the enforcement of all abortion-prohibition laws, but I cannot refrain from mentioning it in passing. Abortion, it is said, is a crime. Distinguishing between the principal and the accessory to a crime as we do in law, who is the principal in the crime of abortion? Clearly the woman. It is she who wills the crime."

"Who is punished? Only the accessory, the physician. Never the principal."

"In one hundred years of abortion-prohibitions in the United States never once has the principal - the woman herself - been punished for the crime of abortion. Threatened, yes. Badgered by the police, yes. They want to make her reveal the name of the accessory. But the woman is never punished."

"What kind of crime is it for which we punish only the accessory to the crime and never the principal? Could it be - I don't say that it is - but just could it be that we don't believe, deep in our hearts, that abortion is a crime? What other explanation can there be for our odd conduct?"

"But I said I would not linger over this peculiarity of the law. I have a much more fundamental issue to explore with the court.

Mr. Sequitur, Margaret's attorney - a pudgy little man - mopped his florid face with a silk handkerchief and strolled back to his table. On a cue, his assistant lifted a box from the floor, a box big enough to hold an inflated basketball. Sequitur, placing his hand on the top, turned to the judge.

"If you will permit it, Your Honor, I have a little demonstration for the court." He turned again to the box and very deliberately untied it and opened it. He reached in and started to draw something out. A hush had fallen over the courtroom. All eyes were on the lawyer's hands. Sequitur, sensing the tension, thoughtfully removed his hands from the box and turned to the judge again.

"Before I go on with the demonstration, I must prepare the ground. You know that it is possible to transplant a fertilized egg from the womb of one woman to the womb of another. In this way it is sometimes possible to bring the blessings of motherhood to a woman who would otherwise be fruitless. This is a fine thing, but unfortunately it is difficult to get the fertilized egg in just the right condition for transplanting it into another womb."

274

"Sterility specialists have long recognized that what is really needed is a way of nourishing and maintaining a woman's ovaries in the laboratory, in "tissue Culture" as they call it. This is easier said than done. Thousands of man hours have gone into this work, without success.

"Today it is my great privilege to announce, for the first time in public, a magnificent success in this humanitarian effort. The medical announcement will appear in the New England Journal of Medicine next month. I am proud to say that it is scientists in our own Huxley University, led by the brilliant Dr. Bokanovsky, who have achieved this stunning success."

"Dr. Bokanovsky's group have found how to maintain a female ovary indefinitely in a culture apparatus in the laboratory. More; they have learned how to stimulate an ovary so that it will turn out eggs at a rate close to that at which a testicle turns out spermatozoa. Putting eggs and spermatazoa together they produce fertilized eggs ready for implanting in the waiting wombs of women yearning for motherhood. The Fertility Laboratory of Huxley University is now prepared to make every woman in the world happy with her very own baby. We may confidently expect the Nobel Prize to be awarded for this great accomplishment."

Sequitur paused and drank some water from a glass. Turning to the bench again, he continued.

"Dr. Bokanovsky, learning of this trial, has very generously lent me some of his material. I have here in this flask" - Sequitur reached into the box and pulled out a two-liter Erlenmeyer flask with a plastic cap on it - "a suspension of living human eggs, all fertilized and ready to be transplanted into expectant mothers."

The attorney sloshed the liquid around in the half-filled flask. The fluid was milky and just slightly pink. Sequitur paced back and forth, thoughtfully juggling the flask as he walked.

"How many fertilized eggs do you suppose there are in here? Dr. Bokanovsky has carefully sampled this flask and made the calculations. There are, he tells me, two times ten to the thirteenth fertilized eggs in this little vessel. In numbers more familiar to most of us - certainly to me - that's twenty trillion. That sounds like a lot. How many is it? What can we compare this large number with?"

"I think our best course is to compare it with the toatl number of people who have ever lived on this old planet of ours. Twenty years ago the demographer Nathan Keyfitz calculated this was 77 billion. With the continued burgeoning of the population I am told this number stands today at 80 billion. That is, all the people who have ever lived, amount to only 80 billion."

"According to the Twenty-Eighth Amendment every fertilized egg is a human being, in the full meaning of the law. I have, then, in this flask, twenty trillion human beings - two hundred and fifty times as many as have ever lived before on earth. Now . . .

Sequitur removed the lid. "Now . . ."

Quickly he inverted the flask , and with a swinging motion sprayed the contents in a semicircular swath on the floor. The audience gasped. The judge, his mouth open, half rose to admonish the attorney. But Sequitur, his voice loud and insistent, continued rapidly, precluding interruption.

"Bear with me! Bear with me! I know I have sullied the dignity of this courtroom, but I will make amends. Bear with me! My argument is far more serious than any minor disorder I may have created."

"A moment ago this flask had twenty trillion living human beings in it. Now they are spread out all over this courtroom floor. They are still alive. But they won't be for long. The most heroic efforts we could possibly mount would not save them. They will die."

"And who killed them? I killed them. I, John Sequitur, killed them! In front of your very eyes, I have killed two hundred and fifty times as many people as have ever lived on earth. Adolph Hitler and Genhis Khan were pikers compared to me. I, John Sequitur, am the greatest murderer of all time."

"The law, it has been said, does not concern itself with trifles. My client snuffed out the life of one human embryo.

276

The Twenty-Eighth Amendment says that every woman's embryo is a human being from the moment of conception, and that my client is a murderer. I, my client's attorney, have just snuffed out the lives of twenty trillion human beings. So says the Twenty-eighth Amendment.

"Do not concern yourself with trifles. Your honor. Release my client - and charge me with murder. Mass murder."

Garrett Hardin,
Mandatory Motherhood

* APPENDIX B *

ABORTION RIGHTS ORGANIZATIONS -

American Civil Liberties Union
132 West 43rd Street
New York, N.Y. 10036
(212) 944-9800

Catholics For A Free Choice
2008 17th Street, N.W.
Washington, D.C. 20009
(202) 638-1706

National Abortion Federation
900 Pennsylvania Avenue, S.E.
Washington, D.C. 20003
(202) 546-9060

National Abortion Rights Action League
1424 K Street, N.W.
Washington, D.C. 20005
(202) 347-7774

National Organization For Women
1401 New York Avenue, N.W.
Washington, D.C. 20005-2102
(202) 347-2279

Planned Parenthood Federation of America*
810 Seventh Avenue
New York, N.Y. 10019
(800) 223-3303

Religious Coalition For Abortion Rights
100 Maryland Avenue, N.E.
Washington, D.C. 20002
(202) 543-7032

LOCAL CLINICS AND WOMEN'S SERVICES -

For a listing of women's clinics in your area call Planned
Parenthood, or look in the Yellow Pages of your local
telephone book under the following categories: Clinics,
Family Planning Information Centers, Birth Control
Information Centers, Women's Organizations &
Services, Physicians & Surgeons, D.O.

* 761 clinics in U.S.

* BIBLIOGRAPHY *

CHAPTER ONE -

1. Confucius. The Analects. Penguin Classics. Penguin Books. 1979.
2. Gerber, Alex, M.D. Science and The Law Agree: A Fetus is not a Baby. Los Angeles Times.
3. Purpura, Dominick. M.D. Humanist Mag. May 1986. p.37.
4. Burnhill, Michael, M,D. Newsweek Magazine. Jan 14, 1985 p. 37.
5. Stavis, Richard. M.D. Ibid. p. 37.
6. Talbot, Michael. Beyond The Quantum. Macmillan Publishing Company. New York. 1986.
7. Lilly, John. On Satori. Magical Blend Magazine #17. 1987. pp. 13.
8. Charon, Jean. The Unknown Spirit. Mary Clinton - A Physicist Looks At Light. Magical Blend Magazine #15.
9. Roberts, Jane. The Seth Material. Bantam Books. New York. 1970. pp. 320-321.
10. The Bible. I Corinthians 15:44.
11. Meyer, Marvin W. The Secret Teachings of Jesus - Four Gnostic Gospels. Random House. New York. 1984 p. 82
12. Katha Upanishad.
13. The Bible. The Book of Genesis, Chapter 2, verse 7.
14. Kirkegaard, Soren. E.F. Schumacher. Small is Beautiful. p. 85.
15. Ni, Hua-Ching. The Complete Works of Lao Tzu. The Shrine of The Eternal Breath of Tao. Malibu, Ca. 1979. p. 195.
16. Flynn, Frederick. Natural Law and the Problem of Over-Population. The Catholic Messenger, 78(30):6.
17. Fisher, Joe. The Case For Reincarnation. Bantam New Age Books - William Collins. Ontario, Canada. 1984. p. 68.
18. Ibid. p. 69.
19. Rajneesh, Bhagwan Shree. Philosophia Ultima - Discourses on the Mandukya Upanishad. Rajneesh Foundation International, Poona, India. 1983
20. Wambach, Helen, Dr. Life Before Life. Bantam Books. New York. 1979.
20. Swami Prabhavananda and Christopher Isherwood. The Song of God. Bhagavad-Gita. Mento. New York 1944. p. 50.
22. Stuphen, Dick. You Were Born To Be Together. Simon & Schuster. New York. 1976 p. 232.

281

23. Schlotterbeck, Karl. Living Your Past Lives. Ballantine Books. New York. 1987.
24. Buddha, The Dhammapada.
25. Websters Treasury of Relevant Quotations. Edward Murphy. Crown Publishers. New York. 1978
26. Perkins, James Scudday. Experiencing Reincarnation. The Theosophical Publishing House. London. 1977 pp. 6-11.
27. Ibid. pp. 42-43.
28. Cranston, Sylvia and Carey Williams. Reincarnation - A New Horizon in Science, Religion and Society. Julian Press. New York. 1984. pp. 138-139.
29. Wilson, Colin. Afterlife. Doubleday & Company. Garden City, N.Y. 1987.
30. Percival, Harold Waldwin. Thinking and Destiny - Beoing the Science of Man. The Word Foundation. Dallas. 1946. p. 44.
31. Schlotterbeck, Karl. op. cit.
32. Seth (Roberts, Jane). op. cit. p. 546.
33. Emmanuel. (Rodegast, Pat & Stanton, Judith.) Emmanuel's Book. Bantam New Age Books. New York. 1985. p. 227.
34. Aurelius, Marcus. Meditations. Penguin Classics - Penguin Books. Middlesex, England. 1964. p. 50.
35. Seth (Roberts, Jane) op. cit. p. 492.
36. Perkins, op. cit.
37. Whitton, Joel L., M.D., and Joel Fisher. Life Between Life. Doubleday And Company. New York. 1986. pp. 12-13.
38. Ibid. pp. 20-21.
39. Wambach. op. cit. p. 99.
40. Stearn, Jess. Edgar Cayce - The Sleeping Prophet. Bantam Books. 1967. p. 260.
41. Cannon, Dr. Alexander. The Power Within.
42. Webster's. op. cit.
43. Fisher, Joe. The Case For Reincarnation. Bantam New Age Books. October 1985. p. 43.
44. Sri Ramana Maharshi. Be As You Are - The Teachings of Sri Ramana Maharshi. Arkana Paperbacks. London 1985.
45. Watts, Alan. "Out of the Trap" Lecture series. KPFA.
46. Seth (Roberts, Jane) The Unknown Reality. p. 669.
47. Kenyon, Edwin. The Dilemma of Abortion. Faber and Faber. London. 1986.
48. Emmanuel. op. cit. p. 125.
49. Seth. op. cit. pp. 500-501.

CHAPTER TWO -

1. Genesis 3:22.
2. Ephesians 4:6.
3. Genesis 3:2,5.
4. United Press International.

5. Dr. John Rock. Los Angeles Times.
6. The Bible. Phillippians 2:5,6
7. United Nations. The Population Debate: Dimensions and Perspectives. John Durand "Historical Estimates of World Population." Population and Development Review Vol.3, No. 3 (sept. '77) pp. 253-296.
8. Mumford, Stephen. The Humanist - Population Growth and Global Security. Jan-Feb 1981, p. 19.
9. Brown, Lester. State of The World - 1987 WorldWatch INstitute report. Harmonist Magazine Vol 2. 1987.
10. Ni, Hua-Ching. op. cit.
11. Wright, A. The Limits of Mankind.
12. Mumford. op. cit. p. 15.
13. Statement. United Presbyterian Church. 182nd Assembly.
14. Peter's Quotations. op. cit. p. 528
15. Ibid. pp. 45
16. Hardin, Garrett. Stalking the Wild Taboo. William Kaufman Inc, Los Altos, California 1973. p. 29.
17. Hardin, Garrett. Mandatory Motherhood. Beacon Press. Boston. 1974.
18. Forssman, Hans & Thuwe. The Abortion Experience.
19. Hardin, Garrett. Biological Insights into Abortion.
20. Doerr, Edd. Humanist Magazine. May/June '86. p. 37.
21. Newsweek Magazine. January 14, 1985. p. 26.
22. David, Henry. Abortion in Psychological Perspective. Policy Review. May 1985. p. 20.
23. Ibid.
24. Lieberman, Dr. James E. & Ellen Peck. Sex & Birth Control - A Guide For The Young. Harper & Row. New York. 1981 p. 125.
25. Gerber, Alex. M.D. op. cit.
26. Santa Ana Register. February 1, 1987.
27. Hardin, Garrett. Stalking The Wild Taboo. William Kaufman Inc. Los Altos, Ca. 1973. p. 29.
28. Los Angeles Times. August 4, 1985.
29. Los Angeles Times. May 3, 1987
30. USA Today Editorial. March 20, 1985
31. Hardin, Garrett. op. cit. pp. 79
32. Time Magazine. December 9, 1985.
33. Lippman, Walter. A Preface To Morals. Time-Life Books. New York. 1929. p. 287.
34. USA Today. op. cit.
35. Time Magazine. Dec. 9, 1985.
36. Plato, The Republic, 5,461C; Will Durant, The Story of Philosophy. New York, Simon & Schuster. p. 31.
37. Mumford. op. cit. pp. 12-13.
38. Height, Dorothy I. What Must Be Done About Children Having Children. Ebony Magazine. Mar. 1985. p. 78.
39. Webster's Quotations. op. cit. p. 284

40. Ibid.
41. Ibid.
42. Corea, Genoveffa. The Mother Machine.
43. Parabola. High Resolve: An interview with Tara Tulke, Rimpoche. Vol 11, #3, Aug. 1986. pp 44-45.
44. Los Angeles Times. May 19, 1987. p. 25
45. Parabola. Modes of Meaning and Experience: Viraha and Vilaiyatal. David Dean Schulman. Vol.11 #3, 1986. p. 11.
46. Meyer, Marvin. op. cit. pp. 64-65.
47. Sanford, John A. The kingdom Within. Harper & Row, San Francisco. Rev. 1987 ed. p. 132.
48. Hatch, Michael. Snata Ana Register — Martin J. Smith. November 8, 1987. pp. 1.
49. Peter's Quotations. op. cit.
50. Devereoux, George. A Study of Abortion in Primitive Societies. INternational University Press. New York. 1955. pp. 7-20
51. Walker, Barbara. The Woman's Encyclopedia of Myths And Secrets. Harper & Row. San Francisco. 1983. pp. 104-105.
52. Seth. (Roberts, Jane). The Nature of The Psyche. Bantam Books. New York. 1979. pp. 68-69.
53. Aristophanes. The Complete Plays - Lysistrata. Bantam Books. New York. 1962. p. 295.
54. MacLean's. "Chemistry and Abortion" May 27,'85. p. 58.

CHAPTER THREE -

1. Hill, A. V. "Promethean Ethics." University of Washington Press. Seattle 1980.
2. Flynn, Frederick. op. cit.
3. Ibid.
4. Demographics Unveiled. Zero Population Growth.
5. United Nations Bulletin.
6. Hardin, Garrett. Population, Evolution and Birth Control. W.H. Freeman & Co. San Francisco 1964.
7. Mumford, Stephen. American Democracy & The Vatican: Population Growth & National Security. Humanist Press. Amherst, New York. 1984. pp. 88-89.
8. Ibid.
9. World Watch Institute. UPI 1986.
10. Ehrlich, Paul & Anne. The Population Bomb. Ballantine Books. New York. 1979. p. 300.
11. Brown, Lester. World Watch Institute. Los Angeles Times Feb. 19, 1986.
12. Aristophanes. op. cit. p. 292
13. Huston, Perdita. Ms. Magazine. "If Women had a Foreign Policy" March 1985. p. 49.
14. World Council on Population. 1984.

15. Los Angeles Times. Jim Mann. Post-Mao China.
16. Time Mag. Dec. 9, 1985.
17. Mumford. op. cit.
18. Sayers, Dorothy L. Creed or Chaos. E.F. Schumacher. Small is Beautiful. p. 37.
19. Doerr, Edward. The Humanist. July-Aug 1985. p. 41.
20. Ken Brower. Ehrlich, Paul and Anne. Extinction. Ballantine. New York. 1981. p. 300.
21. Hardin, Garrett. Population, Evolution and Birth Control. W.H. Freeman & Co. San Francisco 1964.
22. Hardin. Garrett. op. cit.
23. World Conservation Strategy Newsletter.
24. Hardin, Garrett. op. cit.
25. Hans Fei-Tzu. The Zen Teaching of Hui Hai. John Blofeld. Rider - Samuel Wiser Inc. Ney York.
26. Haring, Bernard. Medical Ethics. Notre Dame Fides Publishers. p.119. 26. Mumford. op. cit.
27. Mumford. op. cit.
28. National Geographic Magazine. March 1987. p. 363.
29. Mumford. op. cit.
30. Daniel C. Maguire. MS. Magazine. Mar '86. p. 98.
31. Hardin, Garrett. op. cit.
32. Los Angeles Times.
33. Mumford. op. cit.
34. Ibid.

CHAPTER FOUR -

1. Pope John Paul II. L.A. Times. Jan. 28 '85.
2. Peter's Quotations. op. cit.
3. Swomley, John M. Theology And Politics. Religious Coalition for Abortion Rights, Wash. D.C. pp. 4.
4. The Bible. Luke 6:43
5. Crist, Takey Dr. & Joseph Allen. We Are The Women. Institute for Women Health Care. Jacksonville, N.C.
6. Simmons, Dr. Paul D. A Theological Response to Fundamentalism on Abortion. R.C.A.R. Wash. D.C. p. 7.
7. Hardin, Garrett. op. cit.
8. Latter Day Saints. We Affirm. R.C.A.R. p. 6.
9. Ibid. p. 7.
10. Ibid. p. 1.
11. Reuther, Rosemary Radford. Women-Church. Harper & Row. San Francisco. 1985. pp 139.
12. Nikos Kantzantzakis, Report To Greco
13. Emmanuel. op. cit. p. 227.
14. Greeley, Andrew. Omni Magazine. Jan. 1987 p. 98.

15. Evans-Wentz, W.Y. The Tibetan Book of the Great liberation. Oxford Univ. Press. 1954. pp. 48-49.
16. Mumford. op cit.
17. Robinson, James. The Nag Hammadi Library.
18. Ibid.
19. Ibid.
20. Kenyon. Edwin. op. cit.
21. Ibid.
22. Conor Cruise O'Brien.
23. Watts, Alan. Beyond Theology. Meridian Books - World Publishing Co. New York. p. 176
24. Sanford, John. op. cit. pp. 110-111.
25. Peter's Quotations. op. cit. p. 202
26. Watts, Alan. op. cit. pp. 86-87
27. Hamblin, Dora Jane. Has the Garden of Eden been located at Last? Smithsonian Magazine. May 1987. pp. 127-133.
28. The Bible. Genesis 3:16
29. Walker, Barbara. op. cit.
30. The Beble. Romans 6:14
31. Swomley, John M. Six Ethical Questions. R.C.A.R., Washington, D.C. pp. 4.
32. The Bible. Luke 17:21
33. Tomlin, Lily. The Quotable Woman. op. cit.
34. Reuther, Rosemary Radford. op. cit.
35. Krishhnamurti J. The Penguin Krishnamurti Reader. Edited by Mary Lutyens. Penguin Books. 1970. p. 187
36. Mumford, Stephen. op. cit.
37. Ibid.
38. Ibid.
39. Walker, Barbara. op. cit. p. 212.

CHAPTER FIVE -

1. Gardner, R.F.R. Abortion - The Personal Dilemma. W. B. Eerdmans Publishing Co. Grand Rapids, MI. 1972. p. 119.
2. Hardin, Garrett. The Case For Legalized Abortion. op. cit. pp. 123.
3. Walker, Barbara. op. cit. pp. 115.
4. Simmons, Paul D. A theological Response to Fundamentalism on the Abortion Issue. R.C.A.R. Washington D.C. pp. 12.
5. Hardin, Garrett. op. cit.
6. The Bible. Ecclesiates 3:2
7. Sumner, L.W. Abortion and Moral Theory. Princeton University Press. 1982. p. 150.
8. Blackmun, Chief Justice. Roe Vs. Wade. 1973.
9. The Bible. Galatians 3:16-17
10. Ceausescu, Nicolae. Omni Magazine, Continuum. June 1987.

11. Hitler, Adolph. Quoted in The People's Almanac #3. David Wallechinsky & Irving Wallace. Bantam Books. N.Y. 1981. p. 31.
12. Webster's. Quotations. op. cit.
13. Peter's Quotations. op. cit.
14. Doerr, Edd. op. cit.
15. Peter's Quotations. op. cit.
16. Flynn, Frederick. op. cit.
17. Thompson, Judith Jarvis. "A Defense of Abortion" in the Problem of Abortion, ed. Joel Feinberg. Wadsworth. 1973 pp. 122-23.
18. Gallagher, Janet. The Fetus & The Law. Ms. Mag. Sept. 1984.
19. Ibid.
20. Peter's Quotations. op. cit. pp. 45.
21. Walker Barbara. op. cit. pp. 105.
22. Swomley, John. op. cit. pp. 7.
23. Hiller, Anthony. Go Forth & Multiply - Like Rabbits? Humanist Magazine. Nov-Dec 1984. pp. 17.
24. Schumacher. E.F. Small is Beautiful. Harper & Row. New York. 1973. pp. 72

CHAPTER SIX -

1. Peter's Quotations. op. cit.
2. Schempp, Ed. Buyers Guide to Gods. General Religions Int. 1986. Barrington, New Jersey. pp 66.
3. Spake, Amanda. Ms. Magazine. "Propaganda War over Abortion" March 1986, pg 98

CHAPTER SEVEN -

1. J. Breslin. Los Angeles Herald-Examiner. Sept. 16, 1987.
2. R. Hymers. Los Angeles Times.
3. Meyer, Marvin. op. cit.
4. Ni, Hua-Ching. op. cit.
5. Blofeld, John. The Zen Teachings of Hui Hai. Rider/S. Weiser. New York. pp. 98.
6. Scheidler, J. USA Today. Dec. 2, 1985.
7. Ni, Hua-Ching. op. cit.
8. Sanford, John. op. cit. pp. 104
9. S. Tisdale. We Do Abortion Here. Harper's Mag. Oct '87.
10. Chang-Tzu. Nan-Hua Ching. 5th Cent. B.C.
11. Los Angeles Times. Jan 11, 1985.
12. Peter's Quotations. op. cit.
13. Santa Ana Register. Fundamentalists Ache for Armageddon. Allan C. Brownfeld. May 17, 1987.
14. Schempp. op. cit.
15. L.A. Times. Abortion and Religion. R. Chandler.

16. Donna Ruscavage. The Humanist. Feb. 1981. pp. 57.
17. Mario Cuomo. Time Magazine. Sept. 24, 1984.

CHAPTER EIGHT -

1.   Time Magazine. Jan. 7, 1985 pp. 83.
2.   Ibid.
3.   The Bible. I Corinthians 14:34
4.   Cetron, Marvin and Thomas O'Toole. Encounters with The Future. McGraw-Hill. New York. 1982. pp 176.
5.   Pope John Paul II. L.A. Times. Sept 16, 1987.
6.   Los Angeles Times.
7.   Harvey Brett. Sisterhood is Subversive. Village Voice. Jan 27,1987. pp. 26.
8.   Time Magazine. Feb. 4, 1985.
9.   Ibid.
10. Ruether, Rosemary Radford. op. cit. pp. 150.
11. Ibid.
12. Ibid.
13. Ibid.
14. Ibid.
15. Ibid.
16. Reuther. Ibid.
17. Halifax. Joan. Shaman - The Wounded Healer.
18. Buddha. The dhammapadda.
19. Rajneesh, Bhagwan Shree. The Book - An Introduction to The Teachings of Bhagwan Shree Rajneesh. Rajneesh Foundation International. Poona, India. 1984.
20. Chandrasekhar, S. Abortion In A Crowded World. Univ. of Washington Press. Seattle. 1974. p. 117.